SUBMARINE WARFARE

"DAVID AND GOLIATH"
The Russian battleship "Retvisan" (12,700 tons), and the U. S. submarine "Holland"
(75 tons)

SUBMARINE WARFARE

PAST AND PRESENT

BY

HERBERT C. FYFE

(SOMETIME LIBRARIAN OF THE ROYAL INSTITUTION, LONDON)

WITH AN INTRODUCTION BY

ADMIRAL THE HON. SIR EDMUND FREMANTLE, G.C.B., C.M.G.

SECOND EDITION, REVISED

BY

JOHN LEYLAND

WITH FIFTY-FOUR ILLUSTRATIONS

LONDON

E. GRANT RICHARDS

1907

PREFACE TO THE SECOND EDITION

*A demand having arisen in this country and the United
States for a second edition of the late Mr. Herbert C. Fyfe's
"Submarine Warfare," the publishers asked me to undertake the revision of the book. The request came at a time
when I was otherwise much occupied, but it seemed
undesirable that the public demand should go unsatisfied,
and thus the new edition appears. It was a delicate matter
to revise the work of a dead writer, and the volume remains
in plan, character, and scope what the author made it.
Since the first edition appeared, the second chapter, on
"The Place of the Submarine in Warfare," had lost its
value, and two new chapters take its place in the present
edition. All the other chapters are retained. The text has
been revised, not with the purpose of altering it in any way,
but of removing matter which had lost interest, and of
introducing some new facts. Nothing has been omitted that
could be retained. Few subjects are so difficult to write
about as submarine navigation, and therefore it may be well
to remark that no matter has been introduced into the
present edition except upon the authority of constructors
and officers experienced in the working of submarines. Sir*

Edmund Fremantle has kindly revised the introduction which he wrote for the first edition, and the chapter on the "Probable Future of Submarine Boat Construction," by the late Sir Edward J. Reed, M.P., has been retained as of value, though so much new experience has been gained since it was written. It only remains to say that several illustrations have been added, depicting the newer classes of boats.

J. L.

PREFACE TO THE FIRST EDITION
(1902)

THERE exists no popular work in the English language on submarine warfare, and only one which deals exclusively with submarine boats. This was written fifteen years ago by Lieutenant G. W. Hovgaard, of the Danish Navy. It is a little book of ninety-eight pages, and out of these forty only are given to the " History and Development of Submarine Boats." The rest of the volume is taken up with a description of a vessel imagined by the author, but never constructed. Lieutenant Sleeman's " Torpedoes and Torpedo Warfare " takes no account of under-water craft ; whilst Lieutenant G. E. Armstrong, in his little book, " Torpedoes and Torpedo Vessels," devotes only eighteen pages out of three hundred and six to " Submarines and Submersibles."

Having always taken a keen interest in submarine boats, the writer some two years ago commenced the compilation of the present work. His aim has been to produce a book which should be essentially of a popular character and should appeal to those who have neither the time nor the inclination to pursue the subject very deeply. It necessarily contains a certain amount of detailed description, but the aim has been to avoid technicalities as far as possible. That the book may appeal to the general public, and that it may

ix

also be found worthy of a place on the shelves of the student of naval history and naval warfare, is the author's wish, and he trusts that a volume will not be unacceptable that traces the story of under-water warfare from the earliest times to the present day, that endeavours to explain how a submarine boat is worked, and that attempts to arrive at some conclusions respecting a mode of fighting which may possibly figure largely in future battles on the seas.

Interest in the navy and in naval matters is fortunately greater than it used to be, but there is still a vast amount of ignorance existing in the minds of the public respecting our warships and our sailors. When an explosion occurred recently in the Royal Sovereign a man in the street remarked to his friend, " How lucky it didn't happen when we went to Margate on her last summer ! " The navy is certainly not so much in the public eye as is the army ; still, it should be the desire of every Briton to know even a little about the service for which he pays so much. Many people seem to imagine that torpedo-boats do their work below the waves, and have but very hazy notions respecting the working of the torpedo or the functions of the destroyer.

It was recently remarked to the writer by one who has had a large experience in catering for the mental needs of the British public that we were not a mechanical nation, and that while Americans would naturally be interested in such a subject as submarine warfare, Britons would only display an apathetic attitude towards it. Perhaps the general lack of interest in scientific matters is due to the fact that little trouble is taken to place them before readers in an attractive form. There is no doubt that the Germans, the French, and the Americans are far more alive to the importance of science, and are far more ready to discuss inventions, discoveries, and scientific topics than we are ourselves.

That this work will appeal to a very large class of readers the writer has little hope. He trusts, however, that those who do read it will be encouraged to pursue the subject a little more deeply, and that inventive minds may be induced to apply their ingenuity to the designing of weapons for under-water warfare.

When we decided to add submarines to our navy, we had to adopt the design of an American, Mr. Holland, because no other was then available. Similarly, the system of wireless telegraphy used in our men-of-war is the invention of an Italian.

" We have started," says a well-known English professor, " all the branches of engineering ; we have invented nearly all the important things, but the great development of these things has gone out of the hands of the amateurs of our nation. It is because our statesmen are Gallios who ' care for none of these things,' because they know nothing of science."

It was an Englishman who invented the Whitehead torpedo ; it was in the brain of an Englishman that the idea of the torpedo-boat destroyer was evolved. Are there not those who will bring their inventive talent to bear on the perfecting of the diving torpedo-boat and of the many contrivances that are needed to make it an efficient weapon of offence and defence ?

It may be said that the encouragement given to the inventor by the Admiralty is so scanty as to make him shy of offering them his ideas. Let us hope, now that Lord Selborne and Mr. Arnold-Forster are at the Admiralty, that the bad old days when inventors were snubbed, and novel ideas ridiculed, have gone, never to return. The submersible craft of to-day is no longer an ingenious toy ; it is a practical engine of warfare of no mean value. But there is vast room for improvement in its design. It must be endowed with more speed, its longitudinal stability must be improved, and its appliances for under-water vision perfected. Are there not Britons willing to devote their energies to the realization of the ideal submarine ?

The author has derived his information from a great many sources, some of which are mentioned in the brief Bibliography at the end of the book.

He desires to express his thanks to Messrs. Vickers Sons and Maxim, the Holland Torpedo-boat Company, Mr. P W. D'Alton, Lieutenant A. T. Dawson, late R.N., Mr. Simon Lake, and others, for information kindly given him respecting various boats and for photographs. To Mr. Alan H. Burgoyne his thanks are due for permission to use some of his original sketches.

ROYAL SOCIETIES' CLUB,
    ST. JAMES STREET, S.W.

CONTENTS

CONTENTS

PART III

LIST OF ILLUSTRATIONS

INTRODUCTION

BY

ADMIRAL THE HON. SIR E. R. FREMANTLE,
G.C.B., C.M.G.

Rear-Admiral of the United Kingdom

THE natural attitude of the Naval mind towards submarines is the same now as that expressed by Lord St. Vincent when Fulton invented the notorious " catamaran " expedition.

Fulton had been trying some experiments before Pitt, who favoured the project, to which Lord St. Vincent, then First Lord of the Admiralty, was strongly opposed, and he bluntly stated that " Pitt was the greatest fool that ever existed to encourage a mode of war which those who commanded the seas did not want, and which, if successful, would deprive them of it."

It was, our Admiralty argued for some time, " the weapon of the weaker power, and not our concern "; then we were to " watch and wait," which sounded plausible, but was evidently dangerous, and as the success of the French submarines became too evident we were forced to follow suit. As Lord Selborne reminded us when speaking about water-tube boilers, we have too often ignored new inventions and resisted change till we were left well behind in the race, as we were with ironclads, breechloading guns, and other improvements in naval warfare.

The fact is that every successful invention has its infancy of weakness and failure, its adolescence of partial adoption, and doubtful success, and its manhood of completion and achievement. Unfortunately the natural conservatism of a profession, and perhaps of human nature, is apt to deride the early failures, and to prejudice the invention so as to delay its adoption. Every inventor can tell stories of the obstruction he has met with, and often of his ultimate triumph, like Mr. Whitworth and his steam hammer pile-driving competition, when he succeeded in driving piles with his steam hammer in as many minutes as it took hours under the method previously adopted, much to the astonishment of the old hands.

Certainly the submarine has had its period of failure and ridicule, for the attempt to use submarines dates from very ancient days, as Mr. Fyfe's interesting historical *résumé* shows; yet it is only now arriving at the stage of development which forces us to reckon with it as a serious factor in naval warfare.

We need not follow Mr. Fyfe in his early history of the submarine, but leaving James I's somewhat apocryphal voyage under the waters of the Thames, the inventions of Bushnell, Fulton, Warner, and others, we may come to the Confederate diving boat during the War of

Secession. Here we have a real diving boat which, though it drowned three crews, did succeed in destroying the United States sloop *Housatonic*, one of the blockading fleet off Charlestown, though she was herself sunk in the effort, drowning her fourth crew. It is interesting to compare this submarine boat with one of our modern "Hollands."

The following is the description given by Captain Maury, the well-known hydrographer, then at the head of the Confederate torpedo bureau, of this unfortunate craft, or *David*, as she was called. "It was built of boiler iron, about 35 feet long, and was manned by a crew of nine men, eight of whom worked the propeller by hand, the ninth steered the boat and regulated her movements below the surface of the water. She could be submerged at pleasure to any desired depth, or could be propelled on the surface. In smooth, still water she could be exactly controlled, and her speed was about 4 knots."

It is further stated that she could remain submerged for half an hour "without inconvenience to her crew," and in action she was to drag a torpedo under a ship's bottom, which was intended to explode on striking.

Now contrast this rude and dangerous craft with the numerous submarines now in existence belonging to the French and to Great Britain. It is enough to say that last year France had 68 submarines and submersibles built and building, while we had 30.

I need not describe the *Holland* here, but motive power,

speed, radius of action, and torpedo are all essentially different from those employed in the Confederate *David* above referred to, but above all it has been proved that a modern submersible boat like the French *Gustave Zédé*, or *Narval*, or our "Hollands," can remain under water truly " without inconvenience to her crew " for periods of 24 hours or more, so that all the problems connected with submarine navigation may be said to have been solved, except that of seeing under water, for when submerged the submarine is in Cimmerian darkness, and more helpless than an ordinary vessel in the densest of fogs.   It is true that our submarines are fitted with a "periscope," which is usually above water, under which circumstances objects can be fairly observed in certain directions, but recent accidents have proved that it is a very uncertain guide, though it is said to have been much improved recently.   Nor is it likely that invention has said its last word in regard to the submarine now that it is acknowledged to be a weapon of practical value.

On this point it is convenient to call to mind the remarkable development of the Whitehead torpedo since it was first adopted in our Navy rather more than thirty years ago.   It happens that I have been able to refer to an article on torpedoes which I wrote in *Fraser's Magazine* just thirty years ago, in which I described the Whitehead of that day as having a speed of from 7 to $7\frac{1}{2}$ knots, a range of 1000 yards, and a charge of 67 lb. of gun-cotton. Now the speed of our modern Whiteheads is 30 knots, the range 2000 yards, the charge 200 lb. of gun-cotton, and, thanks to the gyroscope, it can be discharged with extraordinary accuracy *

Admitting, then, that the submarine is with us, and that it will remain, let us see what is likely to be its function in war. The submarine compares naturally with the torpedo destroyer or torpedo-boat ; like them it will attack by stealth, and it has neither their speed nor radius of faction. But, whereas searchlights and quick-firing guns are effective weapons against the latter, they are of little use against the submarine, and as all these craft are to act by surprise, the advantage is strongly in favour of the submarine, which can approach with little danger of being discovered, with the periscope only showing, until close to her enemy, thus rendering a close blockade by large vessels impossible.

I have said that the submarine is naturally the weapon of the weaker power, but that it can be used and that it will be used by the stronger power acting on the offensive I see no reason to doubt. It can certainly be employed against ships at anchor unless they are suitably protected, and it can probably render good service in removing obstructions and clearing passages defended by torpedoes. It is unfortunate that the recent war has given us no experience of submarines, though both Russia and Japan possessed a few towards the close of the war.

* This was written as an introduction to Mr. Fyfe's book in 1902, and I am well aware that quite recently great improvements have been made in the speed of the Whitehead torpedo, though they are kept a profound secret.

The question remains as to whether any antidote to the submarine is likely to be effective. It is possible that one may be discovered, but it is not easy to see in what direction we are to look for it, as the submarine differs from other craft in the fact that the possession of any number of similar vessels, by ourselves for instance, affords little or no protection against a few well-handled *Gustave Zédé's* in the hands of our enemies. At the same time they would be of little or no value against torpedo boats or destroyers; and cruisers blockading, moving about at a speed of 10 knots or more, at some distance from a port known to harbour submarines, would have little to fear, as it would only be by a lucky chance that a submarine could approach near enough to them to have a fair shot. It is also worthy of remark that the navigation and pilotage of a submarine, even with her cupola above water, would be by no means easy in shallow water or thick weather, and of the value of the periscope I cannot but feel somewhat sceptical. The French are stated to have found that submarines can be easily discovered from balloons; but this must naturally apply only to daylight and fine weather, and their opportunity will naturally occur in thick weather or at night.

I have offered these remarks to show that though I consider the submarine to be an important weapon, it clearly has its limitations, and I suspect that when we have them fairly under trial we shall find that when these are fully appreciated and the position of the submarine in naval warfare is duly assigned, much of the terror and mystery now surrounding this novel weapon will be removed. Probably it will be found to be a more dangerous and effective torpedo-boat, and will supplant it in great measure.

Mr. Fyfe has done good service in giving us this popular account of submarines, which is a valuable addition to the scanty literature of the subject in the English language.

It must be added, in conclusion, that both the size and speed of submarines have been much improved since Mr. Fyfe's book was written, though the frequent accidents which have taken place, both in this country and in France, will have scarcely tended to give confidence in their reliability as a practical weapon.

THE PROBABLE FUTURE
OF SUBMARINE BOAT CONSTRUCTION

BY THE LATE

SIR EDWARD J. REED, K.C.B., F R.S., M.P.

(Chief Constructor of the Navy 1863-70)

THERE is nothing in the nature of things that I know of to prevent submarine warfare being carried on in the future to a very large extent. This development will probably follow triple lines : (1) Vessels for the defence of ports and harbours, with sufficient means of proceeding outside to give the defence a certain limited power of attack in the approaches ; (2) vessels primarily designed for attack, and therefore capable of proceeding to sea for considerable distances ; and (3) smaller vessels to be taken to sea in ships, as part of their equipment, and capable of being lowered to take part in a battle, and raised again, and re-stowed on board when no longer needed in action. All these types of vessel will need to be endowed with the power of passing easily and quickly from the floating to the submerged condition and back again to the surface when necessary ; but the boats of the second class in the foregoing category will doubtless be developed to an extent as yet anticipated by very few of us, in respect alike of their ability to proceed for great distances below water and of their ability to steam satisfactorily afloat when submergence is needless.

All who are acquainted with the structure of waves, so to speak, will be aware that wave disturbance diminishes very rapidly as we go down below the surface, and will consequently understand that when once we have succeeded in giving submarines a great range of underwater travel we shall have endowed them with the capability of avoiding at pleasure in bad weather the tempestuous surface of the sea, with all the drawbacks to speed which stormy seas impose upon ships, and especially upon comparatively small vessels. In order to bring about this advantage science has to effect, no doubt, immense improvements in the production of storage of air, or of its equivalent; but there is great reason to believe that the demand will bring the supply, as in so many other matters. Nor must it be forgotten that this is a branch of science for the development of which the ship proper, as we have hitherto known it, has offered few, if any, inducements. I do not know how the sight of an ordinary modern ship of war strikes the eyes of others, but for my part I never look at one, with its vast and monstrous assemblage of gaping mouths of funnels, pipes, and cowls, without thinking that our method of supplying breathing gas to men below in a ship is at present of a very elementary and unsatisfactory character. It is certainly the roughest and readiest method that could well be adopted. Nor is it without a sense of satisfaction that one knows that the submarine ship will at least sweep away these ugly and towering excrescences, and force us to resort much more than at present to the chemical and mechanical arts for the ventilation of vessels.

. The development of the sea-going submarine will bring with it, doubtless, many improvements in the vessels which have been first mentioned, viz. vessels for the defence of ports and their approaches. It is not possible yet to say to what extent the " Holland " boats building at Barrow will prove fairly satisfactory, although my acquaintance with this class of vessel for several years past has given me a favourable impression of it—favourable, that is, as furnishing many elements of initial success.* More than this could not be reasonably expected ; nor can we doubt that with the skill of both the Admiralty designers and those of the great manufacturing establishment which has produced the first few vessels concentrated upon this class of boat immense improvements may be confidently anticipated.

Of the third class of vessels before referred to, the " Goubet " boat may be regarded as a commencing type. The principle of this boat appears to be that of carrying and launching torpedoes from external supports, the size and buoyancy of the vessels being very small by comparison with those of vessels which carry their torpedoes inside. M. Goubet appears to go beyond this principle, and to have other ideas, which are mentioned in the text of this work. Suffice it here to say that the idea of relieving the submarine boat from the necessity of carrying

---

* This was written in 1902. Since that time the improved classes of boats built for the British and other navies have amply justified Sir Edward Reed's forecast The Goubet boats to which he referred have passed into the history of experiments in submarine navigation.

its torpedoes with it goes a long way towards furthering the use of submarine torpedo craft carried on the decks, or at the davits of battleships and cruisers.

If one may contrast for a moment the present attempts at aerial navigation with the concurrent attempts at submarine navigation, one quickly sees how terribly the æronaut is handicapped as compared with the underwater sailor. The advantage of the dense medium which the sea offers to the submarine navigator is precisely the same as it has offered from the beginning of time to the surface navigator, and nothing new is needed to sustain the submarine ship; whereas the unhappy man who seeks to navigate the air has to obtain from a medium of extraordinary levity the support necessary for keeping him aloft. The difference between the specific gravity of air (of which ships are full) and of water is so great by comparison between the specific gravity of any gas available for filling aerial ships and that of air, that the problem of the submarinist is easy indeed compared with the other. But it is in the face of this initial and enormous difficulty that the æronauts of to-day have apparently persuaded themselves that they can successfully float their balloon-ship in mid-air, and propel it not only against the rapid tides of the air in which it floats, but also drive it at a good additional speed. When men are to be found capable of committing their fortunes, and even their lives, to navigation of this kind, it is not surprising to find that the far easier problem of navigating the seas beneath the surface has won the attention and the effort of enterprising men. They certainly have chosen, if the humbler, also the more practical and promising field of operation. I doubt not that they have likewise chosen the more fruitful field.

It is worthy of remark that it is once again in connection with the arts of war that a great extension of human progress has been commenced. But for the temptation of gaining equality with, and even mastery over, our possible foes the art of submarine navigation would certainly not have been attracting the attention of some of our best and most scientific men, who are once again eagerly developing—

> " Those dire implements
> Which sombre science with unpitying pains,
> That love of neither man nor God restrains,
> To warring foes presents."

One can only be thankful that the world is so constituted and so ruled that out of seeming evil often comes great good to men.

I have not been asked to say anything of the book with which these lines are associated. I may nevertheless remark that I have had an opportunity of hastily looking through the author's proof-sheets, and have formed the opinion that it is a most timely and highly instructive work, and one which gives to the non-technical world an extremely good review of all that has been done in the way of submarine war-vessels ; while the technical man into whose hands it may come will be compelled, by its great interest and by its clever record of facts, to read every page of it.

THE FIRST SUBMARINE TO FLY THE WHITE ENSIGN

(By permission of the Admiralty and Messrs. Vickers, Sons, and Maxim)

SUBMARINE WARFARE

PART I

CHAPTER I

INTRODUCTORY

"The submarine craft is a miracle of ingenuity, though Nelson and his hearts of oak, fighting only on deck, in God's free air, and with 'the meteor flag of England' fluttering overhead, would have loathed and scorned her burglarious, area-sneak dodges down below."

In modern under-water warfare two weapons are employed, the Mine and the Torpedo. Both are explosive devices, but whilst mines are stationary, torpedoes are endowed with the power of locomotion in some form or another.

The modern submarine boat is in reality a diving torpedo-boat, and, like all other torpedo-craft of the present day, its function is to discharge automobile torpedoes. The submarine boat is sometimes said to be the child of the torpedo-boat. As a matter of fact, the earliest known torpedo-vessel was designed to do its work *under* water.

In 1776 an attack was made on the English frigate *Eagle*, and in 1777 on the English man-of-war *Cerberus*, by a submarine vessel invented by David Bushnell and provided with "torpedoes." Although no injury was inflicted on these ships, three of the crew of a prize schooner

B

astern of the *Cerberus*, in hauling one of Bushnell's drifting torpedoes on board, were killed by its explosion.
Bushnell's craft, however, was a combination of the submarine and the torpedo, a system which never could have
possessed any fighting value.

A few years afterwards Robert Fulton occupied himself with torpedoes, and, like Bushnell, came to the conclusion that a submarine boat was the best suited for
the discharge of his weapons. In time of peace Fulton
showed that his torpedoes could sink ships, but in actual
warfare he failed to accomplish the destruction of any
craft. For a while torpedo-warfare received but scant
attention, but on the outbreak of the American Civil War
the mine and the torpedo "leapt at one bound from the
condition of theory and experiment to become accepted,
once for all, as practical and valuable factors for offence
and defence."

At this period also it is to be noted that the torpedoists considered the under-water vessel the most favourable method of utilising the spar-torpedo, the weapon
of the day. Both Federals and Confederates paid much
attention to submarine navigation, and success attended
the efforts of the latter, for on 17 February, 1864, the
Federal frigate *Housatonic* was sunk off Charleston by
the Confederate diving torpedo-boat *David*, armed with
a spar-torpedo. This is the sole occasion on which an
under-water vessel has ever succeeded in sinking a hostile
craft in actual warfare, and even then it was being
navigated in the awash condition, and not completely
submerged.

The introduction of the automobile or fish-torpedo

led to the building of above-water torpedo vessels and destroyers by all the great Powers ; but the idea of discharging this weapon from a submarine boat occupied the attention of numerous inventors, and amongst others of Mr. Nordenfelt, of machine-gun fame. Greece and Turkey both bought Nordenfelt submarine boats, but although they achieved a certain amount of success, and were certainly the best specimens of under-water fighting vessels then extant, they failed to receive wider recognition owing to their serious disadvantages.

The possibility of utilising the electric accumulator revived the hopes of the advocates of submarine navigation, and towards the end of the eighties France added the first under-water torpedo-boat to her navy : since then her interest in the subject has never abated, and although it would be unfair to attribute to all French naval men and officials the ideas as to the superiority of the torpedo-vessel to the ironclad put forward by a certain class of writers, it cannot be denied that the question of under-water warfare has attracted more attention in France than in any other country. The year after the launch of the first French submarine, the *Gymnote*, in 1888, the *Peral* was built at Carraca for the Spanish Navy ; and in 1896 the U.S. Government purchased the *Holland*, and afterwards put in hand eight boats of the same type enlarged.

When Greece and Turkey purchased Nordenfelt boats there were not wanting those who declared that Great Britain should also add under-water vessels to her navy. The official view was, however, not favourable at the time to such craft. In the early part of 1900 Viscount

Goschen said that while close attention had been given by the Admiralty to the subject of submarine boats, they considered that, even if the practical difficulties attending their use could be overcome, they should be regarded as weapons for " maritime Powers on the defensive." It appeared to him that the reply to this weapon must be looked for in other ways than in building submarine boats ourselves, for it was clear that one submarine-boat could not fight another. It would seem from this that the Admiralty had at the time no very high opinion of the submarine as an offensive weapon. The attitude of the Board was to observe the policy of other Powers and to profit by their experience. As the powers of the submersible were developed, the view that boats of the class are necessarily the weapon of the weaker Power was seen to be untenable, and a bold policy of submarine construction was entered upon, which has carried us far ahead of any Power save France, and will soon, if it be pursued, enable us to outstrip her. The first order was placed, in the autumn of 1900, with Messrs. Vickers, Sons, and Maxim for five of the newest " Holland " boats (63 ft. 6 in. long), they being the agents in Europe for the Holland Torpedo-boat Company of New York, and this being then the only type available. Not till the statement of the First Lord was published on 1 March, 1901, was the fact of the ordering of these boats made public ; the secret had indeed been well kept. Four boats of the new A class (100 ft.) were launched at Barrow in 1903, and nine more followed in the next year of the same type enlarged. Of the still larger B class, ten were launched in 1905. Improvements have been introduced, and there are eleven boats belonging to the programme of 1905–6, twelve to that of 1906–7, two of them being of a larger class, and twelve to that of 1907–8. Evidently there is no sign of a halt in the building of submersible boats, and Italy, Russia, Germany, and Japan have now entered upon an active submarine policy.

He would be a bold man who would prophesy how the question of submarine navigation will stand fifty years hence. Some have declared that the under-water vessel will go the way of the dynamite gun, the circular battle-ship, the aerial torpedo, and other inventions ; others affirm that the warfare of the future will take place neither on land nor on the seas, but in the air and beneath the waves. It was a cautious statement that Lord Goschen made when he announced that we had begun to build submarines. " What the future value of these boats may be in naval warfare can only be a matter of conjecture. The experiments with these boats will assist the Admiralty in assessing their true value. The question of their em-ployment must be studied, and all developments in their mechanism carefully watched by this country." There is now no doubt as to the qualities of submarine craft. The trials of the first boats have given confidence, and the newer classes are of far greater power.

CHAPTER II

NOTWITHSTANDING the progress that has been made in construction, the actual future of submarine and submersible boats is unknown and undetermined. That they will exercise considerable influence no one denies, especially in narrow waters or in seas where they are known to be present, and, perhaps, morally where their presence is suspected. It is nevertheless true that boats of these classes have played no part in recent warfare, and they contributed in no degree to the damage inflicted upon the Russian Navy during the War in the Far East. There are those who say that their use must be restricted, and that the value assigned to them is exaggerated. At the same time, as we have seen, all the great Powers are building vessels of these classes, and larger submersibles will soon be in commission than some thought it was possible to build. The largest, it is true, may as yet be considered as merely experimental, the object being to discover how far increase of size may be compatible with those qualities which are necessary in submersible boats.

Here it may be remarked that the submarine proper, though navigating usually on the surface, is a boat constructed with reference chiefly to her submerged duties, and therefore having engines adapted more especially for

6

navigation below the surface. A submersible, on the other hand—and submersible boats seem likely in most cases to displace submarines—may be said to have her normal place on the surface, and is therefore provided with engines for surface navigation, giving her a greater range of action than is possible with the submarine boat, and yet with secondary motors which permit her to descend below the surface in order that she may deliver her attack. The early French boats were all submarines, propelled solely by electric motors, their speed being comparatively low and their range of action restricted, owing to the accumulators requiring to be recharged. It was not until after some years of experiment that it was decided to apply special engines for surface navigation with electric accumulators for submerged propulsion ; and the French have been building vessels of the submersible class since 1903. The submersible boat became practicable when two systems of propulsion could be employed ; but in the first submersibles, steam engines being used upon the surface with boilers heated by liquid fuel, great difficulties were felt owing to the excessive heat, and to the length of time required to effect submergence. Later boats are all propelled on the surface by explosive motors of various types, while electric motors are installed, actuated by accumulators, when the boats are below the surface. It was, indeed, the invention of the accumulator that made submerged navigation really possible, and the invention of the explosive motor that provided a suitable means of navigation on the surface and of more rapid submergence when the time came for attack ; while power was furnished whereby the accumulators could be recharged. The electric motor has the great advantage of consuming no air and giving off no deleterious gases, and we are now far from the day of steam boilers used in the Nordenfelt boats, which made it so hot that submerged navigation was well nigh impossible.

Although it may be dangerous to forecast the future, it may be said without hesitation that exaggerated claims have been made for the submersible boats. They are still in the experimental stage, though the same may, in a certain sense, be said of every class of warship in which a great new departure is made—as, for example, when water-tube boilers and afterwards turbines were introduced. In 1890 the French possessed only the *Gymnote*, of 30 tons, whereas now they have a large flotilla, the latest boats approximating to a displacement of from 750 to 800 tons. If these boats should be a success, other nations will doubtless follow in the footsteps of the British and French navies. Some exponents of the submersible boat say that there is no reason why it should not gradually become larger and larger, why it should not have an armoured deck, and why an armament should not be provided of quick-firing guns, to be brought into use upon occasions, or for protection against torpedo-boats or destroyers while the submersible is filling its tanks in order to disappear. In short, we are bidden to expect the construction of larger and larger vessels, capable of going at a high rate on the surface, of submerging rapidly, of proceeding at a considerable speed below water, and of directing their course with certainty under complete control; besides possessing safety, offensive power, and habitability, trustworthy means of propulsion, and complete independence of all exterior help whilst in action.

It must be remembered, however, that a submersible boat, like every other warship, presents a compromise of qualities. It is possible that boats of the class may yet carry guns and even be protected by armoured decks, but how the guns are to be mounted, and how provision is to be made for the armoured deck, no one yet can say. There is obviously a compromise between the size of the boat and her efficient use for the purpose for which she is designed, and it may be said that the whole future of boats of the class in their wider employment depends upon this relation between size and efficiency. An important consideration which tends to the limitation of size is that arising from the difficulty of providing driving power for large boats when submerged, secondary batteries or accumulators of enormous weight, difficult to manage and liable to accident, having to be employed. This is undoubtedly a matter of very considerable importance, adding immensely to the original cost, and also to the cost of maintenance. This question of expense underlies the question of submarine development, because if submersible boats are to exercise the influence that is expected, they must be numerous and capable of keeping the sea for reasonable periods.

There is likewise a compromise, related intimately to the question of size, between surface speed and range and submerged speed and range. It is necessary to recognise a distinction between the two speeds, and the future of the submarine in regard to its character and use must depend upon the balance established between surface and submerged speed and range of action. If we demand a maximum speed on the surface with great range of action, we thereby make it impossible to obtain these same factors in the same proportion when the boat is submerged. The two considerations are antagonistic, whether we have regard to speed only or to speed combined with range of action. These considerations are put forward to show that, valuable as submersible boats admittedly are, the problem of a considerable increase in size, combined with augmented offensive and defensive power, is fraught with very great difficulties. The questions involved are, no doubt, highly technical, and could be fully discussed and understood only by those of great technical experience in matters of submarine navigation.

We may now turn to the question of invisibility, which is a primary element in the construction of submarine and submersible boats, and is not, as will be seen, without relation to considerations of size and rapidity of submersions. Any-craft which is incapable, through want of armament or speed, of defending herself from the ship she proposes to attack, or which is pursuing her, must have recourse to this element of invisibility. Thus it is necessary for torpedo-boats and destroyers preparing to attack to hide themselves in the darkness, in order that they may issue unexpectedly from the unknown. It is the same with submersible and submarine boats, which find their chief element of invisibility in their qualities for submergence. It may be regarded as hopeless for a submersible boat to endeavour to make an attack unless she can approach unseen, or be so speedy that she can advance rapidly, deliver her attack, and as rapidly disappear.

The problem of how to obtain a good view of the object without being seen is, of course, one of very great importance, inasmuch as the success or otherwise of an attack must depend very largely, if not entirely, upon this consideration. In all more recent boats, and in all British classes except those which were first built, a high conning-tower is provided which gives a considerable range of vision when the boat is running awash, that is retaining but a small reserve of buoyancy, and ready to be submerged. It was a collision between this high conning-tower and the hull of a passing vessel that led to the disaster when boat A1 went to the bottom while exercising at Spithead. A great object is to keep the conning-tower open, so that the boat can be navigated with ease and be provided with a natural supply of air. Of course, a conning-tower making a considerable wash is very visible, but in the later boats a form is being given to this part of the vessel which diminishes the visibility very largely. When submerged, a boat of this class may be regarded as usually invisible, for only her periscope remains above the surface, and this can be withdrawn when necessary. The latest British boats of the C class are provided with two periscopes. It is by the periscope that the officer is enabled to see what is going on about him, and, with considerable experience and good judgment, satisfactory results are attained. Yet it must be admitted that a great deal depends upon the state of the atmosphere at the time, in regard to light and transparency, as well as to the condition of the surface of the water. We are not, however, at this moment discussing submerged vision, but the question of the invisibility of the boat, which is largely attained through the use of the periscope. Of course, even a periscope which makes a wash may reveal the presence of a submarine boat. A good deal of attention has also to be given to the question of the colour of the boats, and to the covering to be placed upon the periscopes, when boats are used in the daylight, according to whether the sun is shining or the sky is cloudy.

Another very important matter is the question of buoyancy and the reserve of buoyancy, which, like most other factors in the construction of submersible boats, is closely related to the question of size. Very much depends upon the reserve of buoyancy with relation to the mean specific gravity of the water, and the passing from water of one gravity to another. In order to bring the boat to a position of submergence the buoyancy has to be overcome by filling the tanks, and it is obvious that the relation of the reserve of buoyancy to the displacement of the vessel is a matter of the first importance. It is evident also that if a very large volume of water has to be admitted this cannot be done with safety all at once, and yet it is of the utmost moment to abridge the period required for submergence. In this matter very great success has been attained, and the period has been shortened from a quarter of an hour or more to a very few minutes.

The seagoing qualities of submersible boats are now much greater than in the original boats of the class. Boats frequently behave well in bad weather, and in this respect, since they can be submerged or be partially submerged, present advantages over vessels which remain upon the surface. The boats answer well when running upon the surface, and unless the sea is very rough the conning-tower is kept open.   Here, however, as the experience of disasters has shown, the utmost care is necessary.   A certain tendency may be manifested when the boat is going at speed to run downwards, and therefore the question of keeping open or closed the manhole at the top is one requiring great judgment and constant watchfulness.

Cribb, Southsea

SUBMARINE A 12 OF THE SECOND BRITISH TYPE

Below the surface the depth of a submarine boat can now be kept with the most absolute accuracy, without a deviation of more than six inches.   It is obviously of great importance that submerged vessels should maintain their level at a constant depth, and though this has been a matter of considerable difficulty in the past, the diffi-

culties have been mostly overcome. In regard to stability, submerged boats are unlike all other classes of
vessels, for a vessel wholly submerged gives exactly the
same resistance to inclination in whatever direction it may
be attempted to incline her. · She can be moved with
equal ease—longitudinally, transversely, or obliquely ;
and, in relation to this matter and to the question of speed
below the surface, there are risks to be avoided of going
to considerable depths in a very short time, which may
happen if high speeds are attempted, and there is any
departure from an even keel.

These various considerations all tend to show that,
though submarine navigation presents problems of the
utmost difficulty and complexity, a great advance has
latterly been made in all that relates to this branch of
navigation. Both the surface and submerged motors are
now serviceable and satisfactory, though doubtless improvements will be made. The speed must continue to
be relatively low, especially in the submerged position,
and the range of action must be comparatively limited.

One notable fact is that up to the present time no
satisfactory means has been discovered of attacking submerged boat or boats in the awash condition. It is possible
that torpedo-boats or destroyers may yet carry small torpedoes, specially adapted for discharging at submarine
boats, but up to the present time, so long as boats of the
class remain invisible, or have the means of securing invisibility by submergence, they enjoy an immunity from
attack which is not possessed by any other class of vessels.
In short, invisibility is the very *raison d'être* of the submarine and submersible boat.

CHAPTER III

THE RELATIVE VALUE AND POWERS OF SUBMARINES

THE French, who took the lead and still hold it in the development of the means of submarine warfare, have, perhaps, the best right to speak upon its methods and possibilities. We must guard ourselves, on the one hand, from being induced by enthusiasts or imaginative writers to exaggerate the value of that which is good without exaggeration; while, on the other, we avoid the fatal tendency to despise what it would be dangerous or even fatal to despise. We must not think, because submarine and submersible boats are being built by all the great Powers, that therefore the battleship is doomed to decline, for we see that, just as submarine craft are constructed in larger numbers, so are battleships being built of greater size, thus illustrating the permanent value of the type upon which we depend to hold command of the sea.

The late Vice-Admiral Colomb, not long before he died, made some remarks at the Royal United Service Institution which may be cited in this place appropriately in relation to the attitude of not a few people towards preparations for submarine warfare. Of all men he had studied best the methods of warfare in old and modern time; from him we derive many of the conceptions which now rule our naval policy; to his writings we are accus-

tomed to appeal for the true philosophy of naval warfare
On the occasion referred to he said that all those who had
taken part officially in the providing of naval or military
matériel stood in relation thereto somewhat in the position
of a father towards his children.   They might be expected
therefore to regard what they had created with a certain
jealousy of affection, which might prove destructive, in
some degree, of their soundness of judgment.   He observed that there were many people directly interested,
in relation to this matter, in preserving the *status quo*, or
as conservatives in principle, and he added that, of all
these groups, the most important was that inert but
powerful mass of men who took things as they found them,
without reasoning as to why they existed, without observing their development or decline, and without applying
their critical faculties to discover the relation which they
might have to their changing surroundings.   People of
this class would accept a series of small changes all tending
towards the inevitable result, or even important modifications, if it were not pointed out to them that these
changes were incompatible with the old state of things.
Admiral Colomb was speaking at a time when submarine
navigation was in its infancy, and he had in his mind the
operations of destroyers or torpedo-boats rather than of
submarine vessels.

   But he described, nevertheless, the attitude of mind of
many of those who have begun by ignoring, and ended by
despising, the possibilities of submarine warfare.   There
have been those who thought that the introduction of
boats of the new class would end in the disappearance of
the battleship altogether, and many persons in France

hold this view at the present time. Even that distinguished author and thinker, the Admiral Jurien de la Gravière, writing before the submarine had become a practical engine of warfare, and having in his mind flotillas of destroyers and torpedo-boats, prognosticated the ultimate disappearance of the battleship, and made a remarkable historical analogy to illustrate the coming importance of the flotillas. He said that the military tactics of the Greeks were changed when the conquest of India brought elephants into the line of battle, and in the same way armoured vessels would long play the part in naval warfare which Antigonus, Seleucus, and Eumenes attributed to the monsters disciplined by Taxiles and Porus on the plains of Asia Minor. The elephants kept for nearly a century their place in the line of battle; they retired before the Roman legion; and armoured vessels, said the admiral, would end by disappearing also, though the hour had not yet come. The flotilla, as he conceived it, was composed of vessels of small dimensions, costing comparatively little. If he concentrated them, the colossi would vanish at their approach; if he dispersed them, a whole mercantile marine would be alarmed. Do not count losses, he added; the great art, the principal strength of warfare of this kind, consists in fearing nothing and in making sacrifices without scruple. "He is dead all the same," said the assassin of the Duc de Guise when put to the torture. Alluding to the torpedo in *Les Gueux de Mer*, the admiral said that the engine of gigantic destruction compressed into so small a space had its place properly only in the hands of desperate men. If it were subjected to calculation, or to the thought of personal safety, it

c

would deceive those who placed their hopes in it. Whether it was called a fire-ship or torpedo, it was an instrument of the *guerre à outrance*. "Confided to a fanatic, a patriot, or a sectary, it will rarely be found to fail."

But, though we may regard submarine warfare in the light presented, for the operations of torpedo flotillas, by this eminent French admiral, it is not necessary—indeed, it is very undesirable—to exaggerate the value or distort the function of the submersible, or to conclude, because these flotillas may issue from an enemy's ports, that what Jurien de la Gravière called the *marine des millions flottants* is therefore at an end. So experienced and enthusiastic an officer as Admiral Fournier, chief of the French Submarine Service, holds the very contrary. In his report on the French manœuvres of 1906, which is likely to be regarded for years as a most important contribution to the subject of submarine warfare, he said that it might be expected to find the battleship and the submersible weighed against one another in the balance or placed in opposition. It was therefore opportune to demonstrate that, far from mutually excluding one another in the conditions of modern naval warfare, these two types of vessels were eminently fitted, because of their extreme difference, to render help and assistance to one another. He alluded to the excellent results of associating a numerous flotilla of submersibles with a battle fleet, and he added that henceforth a fighting fleet would only attain its full value if associated with submersibles.

To discuss the subject of the employment and tactics of submarine and submersible boats is not the purpose here, but a few remarks based upon the opinions of some high authorities may be given. It has been proposed that submarine boats might even be carried on board battleships or transports specially constructed, so that they might take a part in fleet engagements. Owing, however, to the great difficulties that would attend the launching and hoisting in of boats in these conditions, it does not appear that any advance has been made or is contemplated in this direction. But it is, of course, possible that situations may occur in which submersible boats may be found in company with fleets at sea, and may find their opportunities in the naval battles of the future.

Undoubtedly the chief value of submarine craft is in the operations of coast defence : (1) in preventing blockade or bombardment ; (2) in making the disembarkation of. troops impossible or exceedingly perilous ; and (3) in forbidding the passage of narrow waterways to fleets or squadrons. It is possible that if the Russians had had submarines at Port Arthur the history of the late war might have been differently written. We may take it for granted that close blockades of ports, which played such a large part in the old wars, are now for ever impossible, and that observing blockades can alone be maintained. Admiral Fournier has pointed out the great superiority possessed by the mobile defence of a port by means of submarines over a fixed defence by means of batteries. The latter, even if sufficient for defence, could not resist an attack without considerable damage being done, whereas submarines should render the attack almost impossible. In the manœuvres to which reference was made, the submarine boats, both at Bizerta and Marseilles, were brilliantly successful. On the first two days each boat was successful twice, and on the third day three times, in torpedoing the bombarding vessels, which would never have made their attack in real warfare. Vessels bombarding or attempting to disembark troops would be so exposed to the menace of these small vessels that they would desist from any attempt if they were present. In short, the submersible boat is in these circumstances so powerful an offensive engine of warfare that it may hold at its mercy the vessels which would attempt this kind of attack. It has long been held by naval tacticians and strategists that the days of the close blockades are over, and that we shall never again see an inshore squadron closely watching the issue from an adversary's port with a battle squadron within signalling distance or within easy means of communication. It is true that observation can now be conducted from a much greater distance, and that indications of the direction taken by an adversary issuing from his port-may be communicated to a fleet at a distance in order that measures may be taken to bring him to action. Meanwhile we may be assured that submarine flotillas will render doubly impossible the old methods of warfare, which perhaps torpedo flotillas had rendered impossible before.

Apart from the tactics to be employed by submarine boats in the prevention of blockade and bombardment, they are destined to take a large part in the wider work of coast defence, adding immensely to the difficulties and dangers of attempts to disembark troops in places where submarine boats may be present or where their presence may be suspected. Submersibles have a much greater range of action than submarines properly so-called, and can therefore range along the coasts in order to attack fleets or squadrons of transports engaged in operations intended to bring about the disembarkation of troops. Admiral Fournier says, in fact, that a flotilla of submersibles would have effective means of action, and would prove the surest agency for rendering impossible or disastrous all attempts to disembark invading troops. In this way they should render it impossible for troops to land in the neighbourhood of naval ports or bases with the object of attacking them from the landward side. Admiral Fournier, indeed, speaks of the possibility of divisions of sea-going submersibles, supported by destroyers, issuing from the French ports or from Algiers and Tunis, in order to make cruises in the basins of the North Sea, the Channel, and the Western Mediterranean, thus adding immensely to the strength of the strategic position of his country. What is possible to one navy may certainly be possible to another, and it is probably as much with regard to the defence of our coasts as to the menacing of an enemy's fleets that the British Admiralty has entered upon its vigorous policy in the building of submersible boats.

That vessels of this class are destined to make infinitely more difficult and dangerous the navigation by battle squadrons of narrow waters, such as the Straits of Dover, is certain. The French are accustomed to consider mostly the danger with which they are menaced by Germany, and they depend chiefly upon their flotilla of destroyers and submarines to prevent the German fleet from passing through the Straits of Dover and meeting the French fleet before it has had time to concentrate. In the same way we might be quite sure that a German

fleet would not venture into the Channel, in face of our
submarine base at Dover, while its presence in the North
Sea would be rendered infinitely more dangerous.   It may
be that the moral influence in such cases will be greater
than the real effect.   We may consider also the peril that
might attend the return of a squadron to its own ports,
perhaps steaming slowly owing to damage suffered in
action, if submarine boats were known to be awaiting its
arrival in the approaches.

Officers of submarine craft in the British and French
navies have gained very greatly in the skill and the certainty with which they handle these vessels, and this is
true notwithstanding the disaster to the British A1, and
the catastrophes which overtook the *Farfadet* and *Lutin*
of the French.   Upon the progress in the British Navy
little light is thrown, though that great progress is being
made is beyond all doubt. The French are less reticent,
and Admiral Fournier in his report says that the successes attained by French boats have caused surprise in
naval circles because few are abreast of the progress
that has been realised.   It was assumed that the visibility of the periscope above the surface would reveal the
presence of an assailant, and would enable the menaced
vessel to escape ; but this, we are told, is not at all the
case.   A few years ago submersion was not easily or
quickly accomplished, and the periscope being fixed, it
was often observed by the vessels about to be attacked.
But nowadays the situation has changed.   The new periscopes, discreetly used, enable a better view to be obtained than was before possible, and the skill with which
French boats can approach an enemy without being dis-

covered is an indication of the great advance which has been made. It is, indeed, the ability to remain invisible in the approach which marks the skill of the commander of a submarine or submersible boat. In ordinary cases it is necessary only to allow the top of the periscopic apparatus to appear above the surface in order to ascertain the locality of the enemy. Then, withdrawing it, the boat advances, takes another observation, and so nears her mark, projecting the tube to take a final observation when the torpedo is ready to be discharged. All this, no doubt, is a matter of great skill, and only with long experience is proficiency attained.

As to the best way of escaping from submarine boats intending to attack, speed is no doubt highly important, combined with rapid turning power, and safety may be found in movement. It is maintained by some that the chances would be against the escape of a ship if she were already within range of a submersible which had taken measures to destroy her, but obviously this can only be a matter of opinion. Two methods have been proposed, one being to steam away as rapidly as possible outside the torpedo range of the assailant, while the other is to steam directly towards the boat with the object of running her down. Admiral Fournier says that the first of these is the only prudent method, if it be possible. As to the bolder plan, he thinks that its chances of success would be remote, and that the manœuvre might end in disaster. For the success of the submersible, the first requisite is that her enemy should be stationary, or that her course should bring her past the boat within torpedo range. It is also of immense importance for the boat to remain unseen, and of equal importance for her to see clearly, for if the enemy turn away the direction for firing the torpedoes would be quite different from what it would be if she stood straight on. The closer the submarine can approach to the enemy the better her chance ; but she must keep on the enemy's bow, for, if left astern, she can do nothing. Therefore speed is important for a ship passing through waters likely to be infested with submarine boats, and it may be assumed that a ship has a distinct and definite area of danger before her extending probably about three points on either bow. It is possible that a couple of destroyers steaming ahead, a little on the port and starboard bow, might discover submarine boats and give warning. Perhaps, also, some contrivance for the destruction of submarine boats may yet be discovered.

Enough has now been said to illustrate the methods which are open to the submarine boats, and to suggest the course which may be taken to evade them. They will operate chiefly in the neighbourhood of ports or in narrow waters, and are not likely to be encountered in the open sea. It is also possible that in the early days of a war they might be much in evidence, but that, through disaster and the dangers to which they would be subjected, their menace would grow less, and if the war were continued long it might disappear. But that the submersible boat is an engine of war to which very great importance is now properly attached, and which no maritime nation can afford to neglect, is abundantly proved.

THE ILL-FATED SUBMARINE A 1

Running trials after being repaired and refitted

Cribb, Southsea

CHAPTER IV

THE MORALITY OF SUBMARINE WARFARE

"War's a brain-spattering, wind-pipe slitting art. It is not to be 'humanised,' but only abolished one fine day when nations have cut their wisdom teeth."

"Inter arma silent leges."

"All's fair in love and war."

"The sea-fights of the future, with improved ships, guns, and range-finders, may be fought at ranges almost beyond the ken of unaided human vision. It is to be hoped that before that time arrives the progress of civilisation, intellect, and humanity will have consigned all weapons of war to the museum of the antiquary, and that other methods than war may have been discovered for preserving the peace and virility of men and nations."

In the early years of the nineteenth century the writer of an article in the *Naval Chronicle*, devoted to a consideration of Fulton's schemes, stigmatised his torpedoes and submarine boats as "revolting to every noble principle," their projector as a "crafty, murderous ruffian," and his patrons as "openly stooping from their lofty stations to superintend the construction of such detestable machines, that promised destruction to maritime establishments." He went on to protest against the policy of encouraging inventions that tended to innovate on the triumphant system of naval warfare in which England excelled, and he concluded thus :—

"Guy Fawkes is got afloat, battles in future may be fought under water ; our invincible ships of the line may give place to horrible and unknown structures, our projects to catamarans, our pilots to divers, our hardy, dauntless tars to *submarine assassins ;* coffers, rockets, catamarans, infernals, water-worms, and fire-devils ! How honourable ! how fascinating is such an enumeration ' How glorious, how fortunate for Britain are discoveries like these ! How less worthy of being adopted by a people made wanton by naval victories, by a nation whose empire are the seas ' "

It is quite evident that even in this advanced Twentieth Century there exist many Britons who in their heart of heart agree with this writer, and who cherish the idea, though they may not openly express it, that there is something mean and underhanded, something dishonourable and " un-English " in all methods of under-water warfare. The Englishman prides himself on being a lover of fair play, and so long as the odds are more or less equal he is ready to enjoy any contest or sport. The average Englishman is neither a hot-headed Jingoist nor a peace-at-any-price humanitarian ; he regards wars as unfortunate necessities of modern civilization, and he likes to see them waged fairly and squarely, each side observing the rules of the game. As regards warfare on land, it must be confessed that he has had to correct some of his ideas since the Boer war. He would have preferred the enemy to come out into the open and fight like men. Instead of this, they took every precaution to avoid being seen, and our army found that it had to face an invisible foe. From the Boers we have learnt the lesson of the value of cover and entrenchments, and now officers and men, however much they may dislike it, are forced to seek and utilise cover whenever possible, making it their aim to hit their opponents and to avoid being hit themselves.

"Let us admit it fairly as a business people should—
We have had no end of a lesson, it will do us no end of good."

In naval warfare we have had an opportunity of learning lessons in the light of actual experience, for there has been the first big battle on the seas since Trafalgar ; but no light has been thrown upon the newest engine of warfare. It is thus possible for men to hold different opinions as to the value of submarine fighting, and we consequently find that there are numerous people who, whilst they would not go so far as to declare mines, torpedoes, and submarine boats unlawful, yet consider them as methods better fitted to the requirements of other nations than to those of the Mistress of the Seas.

Modern submarine warfare was introduced by two Americans, David Bushnell and Robert Fulton, and forced itself into prominence during the American War of Independence. The spar-torpedo originated in America ; the Whitehead torpedo was first adopted by the Austrian Government ; and Norway, Sweden, Denmark, France, and Austria all began to build torpedo-boats before Great Britain condescended to add them to her Navy.

As to submarine vessels, Greece and Turkey purchased Nordenfelt boats in 1887. France built her first boat in 1888, and the United States purchased their first submarine, the *Holland*, in 1900. Great Britain followed other nations in the matter of mines, torpedoes, and submarine boats, and adopted such methods of warfare because other nations forced her to do so, profiting by their experience.

Before the advent of the torpedo-boat Great Britain was secure in her position of Mistress of the Seas, so long as she possessed more line-of-battle ships than any other nation. The arrival of the torpedo-boat, the destroyer, and the submarine, all armed with the Whitehead torpedo, has given weaker nations the chance of attacking our iron-clads with new weapons, and there are even those who affirm that the battleship is doomed, and must give way to a different type of craft.

The whole trend of modern invention may prove to the advantage of weaker nations. Earl St. Vincent described under-water methods as " a mode of war which they, who commanded the seas, did not want, and which, if success-ful, would deprive them of it." It is quite true that Great Britain would sooner trust to her guns and her line-of-battle ships than to her torpedoes and torpedo craft in actions on the high seas, but owing to other nations—admittedly weaker—having adopted the tor-pedo, she had no choice but to adopt it also in order to maintain her naval supremacy. So long as she provides herself not only with methods of submarine attack, but also with means of warding off the under-water attacks of the enemy, other nations are not likely to wrest the command of the seas from her.

It is idle to lament the advancement of Science. Man is an inventive animal, and is ever trying to inaugurate new devices and improve on old ones. For hundreds of years the sailing ship held the field, and guns and cannon underwent but little change. During the " Wonderful Century," however, changes began in earnest. The wooden sailing ship disappeared, and the steam-driven ironclad took its place, whilst rifled ordnance, high explosive shells, and powerful propellants were introduced.

The fish torpedo made its appearance, and the swift torpedo vessel followed in its wake, and we have now submarine boats and turbine-driven men-of-war, and are threatened with aerial machines for the launching of aerial torpedoes both on armies and on fleets.

What the future has in store none can foresee, and until the next great struggle between first-class Powers the value of this modern engine of warfare may remain doubtful. All that is certain at present is that Great Britain cannot afford to dispense with submarine boats, and has no intention of doing so.

We may seem to have wandered a long way from the "morality of submarine warfare," but our purpose has been to show that when certain people argue—as they have done seriously — that torpedo warfare should be declared contrary to the laws and customs of war, they are, to a certain extent, influenced by the fact that the torpedo is a weapon which Great Britain could very well do without, provided it was taboo by other nations.

No one, not even a member of the Peace Society, would urge the suppression of the Lee-Metford or the quick-firer, because Great Britain relies on these for the maintenance of her place in the front rank of the nations of the world, and the argument as to the " illegitimacy " of the torpedo depends largely on the fact that other nations gain and Great Britain loses by its adoption.

There have been persons who have argued in favour of giving no quarter to crews of torpedo-boats and sub-

marines that might fall into our hands, and have suggested that we could explain such action to the other
Powers, to whose advantage it is to use such weapons,
by saying that though we had been driven to employ such
methods we were forced to treat the practice with severity.
Such a course of action would cut both ways, and we suspect our own torpedoists would be very much averse to it.

Strange engines of warfare and new modes of fighting
are received by the bulk of a nation, whose instincts are
conservative and whose minds are incapable of imagining
a state of things other than that which prevails at the
moment, in much the same way as are new inventions.
They are first of all scouted as impossible : then, if
possible, of no utility , and finally, when they have been
universally adopted, they are declared to be no novelties
at all.   Just as many old ladies have been heard to declare that they will never travel by the Twopenny Tube,
so nations have been known to disclaim all intention of
using particular weapons.   Yet after a time we find the
old ladies in the Tube and the nations employing the
weapons.   Familiarity breeds contempt.

The earliest man—*Homo sapiens*—fought with his fists,
his legs, and his teeth.   Gradually he made for himself
weapons, deriving his first instruction in their manufacture by observing the ways in which the animal creation
fought one another.   His earliest weapons were made of
wood, bone, and stone, and in due course there were
evolved the spear, the waddy, the boomerang, the hatchet,
the tomahawk, the bow and arrow, the pike, the lance,
the axe, the sword, and other implements.

It is exceedingly probable that the adoption of a new

engine of warfare by a tribe would be condemned by another tribe—to whom it had not occurred to use it—as illegitimate ; but it is equally probable that, while sturdily protesting against the use of one weapon, the tribe would be slyly endeavouring to procure one more deadly still.

The first great revolution in the art of war was the introduction of gunpowder, both as a propelling agent and also as a charge for shells and bombs. Although the explosive nature of saltpetre when mixed with carbon and charcoal was doubtless known to the Chinese some centuries before the Christian era, our first knowledge of the use of gunpowder as a military agent dates from the seventh century, when it was used by the Byzantine emperors under the name of " Greek fire " in the defence of Constantinople against the Saracens.

" Greek fire," the invention of which is commonly attributed to Callinicus in 668 A.D., consisted probably of pounded resin or bitumen, sulphur, naphtha, and nitre. There were three ways of employing it : it was poured out burning from ladles on besiegers, it was projected out of tubes to a distance, and it was shot from *balistæ* burning on tow, tied to arrows. Its effect was probably rather moral than material.

Geoffrey de Vinesauf, in an account of a naval battle in the time of Richard I, writes thus of Greek fire : " The fire, with a deadly stench and livid flames, consumes flint and iron ; and, unquenchable by water, can only be extinguished by sand or vinegar. What more direful than a naval conflict ! What more fatal, when so various a fate envolves the combatants, for they are

D

either burnt and writhe in the flames, shipwrecked and
swallowed up by the waves, or wounded and perish by
arms ? "

Despite the lamentations of the humanitarians of the
time, Greek fire and serpents (missiles resembling rockets
charged with and impelled by the slow explosion of a
certain mixture) continued to be used in the Navy until
the reign of Richard III.

· Another favourite method of naval warfare was the
" fire-ship." Falkiner, an old writer, tells us that fire-
ships were used by the Rhodians in 190 B.C. They were
certainly used by the Greeks ; they were employed by
ourselves against the Armada, and they first appeared
in our Navy List in the year 1675 ; they were used in the
Dutch and French wars at the close of that century, but
probably fell into disuse in the eighteenth. It is·quite
clear that with the French, as well as with ourselves, the
crews of fire-ships did not expect quarter. Admiral
Gambier deprecated fire-ships as being a " horrible and
anti-Christian mode of warfare " ; while Lord Cochrane
said that if any attempts were made upon the British
squadron by fire-ships they would be " boarded by the
numerous row-boats on guard, the crews murdered, and
the fire-ships turned in a harmless direction."

Lord Dunsany appeared to think that this apparently
cruel rule of no quarter to the crews of fire - ships
worked well for humanity in practice, and he seemed to
be in favour of its being extended to the crews of torpedo-
boats and submarines. His Lordship pointed out, in a
lecture at the Royal United Service Institution, that the
crews of fire-ships did not stick to their ships till the

moment of explosion, but after firing the fuse made their escape in boats, which boats, as they passed through the enemy's lines, would naturally become targets, and if meanwhile some ship clasped in the deadly embrace of the fire-ship had exploded, it was all the more likely that the fugitives would be the objects of unsparing vengeance.

"Probably then the vague but fatal epithet 'un-English' came to attach to men who used a deadly weapon, but withdrew themselves (sometimes too quickly) from the fray. I cannot produce evidence of the facts, but I believe that officers serving in fire-ships did not stand high with their brother officers. Yet before the close of the great war officers of the greatest courage and repute were eager to serve in boats of this class."

The first use of gunpowder as a propelling agent was in Spain in the twelfth century, at which period both the Moors and the Christians used artillery. It was first employed in warfare in England in 1327 by Edward III in his war against the Scotch, the cannon from which the shot was fired being termed "Crakys of war."

There is abundant evidence that the use of artillery in battle was at first thought to be improper. When cannon was employed at Chioggia in the fourteenth century all Italy made complaint against this manifest contravention of fair warfare ; the ruling classes, seeing their armour, lances, and knightly prowess rendered useless, vigorously opposed the newly-invented arms, declaring that they were calculated to extinguish personal bravery. Perhaps this sentiment may have had some weight with our Navy, for it was not until towards the close of the sixteenth

century that artillery finally assumed the position of the
dominant arm in the service and that musketry fire altogether displaced the arrow and the bolt.

Shells appear to have been first used by the Sultan of
Gujarat in 1480, and they were in general use about the
middle of the seventeenth century.

There is no doubt whatever that shells and bombs were
considered highly immoral by the side which did *not* employ them.   To those accustomed only to fire solid shot
there must have been something very terrifying in the
hurling of shells filled with explosives which when they
burst slew those round about and set fire to dwellings and
ships.

When the *Bomb Ketch,* a ship firing bombs and shells,
was introduced into our navy in the seventeenth century,
the French were particularly angered by the "inhumanity" of the English in firing "inflammable fire balls
and shells."—Again, in the eighteenth century we find
the Maréchal de Conflans issuing an order against the use
of hollow shot or incendiary shell because they "were not
generally used by polite nations, and the French ought
to fight according to the laws of honour."

At the battle of the Nile in 1798 the French flagship
L'Orient took fire and blew up, and it has been said that
when the French sailors reproached the English for using
incendiary missiles the latter repudiated the charge, and
mentioned that they had found such unlawful weapons in
one of the prizes they had taken, and that thus the hollow-
ness of the French regard for humane warfare was demonstrated.

Whilst Great Britain did not scruple to fire lyddite

shells at the Boers, their wives, and their children at
Paardeberg, she prided herself on her abstention from the
use of explosive or expanding bullets, and much abuse
was heaped on the Boers for their employment of such.
It may, however, be doubted whether a bullet which kills
you right off at once, or, at any rate, which disables you
permanently for a long time, is not preferable to one
which is of so mild a nature that you can be shot over
and over again, alternating your appearances on the
battlefield with visits to the hospital.

A lecture on " Explosive Bullets and their Application
to Military Purposes " was delivered before the Royal
United Service Institution in 1868 by Major G. V. Fosbery, the first officer to use these projectiles in the field,
systematically and to any large extent, against some of the
mountain tribes of the North-West frontier of India.
The lecturer tells us that the natives considered them unfair on two grounds—firstly, because they exploded in
an objectionable way; secondly, because there was nothing
they could collect of them afterwards, as in the case of
ordinary bullets. But more civilised people complained
of the use of "rifle shell" on the ground of their Satanic
nature, and to these Major Fosbery replied as follows :

" The arguments which condemn a warlike instrument
simply on the grounds of its destructiveness to life, provided that it neither adds keen agony to wounds nor new
terrors to death itself, are, if logically pursued, simply
retrogressive, and even if not recommending by implica-
tion a return to the bow and arrow, at all events point
to the old times of protracted wars and deaths from
fatigue and disease far exceeding in number those caused

by the weapons of an enemy. We can therefore afford
to set these on one side, or rather we are bound to neglect
them altogether and seriously consider any invention
which under the conditions above laid down promises us
a more certainly destructive fire than that attainable
cœteris paribus by the arms at present included in our
war material "

In spite of opinions such as these the humanitarians
have won the day, and explosive bullets are now taboo
by Great Britain. The great Duke of Wellington used to
say that he should not like to see the bullet reduced in
size, because it broke the bone, and the object of war was
either to kill your man or else put him in hospital and
keep him there. With the Mauser and the Lee-Metford
neither of these results is attained.

. The prototypes of the modern submarine torpedo,
although they were employed on the surface of the water
and not below,-were the " machine," the " infernal," the
" catamaran," the " powder vessel," etc.

" Machines " may be best described as fire-ships specially arranged so as to explode very destructively when
alongside one of the enemy's vessels. They are first
found in the British Navy in the seventeenth century,
but were soon discontinued—not, we are afraid, on humanitarian grounds, but because Bushnell and Fulton pointed
the way to the more convenient explosive device known
as the " torpedo."

In the year 1650 Prince Rupert made an attempt to
b'ow up the English Vice-Admiral in the *Leopard* by a
species of " infernal." He sent a couple of negroes and
one of his seamen in Portuguese dress alongside the

Leopard in a shore boat. They carried with them what purported to be a barrel of oil, but the barrel really held an infernal machine to be fired by a pistol attachment, the trigger of which could be pulled by a string passing through the bung. The story goes that one of the crew of the boat, finding the lower deck ports closed, " uttered an exclamation " in English. This betrayed them, but Blake refused to take vengeance on them, though the trick was one he would himself have scorned to play on his adversary.

During the war between Great Britain and the United States in 1812 the *Ramillies*, of seventy-four guns, was so unfortunate as to be the object of attack both by a diving vessel carrying torpedoes and by a powder-ship. The *Ramillies* was lying off New London at anchor and maintaining the blockade. As she was known to be short of provisions, the Americans fitted out a schooner and filled the hold with powder, covering it over in the hatchways with barrels of flour. By means of an ingenious piece of clockwork attached to a gun-lock and a train leading to the powder its explosion was ensured at the intended time. The *Ramillies*, suspecting nothing, but thanking Heaven for the gift, captured the vessel, and the crew escaped to land. By some extraordinary chance (or was it destiny ?) the schooner was ordered to anchor near another prize some distance from the *Ramillies*, so that when the clockwork reached the fatal hour, 2.30, the charge exploded and blew up, not the *Ramillies* with her captain, Sir Thomas Hardy, and crew of six hundred men, but only the prize crew who were in the schooner.

The naval historian James could not trust himself to

comment upon " this most atrocious proceeding " ; whilst a naval officer wrote : " A quantity of arsenic in the flour would have been so perfectly compatible with the rest of the contrivance that we wonder it was not resorted to. Should actions like this receive the sanction of Governments, the science of war and the laws of nations will degenerate into the barbarity of the Algerians, and pillage will take the place of kindness and humanity to our enemies."

During the American Civil War a species of weapon known as a " coal torpedo " was employed. This consisted of a hollow lump of iron, filled with a charge of dynamite. It was rubbed over with coal-tar and dust, and exactly resembled a large lump of coal. Lord Dunsany thought that this certainly seemed to be on the verge of lawful, if not beyond it.

At the close of the eighteenth century David Bushnell inaugurated the era of submarine warfare by devising cases filled with explosives, arranged to go off at a set time by clockwork. To enable these cases to be affixed to the sides of vessels Bushnell invented the first boat capable of diving beneath the waves of which we have any definite details. His attempts to blow up the *Eagle* in 1776 by a case fastened on her bottom, and the *Cerberus* in 1777 by means of a towing torpedo, failed, owing more to the lack of skill on the part of the operator, Serjeant Ezra Lee, than to any defect in the apparatus employed. Nor was Bushnell successful in his effort to destroy vessels in the Delaware by the aid of a number of kegs filled with powder and set adrift.

The introduction of gunpowder, of Greek fire, of fire-

Crib, Shelltea

SUBMARINE B 2 OF THE THIRD BRITISH TYPE

ships, of artillery, of shells, of bombs, of machines, of infernals, of catamarans, of powder-vessels, having, as has been shown, been at one time or another denounced as immoral by certain " humanitarians," it was but natural that a secret contrivance for bringing about a terrific explosion *beneath* an unsuspecting ship's crew should have been believed to be an invention of the Evil One ; and history affords proof that the novel modes of fighting introduced by Bushnell and Fulton were regarded with great disfavour by naval men, who considered the innovators as men " who would discredit the glorious traditions of our Navy, and substitute a set of catamarans for the noble frigates that had carried our flag to victory and were the pride of the nation " ; by humanitarians, who regarded the torpedoes as a " dishonest and cowardly system of warfare " ; and by the public generally, who denounced the nations who attempted to compass the destruction of British ships of the line by dastardly tricks which England would never stoop to employ.

In a work written by James Kelly, and published in 1818, the author comments with great severity on " some infamous and insidious attempts to destroy British men-of-war upon the coasts of America by torpedoes and other explosive machinery." This refers to the attacks on the *Ramillies* by one of Fulton's boats, attacks which failed, but which caused Sir Thomas Hardy to notify the American Government that he had ordered on board from fifty to one hundred American prisoners of war, " who, in the event of the effort to destroy the ship by torpedoes or other infernal inventions being successful, would share the fate of himself and his crew." So frightened were the

relations and friends of prisoners of war by these threats
that public meetings were held, and petitions were presented to the American executive against the further
employment of torpedoes in the ordinary course of
warfare.

Those who endeavoured to perfect a system of submarine mining for the defence of harbours and coasts were
abused in the same way that Bushnell and Fulton had
been. Samuel Colt, the inventor of the pistol which bore
his name, and one of the first to experiment with mines
fired from shore by means of an electric current, was
roundly denounced by John Quincy Adams, who dubbed
him "that Guy Fawkes afloat."

At the time of the Crimean War the popular term
"infernal machine" was applied to the submarine mines
laid down by the Russians to defend the approaches to
Cronstadt. In the seventies Lieut.-Col. Martin endeavoured to establish, on the grounds of humanity, an
international anti-torpedo association ; while even now
there are people found to protest against the employment of certain forms of torpedoes, as witness the following letter published a few years ago in the *Engineer*. The
author, Mr. Reginald Bolton, declared that while no one
could object to the defensive lay torpedo or the spar
torpedo, the same could not be said of the "Whitehead,"
"Brennan," or "Edison."

"Surely," he urged, "our forefathers' code of morality
in warfare should not be in advance of our own. All
civilised nations have debarred the brutal explosive
bullet, and why not the equally mean submarine torpedo ?
If such a remedy as Commodore Hardy's were to be

applied by any nation, could its opponent complain, and is there anything in the practice of morality to prevent, say, a thousand prisoners' lives being presented as a bar to the use of an implement which was acknowledged to be a disgrace to its employers not less than eighty years ago?"

The methods of warfare which have most aroused the ire of humanitarians and " blatant platform orators, with their vulgar party cries of eternal peace," are those which depend for their success on secrecy or deceit. Powder-vessels, coal torpedoes, *et hoc genus omne*, are condemned because they pretend to be what in reality they are not, and torpedoes and submarine boats because they advance in secrecy without giving the enemy any chance of firing at them or of protecting themselves against their insidious attacks beneath the water-line.

The arguments of the humanitarians, who are doubtless well meaning enough, are inconsistent, because, while they raise no protest against certain modes of conducting war, they unreservedly condemn other methods—mainly, it must be observed, because of their novelty. Such a class of person resembles the Quaker who found himself in a vessel engaged in a conflict with another vessel. He resolutely refused to assist in fighting the guns, but at last, when the enemy attempted to board, he collared the leader and pitched him into the sea, saying as he did so, " Friend, thou hast no business here."

Major Fosbery, in his lecture on explosive bullets, asked whether any of the deaths due to fighting were, strictly speaking, humane, and if they were not, what was this humanity of which so much was made? " Have we not heard that in the dark ages humanity beat out men's brains with a mace, whilst cruelty used the lance, the sword, and the arrow, and that bishops of the period rode into action with the mace so as to kill without shedding blood ? A very nice distinction indeed, as you will admit. In later times, were not Congreve and Shrapnel denounced as monsters for the initiation of inventions in whose perfection we rejoice to-day ? "

Inconsistency, indeed, is the particular failing of Peace propagandists. They not only condemn the use of certain weapons while raising no protest against others equally as destructive of life, but they also pretend to be horrified at deeds committed by the enemy which they themselves would not scruple to do should opportunity offer. Particularly is this the case in savage warfare. Captain Herbert has mentioned a striking instance during the Zulu War. One day the boys were calling in the streets, " Shocking *murder* of a whole British regiment " (it was at Isandlwhana), and a few weeks afterwards the same boys were shouting, " Great *slaughter* of the Zulus." This is akin to the practice of those orators who refer to the "expansion" of England, but to the "encroachment " of Russia.

As to the " inhumanity " of the submarine vessel, Mr. Nordenfelt, it may be noted, would not admit that there was anything especially cruel or horrible in the idea of a diving torpedo-boat. War altogether was cruel and horrible, and caused an enormous amount of pain and suffering, but any invention which tended to shorten a war or to protect common or private property during war would really diminish this suffering on the whole. Humanitarians had urged that there was something especially cruel in the secrecy of the submarine boat, but the whole tendency of war had, he pointed out, moved in this direction ever since the days of old, when Hector and Achilles advanced in front of their respective followers and spent half an hour in abusing their adversary's parents and ancestors before they commenced to fight.

EMERGING TO TAKE BEARINGS

The whole object of modern warfare is to keep the enemy ignorant of your whereabouts and your actions, and to mislead him whenever possible, and for this reason smokeless powder, torpedoes, disappearing guns, etc., have come into use; false attacks are considered admissible, and every advantage is taken of cover and entrenchments. The only "cover" possible in naval warfare is beneath the waves, and it is difficult to see any greater inhumanity in submarine than in military mining, which certainly dates from very early times. If it be lawful to sap and mine before a fortified town, and to blow up an army as it marches unsuspectingly over " mined " ground, it is surely permissible to send ships sky-high by mines and to sink them by torpedoes.

Mr A F. Yarrow has remarked that it seemed strange that an artilleryman behind ten or twenty feet of earthwork, hurling explosive shells at an almost unseen foe, should be held as fighting fairly ; while in the case of the torpedoist, who has the pluck to accompany his missile to within a short distance of his enemy, it should be considered an unfair mode of attack.

Yet so it is, and writers in recent times have placed submarine warfare on a par with guerilla warfare and train-wrecking. "The torpedoing of a single German ironclad by a submarine would almost certainly be followed by a refusal to recognise submarines as belligerents."

The question of the laws and usages of civilised warfare has been the subject of many books and articles, and conferences have been called to endeavour to arrive at some understanding on the subject, but no interdiction of submarine boats has resulted. An International Conference on the " Usages of War," held at Brussels in 1874 at the instance of Alexander II, considered among other things " the means of injuring an enemy," and suggested the prohibition of the use of poison and poisoned weapons, murder by treachery, and murder of a disarmed enemy, projectiles causing unnecessary suffering, and prohibited by the declaration of St. Petersburg in 1818 ; " ruses de guerre " were, however, declared permissible.

In relation to these subjects, it is interesting to note that differences arose at this Conference between the representatives of the large States, possessing great standing armies, and of the minor States with small armies. The former thought that war should be the business of professional trained soldiers, that they, and as a rule they alone, should fight, that war should follow a regular course, and that the worthlessness, from a military point of view, of the sporadic efforts of partisan warfare should be recognised, and that when a battle was won, and the seat of Government was in the possession of an invader, the inhabitants should respect the conquerors as the *de facto* and *de jure* Government. If they interrupted communications and cut off isolated bodies of troops, they were to be dealt with, not as honourable combatants, but as assassins and marauders.

The " Geneva Convention " met at Geneva on 8 August, 1864, and on the 22nd of the same month an International Code was adopted by all civilised powers except the United States. The code mainly concerned itself with the succour of the wounded in time of war, and certain cruel methods of warfare, such as the use of explosive bullets, were condemned, Great Britain agreeing not to use such weapons in war against civilised nations.

The Peace Conference at the Hague was opened on 18 May, 1899. Of the eight proposals submitted for discussion, the second was the prohibition of the use of new arms and explosives, the third the restriction of the use of existing explosives and the prohibition of projectiles and explosives from balloons, and the fourth the prohibition of submarine torpedo-boats and the agreement not to construct boats with rams in the future.

The final act embodying the results of the Conference contained three declarations. (1) Prohibition of the throwing of projectiles and explosives from balloons or any other analogous means This prohibition to be in force for five years. (2) Prohibition of projectiles intended solely to diffuse asphyxiating or deleterious gases. (3) Prohibition of the use of bullets which expand easily in the human body.

It may be noted that Great Britain did not bind herself to accept any of these three declarations.

" The laws of war," wrote Montague Bernard, " are nothing at all but the usages according to which warfare by land and sea is carried on, and the collection of the whole body of usages represents what we call the laws of war. . . . The student of history is apt to be a little puzzled by frequent reference to ' *laws* ' with which he is tacitly assumed to be familiar. What are these laws ? Where are they written ? What authority do they command ? They are a body of *usages*, for the most part conditional, which have arisen principally from motives of convenience and the extension of commerce."

It is, of course, recognised that the only force which supports international law is the appeal to the conscience of the nation, for there is no international tribunal to punish countries for deeds committed in time of war. While it is unlikely that the rough game of war ever will be played (it certainly never has been in the past) in exact conformity with the rules of the jurists, there are certain methods of waging war which England would not employ, and certain acts which she would not commit in the event of hostilities breaking out between herself and a civilised country.

She would not use explosive bullets. She would not fire on undefended towns, and would endeavour to avoid the destruction of non-combatants and their property. She would not poison wells ; she would not endeavour to accomplish the assassination of a commander-in-chief ; she would not abuse a flag of truce ; she would not murder prisoners who behaved themselves, and put to death those who surrendered.

On the other hand, she would consider herself at perfect liberty to employ submarine boats, torpedoes, and mines, both military and naval ; to discharge shells filled with high explosives, whether lyddite, melinite, or other substance, from aerial machines ; to intercept the enemy's messages and to mislead him by sending false ones ; to commence hostilities without issuing a declaration of war * ; to fire on, and if necessary sink, the merchant ships of the enemy ; to starve a garrisoned town ; to erect wire entanglements and similar obstructions ; to offer wrecking lights as navigation lights ; and to employ any " stratagem " or " ruse de guerre " which might serve some useful end. With regard to stratagems, it appears to be quite proper to disguise ships and men, and to use false signals, false colours, and neutral flags, though a British naval officer would probably not fire into his enemy before hauling down his neutral or false colours.

Vice-Admiral Rodney M. Lloyd pointed to the curious anomaly that while in naval warfare all stratagems were admitted, expected, and provided against, in military operations, on the contrary, some acts of a similar kind

* The Romans considered that no war could be just unless it was preceded by a formal declaration.

appeared to be objected to. The Boers, for instance, frequently disguised themselves in British khaki uniforms, and endeavoured to delude sentries and guards.

Some writers refer to this as the "abuse of the khaki uniform" and "the treacherous use of the khaki uniform," but if such things are permitted in naval opera-

BENEATH THE WAVES

tions it is difficult to see why they should be considered immoral if practised on land.

Apropos it may be mentioned that during some Russian naval manœuvres the admiral's ship was destroyed by the following trick. A party of volunteers from other squadrons came alongside the cruiser *Africa*, the flagship, in a Finnish coasting smack, and one of the volunteers, dressed as a peasant, came on board with a telegram.

Whilst the attention of the *Africa's* crew was diverted the other volunteers fastened a small buoy, with the inscription, " Frigate *Prince Pojarsky*," under the stern of the flagship.

Of course, there is a very thin line which separates what is considered fair and what is considered unfair warfare among civilised communities. Lord Dunsany said that he was not perfectly sure that there could not be something said in favour of poisoning wells. " We have heard something about poisoning the air. The French some time ago had what they called *boulets asphyxiants*. These would have utterly poisoned a whole ship's crew. If these missiles may be used, then it comes to this : that it is lawful to poison the air, but not lawful to poison the water."

Lyddite shells were thought rather to resemble these *boulets asphyxiants*, for their stench was reported to be terribly stupefying to those in the immediate neighbourhood when they burst. But whereas explosive shells fired from guns are considered " legitimate," shells fired from rifles are regarded as " illegitimate."

Respecting the question of poisoning wells, Colonel Lonsdale Hale has remarked that so long as this was done openly, and the fact notified in some way to those who would use them, there seemed to be nothing more to be said against this forbidden practice than against the permitted practice of depriving the enemy of good water supply by filling in wells and by cutting off the good water, as the Germans did at Metz and Paris, and reducing their enemy's water supply to the sewage-receiving

Moselle and Seine. If it was permissible to starve one's enemy by denying him solid food, it seemed to him equally permissible to starve him by denying him liquid food.

Wolff and Bynkerhoeck, two of the originators of international law, thought the use of poison in warfare perfectly legitimate. Vattel considered the practice interdicted by the law of nature which did not allow of the multiplying the evils of war beyond all bounds. To get the better of the enemy he must be struck, and if once disabled, what necessity, he asked, was there that he should eventually die of wounds ?

Opinion also differs as to the morality of attacking undefended towns and injuring the property of non-combatants during a war.

The late Admiral Aube, when he was head of the French Admiralty, said the proper way of bringing this country to order was to burn Brighton and Scarborough and a few other places ; and Admiral Sir J. C. Dalrymple Hay, Bart., has remarked that he could not say he thought that he was wrong. According to the latter, the object of each side is to do the greatest possible destruction to the enemy, and also to make him cave in ; the whole of the country is engaged in war, they pay taxes for the war, they encourage their soldiers and sailors to fight courageously, they suffer for the war in various ways, and they urge it on ; and they must expect to suffer accordingly.

Humanitarians affirm that in actual war soldiers and sailors of the Dalrymple Hay school would be too human to act up to their expressed opinions ; the probability is that England would only resort to such measures if the enemy were determined to employ them. Vice-Admiral Bourgois, in his book *Les Torpilleurs*, made a strong protest against the doctrines of those who advocated the bombardment of undefended towns and the sinking without warning of defenceless merchant ships. He urged that the nationality of the vessel should first be verified, and then provision made for the crew and passengers.

Apart from the " Hague enthusiasts," who are for prohibiting the employment of high explosives, aerial torpedoes, and submarine torpedo-boats, there is another class of humanitarians who urge the adoption of all new and deadly engines of warfare, apparently with the idea that if war is made sufficiently terrible no nation would dare fight another. " The more terrible the anticipation of naval war," says a writer, " as fashion and science continue the contest, the less likely will be its realisation."

The late M. Bloch, as we know, considered war to be tactically, strategically, economically, and morally impossible. Since that time the war in the Far East has taken place, larger numbers of men have been put in the field than ever before, and the Russian fleet has been destroyed.

Admiral Porter, of the U.S. Navy, considered that if war was made so dangerous that every combatant would to a certainty be killed, then there would be an end of the business, and the Peace Society could put up their shutters.

The newspapers, especially the halfpenny ones, have often informed us of the discovery of new engines of warfare of terrible potency. Mr. Tesla was going to wipe out the British Fleet by simply touching a button on his

waistcoat or elsewhere.   Mr. Hudson Maxim had devised
a method of throwing aerial torpedoes, carrying each of
them one ton of high explosive, which was so efficacious
that one cruiser lying just out of range of our guns would
destroy all our battleships with the greatest ease.   Dr.
Barton was building an airship which would throw explosives on the enemy below, who would be powerless to
retaliate, and so on.

The wars of the future, so the halfpenny journalists
informed us, would be either waged under the seas or
above the clouds, and we seemed to be approaching the
time imagined by Lord Tennyson, whose swain (in
" Locksley Hall ")—

" Heard the heavens filled with shouting, and there rained a
        ghastly dew
   From the nations' airy navies grappling in the central blue "

If wars ever die out, it will certainly *not* be owing to
the destructive capabilities of the weapons employed.   In
the eyes of old Geoffrey de Vinesauf the naval conflicts
of his time were as terrible as he could well imagine them
to be ; but they have now grown far more terrible ; they
have been witnessed in all their horror, and yet we hear
of no further proposal to modify their fearful character
or forbid the use of submarine boats in war.

Those who are in favour of utilising the latest resources
of science for the purpose of warfare are in reality more
humane in the truest sense of the word than those who
seek to limit nations in their choice of weapons.   Admiral
Sir John Fisher, who was one of those chosen to represent
Great Britain at the Hague Conference, expressed himself strongly on the cruelty of making war on " humane "

or moderate principles; and it is an undoubted fact that, in spite of the deadly nature of modern arms, wars, on land at least, are not so destructive of life, nor do they cause so much misery and suffering, as they did formerly.

We can speak with more certainty with regard to warfare on land than we can to warfare on sea; but though the next great naval fight between two nations will certainly entail terrible suffering on the combatants (as the naval actions in the Far East did), it may be said that on the whole they will neither cause such wholesale misery nor be so protracted as the naval battles of old.

"Every war," said Captain Herbert in an excellent lecture at the Royal United Service Institution on "The Ethics of Warfare," "marks a step. In 1885 the Servians, when they invaded Bulgaria, paid conscientiously in good coin for every fowl or pig seized in farmhouses, for every glass of brandy drunk in village inns; and when the tables were turned, and the Bulgarians invaded Servia, the Bulgarian soldiers and the Servian traders fraternised most cordially in the alehouses of Pirot. To come to the latest European war—that between Turkey and Greece in 1897—we have the testimony of the war correspondents that the behaviour of the Ottoman soldiery was quite exemplary. If things continue in this wise we shall perchance hear in the next century of every rifle discharge being preceded by a conciliatory caution and every bursted shell being followed by a humble apology."

Dr. J. Macdonell has also touched on this important subject. "It must be owned," he said, "that the progress in mitigating the evils of war has been immense— that acts of useless violence which were once habitual

are now exceptional, and are punished or condemned by
military opinion.   Ask those who say, 'Things are much
as they were · the grim realities of war are no better than
before,' to note the matter-of-fact way in which old
writers relate cruelties as the necessary accompaniments
of warfare ; then compare with such passages some of
the many handbooks published by European Governments for the use of their troops.   It has been truly said
that the difference between the methods of the Thirty
Years' War and of the War of the Spanish Succession is
the difference between darkness and twilight ; the difference between warfare as understood by Tilly and Pappen-
heim and that described in modern official Manuals is the
difference between light and darkness.   Everywhere it is
recognised that only effective injuries are justifiable.   The
modern soldier strikes hard ; he doesn't mutilate or
destroy for the love of destruction."

The Rev. Edmund Warre has drawn a vivid picture
of the wretched plight of the slaves labouring at the oars,
who suffered intense discomfort and were in continual
danger.

" In a hot climate, with but very little ventilation, it
must have been exceedingly trying to take part in a
laborious mechanical toil with perhaps some hundred or
two of human beings stark naked and packed so closely
that there was not room, as Cicero says, for even *one* man
more.   The heat, the smells, the toil must · have been
terrible to any one undergoing it against his will—so
terrible as to suggest that even death itself were better
than such drudgery.   A dull, dead feeling of despair must
have crept over man and crew in such a case, and though

the lash might keep them going under ordinary circumstances, such spirits could not be relied upon in times of emergency. Besides the question of discomfort, the actual danger was very great. The crews were liable at any moment to be drowned or burnt, or, in the case of defeat, butchered by the victors—perhaps, as at Sybota, deliberately in cold blood. Conceive the moment of conflict and its horrors when the sharp-pointed beak came crashing through the timbers, smashing them right and left along with the helpless mass of human beings, while the water followed swift upon the blow, perhaps just giving time to the Thranites (the rowers on the topmost of the three benches in the Trireme, who had the most work and the longest oars) to swarm up upon the deck, while the helpless Thalamites (the rowers on the lowest bench) were drowned at once."

Science, although she is continually placing man in possession of weapons more terrible and more destructive than those of the previous generation, really acts for the good of humanity at large, who owe a debt of gratitude to the mechanical geniuses who have evolved modes of warfare which enable war to be waged with as little unpleasantness as possible to the peaceful populations that have no concern with it.

In one respect, at least, modern warfare is certainly more humane than that of olden times, and this is in the treatment of the wounded and the captured. In ancient warfare the fate of the captive was death or slavery, and in early battles no quarter was given, except to personages of great distinction, and the object of both sides was to slay as many of their opponents as possible ; and as surrender only made the prisoner the perquisite of his captor, the fighting was both bloody and fierce. Even as late as 1780 a prisoner was still viewed as the property of the victor, and there was a regular scale or tariff of payments.

One instance, culled from an account of a battle between Christians and Turks, written by Geoffrey de Vinesauf, must suffice.

" Drawing the hostile galley with them to the shore the victors exposed it to be destroyed by our people of both sexes who met it on land. Then our women seized and dragged the Turks by the hair, beheading them and treating them with every indignity and savagely stabbing them, and the weaker their hands so much the more protracted were the pains of death to the vanquished, for they cut off their heads, not with swords, but with knives."

Dr. Macdonell has pointed out that the only notable survival of barbarism in respect to captives was the rule —abrogated apparently in some countries, but retained by us for reasons never satisfactorily explained—that the crews of private vessels captured at sea were treated as prisoners of war.

In the next great fight on the seas, if a submarine boat should be hit by the quick-firing guns of a battleship she is endeavouring to destroy, her crew, provided they are not sunk like rats in a trap, will be picked up by the ironclad's boats and kept as prisoners of war till hostilities are at an end.

We are reminded of some lines in Mr. Kipling's poem, " Kitchener's School "—·

"They terribly carpet the earth with dead, and before their canuou
   cool
   They walk unharmed by twos and threes, and call the living to
   school."

Those who argue in favour of the suppression of under-
water warfare have pointed out that whereas the battleship can save the crew of the torpedo vessel, the latter,
owing to her small size, can only steam away, sending the
big ship to the bottom, and leave the unfortunate crew
to drown or save themselves as best they can, which, with
shell and shot flying about, would not be easy. A way
out of the difficulty has not been found yet.

What, then, is the conclusion of the whole matter ? It
is this. Since the object of war is peace, make war as
deadly as possible ; since your goal is complete conquest,
use all efforts to get it over as quickly as possible. This
is the tendency of all modern warfare on sea. The
destruction is as swift as the consequences are far-
reaching. As a modern writer has said :—

"Save us from the cruel mercies of the weak. War—
that splendid mistress for whose favours we have all
longed since we reached man's estate—must be given her
full attributes and painted in her most deadly colours in
order that the misery, which undoubtedly she brings to
the majority of the population, may extend over as short
a period as possible. Let us make her as deadly as we
can, in the name of humanity and of every good feeling."

CHAPTER V

THE MECHANISM OF THE SUBMARINE, AND
· SUBMARINES OF THE FUTURE

MR H. G. WELLS, in his *Anticipations*, confessed that his imagination, in spite even of spurring, refused to see any sort of submarine doing anything but suffocate its crew and founder at sea. " It must involve physical inconvenience of the most demoralising sort simply to be in one for any length of time. . . . You may of course throw out a torpedo or so with as much chance of hitting vitally as you would have if you were blindfolded, · turned round three times, and told to fire revolver-shots at a charging elephant. . . . Given a derelict ironclad on a still night within sight of land, a carefully handled submarine might succeed in groping its way to it and destroying it ; but then it would be much better to attack such a vessel and capture it boldly with a few desperate men in a tug. At the utmost, the submarine will be used in narrow waters, in rivers, or to fluster or destroy ships in harbour, or with poor-spirited crews—that is to say, it will simply be an added power in the hands of the nation that is predominant at sea. And even then, it can be merely destructive, while a sane and high-spirited fighter will always be dissatisfied if, with an undisputable superiority of force, he fails to take."

Mr. Wells had probably not kept himself in touch with the latest developments of submarine navigation when he wrote this "anticipation." Since that time great advances have taken place. Boats have made, and do make, long passages at sea, submerging and emerging with ease and certainty, and discharging torpedoes with remarkable success both at stationary and moving targets French boats have proceeded from port to port. British boats have behaved remarkably well at sea ; and the state of affairs Mr. Wells anticipated will not come to pass.

The *David* represented the best type of under-water vessel in the sixties, but that she was infinitely inferior to British, French, and American vessels of to-day goes without saying, and it will not be surprising if the submarine of thirty years hence bears the same resemblance to the original *Holland* as the *Holland* does to the *David*.

The ideal submarine boat has a speed as great as that of the fastest torpedo-boat, a very wide range of action, excellent sea-keeping powers, unlimited quantities of air for power and for respiration by the crew ; a means of directing her course by vision upon a moving object whilst herself remaining invisible beneath the surface, and she must be very habitable and comfortable for long periods of time.

The submarine of to-day lacks many of these attributes. She has a comparatively slow rate of speed, whether on the surface or submerged, a narrow range of action, poor sea-keeping powers, though suffering little when submerged, a limited quantity of compressed air, and is practically blind when beneath the waves. Thus she differs greatly from the ideal boat as sketched above, but great progress has been made, and further gradual improvement may be safely predicted.

We propose in this chapter to describe, in simple language, the working of a vessel intended for under-water navigation, and to consider what improvements are likely to take place.

Every submarine boat worked by a crew must of necessity be capable of floating on the surface of the water. This is a self-evident proposition, for the crew must have means of ingress and egress; and the only practical way of entering and leaving the boat is by an opening in the hull when she is on the surface.

We have no doubt that the files of the Patent Office would show that many inventors have designed boats which would sink to a certain depth directly they were placed in the water. While in such a system no time would be lost in submersion, there would undeniably be difficulties in the way of coming to the surface, etc.

The first problem, then, which confronts the designer of a submarine boat is to find the most suitable method of sinking her to the depth at which it is intended to navigate.

The most fundamental law of hydrostatics, which applies to all floating bodies, and is equally true of wholly submerged vessels floating at any depth, as of ships of ordinary form floating on the surface, having only a portion of their volume immersed, is that a ship floating freely and at rest in still water must displace a volume of water having a weight equal to her own weight.

The " displacement " of a vessel is defined as the

weight of water displaced, which is equal to the weight
of the vessel and that of her lading. A ship floating on
the surface " displaces " a certain weight of water, and
in order to force her beneath the surface two methods
are open.

In the first place, her weight is increased by the introduction of water ballast ; thus her " displacement " is
altered, and she sinks until her weight is again equal to
the volume of water displaced.

In the second, the weight of the boat would remain
constant, but the displacement would be altered by the

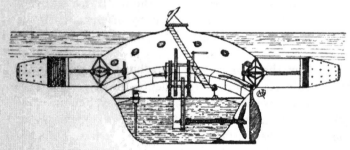

THE SUBMARINE OF ANDRÉ CONSTANTIN (1870)

drawing in of " cylinders " or " drums," the boat thus
sinking until her displacement again equalled her weight.

The first inventor to employ the latter method was
André Constantin, who built a vessel during the siege of
Paris, which was furnished with pistons working in two
cylinders ; on these being drawn in from the interior the
boat sank to the required depth. The actual trials were,
however, not satisfactory. The *Nautilus*, of Messrs.
Campbell and Ash, which underwent some trials in Til-

F

bury Docks in 1888, depended also on the pulling in of cylinders (ten were employed, five on each side of the vessel) for her submersion ; the results were equally discouraging, and some eminent men nearly lost their lives owing to the erratic behaviour of this craft.

No serious ship-constructor would nowadays think of adopting this method of submersion, and we may therefore pass on to consider boats which are brought to the submerged condition by the admission of water into special reservoirs or tanks.

Submarine boats, so far as their immersion is concerned, may be divided into two classes.

1. Those which when submerged possess no floatability.

2. Those which in the same condition possess a small reserve buoyancy or floatability

Modern submarines almost without exception belong to the second division, as this class has been found to possess great advantages over the first.

1. Submarines with no Floatability when Submerged.

Boats upon this plan would possess when submerged a total weight equal to the weight of water displaced, and no margin of buoyancy. During immersion it has been found necessary in such boats to make the weight of the vessel and its contents slightly exceed the weight of water displaced by the total volume of the vessel ; this excess of weight causes a downward motion which rapidly accelerates unless checked, and care must be taken to regulate, either automatically or otherwise, the depth, lest the vessel sink to a depth where the pressure is greater than she can withstand.

M. Goubet, one of the unappreciated pioneers of modern submarine navigation, was a believer in the " no-floata-bility " idea, but it has, for some time past, been regarded with disfavour. Theoretically it is possible to navigate

"GOUBET II"

a submarine whose total weight equals the weight of water displaced so that she keeps at a given level with-out rising or sinking, but the system will not work satis-factorily when put to severe and prolonged tests. It is found to be impossible to obtain perfect equality between the two weights : submarine currents, variations in the weight of water and in atmospheric pressure and temperature, and movements inside the boat, all tending to disturb its equilibrium.

2. Submarines Possessing Floatability when Submerged.

Mr. Nordenfelt realised the superiority of submarines possessing a reserve buoyancy when submerged over

M. GOUBET ABOUT TO GO UNDER WATER IN HIS BOAT

those which possessed no buoyancy, and all the most important of latter-day submarines fall under this division.

It is quite obvious that should any accident happen, such as the entry of water, the failure of the machinery, the asphyxiation of the crew (rendering the detaching of a false keel impossible), etc., the submarine with sufficient reserve buoyancy should at once rise to the surface, barring accidents ; while the boat with no floatability would remain where she was and then gradually commence to sink, owing to the fact that it is almost impossible to prevent water from finding its way, little by little, into the boat.

In submarines which possess floatability when submerged some mechanical means must be resorted to to force them below the surface. The first operation consists in introducing a certain amount of water into the tanks so that the boat is brought to the " awash " condition, with the greater part of the hull below water and only the conning-tower, etc., appearing above the waves, and a sufficiency of water ballast being admitted to overcome the buoyancy as desired, the mechanical means are employed to overcome the buoyant reserve. Complete submersion has been attained in two ways : by screws on vertical shafts employed to " screw " the vessel below the surface, whether at rest or whilst moving, and by horizontal rudders, or planes, used to steer the boat below the surface ; this latter method, which is now almost universally employed, is only applicable to moving vessels.*

IMMERSION BY SCREWS MOUNTED ON A VERTICAL SHAFT.

Just as a ship is driven backwards and forwards in the horizontal plane by means of a screw or screws mounted on a horizontal shaft, so it is possible to drive a vessel up and down the vertical plane by means of one or more

* A system of moving weights was employed by Drzewiecki and other inventors.

screws immersed in the water and mounted on a vertical shaft, the boat by this method being literally " screwed down " into the liquid.

The principle of the vertical screw was adopted·by Bushnell, who, in the description of his submarine vessel, writes : " At the top there was likewise an oar for ascending and descending or continuing at any particular depth. . . . When the skilful operator had obtained an equilibrium (by means of the forcing pumps) he could row upwards and downwards or continue at any particular depth with an oar placed near the top of the vessel, formed upon the principle of the screw, the axis of the oar entering the vessel. By turning the oar one way he raised the vessel, by turning it the other he depressed it."

M. Gaget remarks that " it is very strange that Bushnell should have discovered and concealed with so much care the instrument of propulsion which Sauvage studied and introduced fifty years later." The fact is, of course, that the principle·of the screw-propeller was known in the seventeenth century, and that in May, 1785, Joseph Bramah patented a screw-propeller, identical in general arrangement with those in use to-day. The first practical use of the screw was made by John Stevens, who in 1804 launched a steamboat eighteen feet long by fourteen feet beam with a direct acting high-pressure engine having a tubular boiler and driving a screw with four blades. Although the principle of the screw for ship propulsion was thus recognised at this early period, it was not till the thirties (of the nineteenth century) that the screw-propeller succeeded in attracting the attention of the engineering world.

Professor Tuck in his boat (1884) placed the propeller directly beneath the centre of the hull, so that it should submerge on an even keel.

Mr. Nordenfelt used vertical screws, which at first he fitted inside sponsons, but afterwards in the fore and aft line, and considered it absolutely essential that a diving boat should be kept horizontal when being submerged, as any inclination downwards with the impetus of a heavy boat would, he considered, almost to a certainty

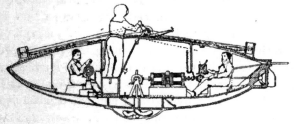

PROFESSOR TUCK'S SUBMARINE (1884)

carry the boat below its safe depth before it could be effectually counteracted by shifting weights. Such a theory was soon shown to be founded on a misapprehension.

Some inventors (Waddington, Baker, etc.) have used four screws operating in pits equidistant from the centre of the boat, two on the upper part and two on the under part ; but all such methods have been discarded in the newest designs.

IMMERSION BY HORIZONTAL RUDDERS.

The ordinary vertical rudder steers the ship either to port or starboard in the horizontal plane, and the horizontal rudder is used similarly to control the submarine's position in the vertical plane. This method of steering a boat beneath the surface by the inclination of horizontal rudders is, of course, only applicable when the boat is moving.

The position that the horizontal rudder or rudders should occupy is a question about which much has been written, and opinion appears to be still divided on the subject. Some hold that they should be placed at the stern, others that they should be placed on either side of the vessel; and these latter again differ as to whether they should be forward, amidship, or aft. In spite of all the arguments in favour of placing the rudders forward, Captain Hovgaard considered that this disposition could hardly be recommended except in very long boats where it might prove a necessity. The *Gustave Zédé* has six diving rudders—two forward, two in the centre, and two aft; whilst in the *Narval* class there are four rudders—two forward and two aft; the *Holland* submarines have aft rudders only.

Control in the Vertical Plane.

That beautiful machine, the Whitehead torpedo, is maintained at a set depth below the surface by means of a pendulum and a hydrostatic valve which regulate the horizontal rudders, and also in its true course by the gyroscope. In the case of the submarine, it is necessary that she should not pass a certain limit when on her downward course, and that she keep so far as is possible the same level throughout her run under water. Boats being unable to withstand the pressure of the surrounding water below a certain depth, automatic means may be provided to prevent the dangerous limit being exceeded.

Though Mr. Nordenfelt thought that a submarine boat could only be submerged on an even keel, modern boats go down and rise at a slight angle, using their horizontal rudders to direct the course downward or upward. The control of the submarine in the vertical plane is accomplished by the manipulation of the rudders, either automatically, by means of some such arrangement as the hydrostatic valve or pendulum, or by hand, and she can be kept on an even keel and prevented from rising to the surface or sinking to the bottom, when running beneath the waves, by the pumping of water from a reservoir situated aft to one situated forward, or vice versa, by the admission of water into trimming tanks, by shifting weights, etc. These operations can be carried out either automatically or by hand-operated mechanism.

It will be readily understood that while it is a comparatively simple matter to force a vessel beneath the surface to a depth previously determined, it has not always been easy to ensure her keeping at this depth during the whole time of submergence, and maintaining throughout the run a perfectly even keel; but in this matter experience has brought high skill, and it is now possible to keep the depth of a submarine boat with great accuracy by hand power, the deviation often not exceeding six inches, so that automatic arrangements are by some considered unnecessary.

One of the greatest difficulties the inventor of submarine boats has to overcome is their lack of longitudinal

stability. Submerged vessels, as has been explained, are
of two classes—those which are equal in weight to the
water they displace, and those which are lighter. Both
classes are subject to various disturbances which tend to
upset their longitudinal stability and send them up to
the surface and down towards the bottom. In a later
chapter mention is made of the difficulties experienced by
those who had to navigate the *Nordenfelt*.

The principal causes of disturbance were summed up
by Captain Hovgaard in a paper entitled, " The Motion
of Submarine Boats in the Vertical Plane," read before
the Institution of Naval Architects at the Annual Meeting
in 1901 ; and Sir William White has more recently discussed the question in the *Times*

1. Faulty use of horizontal rudder.   2. Admission of
water through leakages.   3. Expulsion of foul air and
products of combustion.   3a. Firing of torpedoes and
projectiles.   4. Movements of crew.   5. Existence of free
surfaces of liquid.— 6. Movements of loose weights, such
as fuel.   7. Variations of buoyancy caused by varying
density of sea-water. 8. Grounding and collision. 9. Variations in speed.

Some of the most important of these disturbances may
be briefly discussed

1. Most modern submarines are provided with more
than one pair of horizontal rudders, but if all the rudders
should refuse to act and the boat is running down an inclined plane, the only thing to be done is to blow the
water out of the tanks or detach a weight, and thus
bring the boat to the surface.

2. By the careful construction of the hull, and by strict

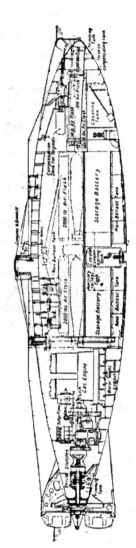

INTERIOR OF THE FIRST BRITISH SUBMARINE (NOS. 1–5)

control of all sea-valves, the admission of water may be prevented. If the boat is stove in and water enters in any quantity, she will inevitably sink. The collision of the conning-tower of A 1 with the hull of the vessel she struck at Spithead, whereby large quantities of water were admitted, and the disasters of the French boats *Farfadet* and *Lutin*, are illustrations of the consequences of such accidents. As a means of escape some inventors have proposed to provide their submarines with detachable boats.

3. Usually the length of the run under water will not be so great that the foul air will need to be got rid of. If necessary, it can be expelled by drawing on the store of compressed air, and as the substances withdrawn will always be small, no change in longitudinal balance need be feared if precautions are taken. As all modern submarines are driven by electricity beneath the surface, the expulsion of products of combustion need not be considered.

3a. In the earliest submarine boats the torpedoes consisted of charges of explosive in cases, which were attached to the outside of the vessel to be attacked, or were towed against her sides.

Those who had little faith in the future of under-water warfare declared that a torpedo could never be fired from a tube in a submerged vessel without disastrous effects. The Nordenfelt boats were certainly not successful in discharging torpedoes, for as a general rule they as nearly as possible stood up vertically on their tails and proceeded to plunge to the bottom stern first on these occasions. However, since then submarines have fired torpedoes quite satisfactorily under water, and the difficulty is no longer felt.

The expulsion of a torpedo from a vessel totally submerged in the water, whether equal to or less than the weight of the water displaced, naturally reduces her weight and tends to send her up towards the surface. This tendency can best be counteracted by the admission of a certain quantity of water ballast into the boat.

The method now usually followed is to allow the surrounding water to enter the tube immediately after the launch of the torpedo, and as the weight of the volume of water admitted will be about equal to that of the missile ejected, the longitudinal stability of the submarine should not be disturbed. When the second torpedo comes to be placed in the tube, the volume of water already in it must of necessity be ejected, and a compensating reservoir may be used to receive it. As each torpedo is fired a certain amount of water, corresponding to the weight of the projectile, must be allowed to enter the compensating reservoir. This may be done automatically.

The *Engineer*, in a leader, on 18 January, 1901, said : " The discharge of a bow torpedo (by a submarine) would be instantly followed by the rise of the bow ; relieved of the weight, the boat would tend to stand on end. If going ahead at the time she would immediately come to the surface to be destroyed. If going astern she would plunge downwards, and the consequences might be equally serious. . . . Torpedoes must be fired when the submarine is at rest."

In spite of this dogma, submarines have repeatedly

fired torpedoes whilst in motion with success, and in modern submarines ample provision is made for the loss of weight occasioned by the discharge of the torpedo.

4. Reference has been made to the fact that when the Nordenfelt boat was moving along on an even keel, and a greaser walked forward a couple of feet in his engine-room, her head would go down a little, the water would surge forward in the tanks, and she would plunge to the bottom, unless checked in time. It has been said that one man going forward in a submarine boat would cause her to dive to a depth of thirty-six feet in one minute. The movements of the crew may be compensated for by automatic arrangements, but the ideal method would be one in which every one would remain immovable at his post during the submerged run. Officers and. men of submarine vessels have now become very skilled in the handling of these craft, and they act with the greatest certainty and success .

Steering Below Water.

Quite early in the history of submarine navigation it was found that the compass was not so reliable when the boat was navigating under water as it was when she was on the surface. This is not to be wondered at, for the compass of a submarine is placed in the interior of a tightly-closed metallic shell, and in close proximity to an electro-motor and powerful currents capable of. influencing it considerably, if not of rendering it altogether useless.

The principal causes of the unreliability of the compass in a submerged boat are :—

1. The currents normally produced by the electric motor.

2. The abnormal currents flowing in certain unknown parts of the hull owing to lack of proper insulation.

3. The permanent or transitory magnetisation of the hull if made of a magnetic metal.

The best position for the compass in a submarine has been a much-debated point, but it is now generally agreed to be in the centre of the hull.

M. Maurice Gaget, in his book *La Navigation Sous-Marine*, stated that so entirely untrustworthy and impracticable had steering by compass in French submarines been found, that the gyroscope had been requisitioned. He inclined to the belief that this instrument was the best indicator of route that had yet been devised, yet he pointed out the want of some reliable method by which the distance made by a submerged boat could be gauged with accuracy.

MOTIVE POWER.

The question of the best method of propulsion for submarine boats must be considered under two heads, namely, propulsion on the surface and below the water.

It will be quite evident that the conditions under which a motor in a submarine works differ according as the boat is running above or beneath the surface ; and we arrive at the conclusion that if the same motor is ever to serve for both conditions special arrangements will have to be made to permit it to work under abnormal conditions.

Every heat engine consumes both air and fuel (whether coal, oil, gas, etc.), and the process of absorption of the fuel is accompanied by the giving out of a certain weight of the substance in the form of gas. If a boat could use such engines beneath the water its weight would be continually modified, and it wou'd be practically impossible to compensate for this change by the addition of water

INSIDE THE "GOUBET"

to the reservoirs. Besides this difficulty, the combustion of the fuel would not only absorb a large quantity of the air which is so precious a quantity in a submerged vessel, but would also set free deleterious gases, which naturally would have prejudicial effects on the health of the crew. It may therefore be asserted that a submarine can only be propelled under water by means of a motor capable of working without combustion or loss of weight. It re-

G

mained therefore to discover the most suitable method fulfilling these conditions.

1. *By Mechanical Means such as Clockwork, Springs, etc.* —The Howell torpedo was driven by means of a heavy flywheel in the interior, which was spun up to 10,000 revolutions a minute before discharging by means of special machinery. While all these methods are practicable, they have been put aside as unsuitable owing to the slowness of the speed which a boat thus propelled could attain.

2. *Compressed Air.*—In order that a submarine may be driven at a high rate of speed for a considerable distance, such a large store of compressed air would have to be carried, if this method were adopted, that little space would be left in the vessel for any other purposes. In addition to this, such a store o˙ compressed air would be a source of danger.

3. *Manual-Power* —The earliest submarines were, of course, driven by hand-power, but no one nowadays would think of adopting this method.

4 *Steam from Heated Water.*—Mr. Nordenfelt propelled his boats beneath the surface by means of the steam given off by the heated water in the cisterns, and this was found sufficient for a distance run of fourteen miles. He disliked accumulators, and this is not to be wondered at, for in his time they were very far from perfect ; were he designing a submarine to-day, however, it is probable that he would choose electricity for sub-surface working.

5. *Chemical Engines.*—Dr. Payerne, d'Allest, and others, by means of a *chaudière pyrotechnique*, burnt, in hermetically closed furnaces, combustibles containing in

themselves the oxygen necessary for their combustion, and got rid of the products of combustion by ingenious devices.

6. *Electricity.*—All modern submarines rely on an electric motor for under-water propulsion, the current being derived from accumulators, and the accumulators being recharged by the gasoline or other engines working a dynamo when on the surface. The ideal primary battery and the ideal accumulator are probably still to seek ; but the latter improves yearly, and there is little doubt that some few years hence the current available will enable the submarine to make long voyages under water with greatly increased speed. It was said that the *Holland* on no fewer than four occasions burned up the armature of her motor, and some device seemed to be wanted to keep the armature cool.

PROPULSION ON THE SURFACE.

While the " Holland " boats for the British and United States navies, and the new types developed from them, are driven on the surface by gasoline engines, this type of motor was not used in the early French boats, a steam engine, fed with liquid fuel, being employed in the *Narval* and vessels of this class ; while in the *Gustave Zédé, Morse,* etc., electricity is the sole motive power both above and below the waves. France avoided the use of gasoline owing to the danger which arises from its presence on board submarine craft. But in the new submersible classes, in which the normal position is on the surface, special sets of engines have, of course, to be provided for surface navigation, while for propulsion submerged storage batteries are brought into operation.

(a) *The Steam Engine.*—In the Nordenfelt boat steam was raised, when running on the surface, by the burning of coal, but since that time the advances made in the employment of liquid fuel have led almost to the exclusive

THE GASOLINE ENGINES OF THE FIRST BRITISH SUBMARINES

employment of this combustible for submarine boat propulsion. The great drawback to the use of the steam engine is the length of time necessary for the unshipping of the chimney, the cooling of the engines, etc., whereby, as in the *Narval* class, submersion is retarded.

(b) *The Oil Engine.*—Various types of these engines are now used in submarine boats, and much better results are

attained than were possible a few years ago ; but there
are still defects which the ingenuity of the engineer will
probably overcome.

Those who make the dogmatic assertion that the submarine boat cannot be very fast because she cannot be
endowed with much power, remind one of the wiseacres
who were so convinced that steamboats would never replace sailing-vessels, nor steam locomotives the horse-
drawn coach.

In the discussion which followed the reading of Mr.
Nordenfelt's paper on Submarine Boats at the Royal
United Service Institution in 1886, Mr. Anderson, c.e ,
stated that it was well known, through the late Mr.
Froude's investigation, that a fish-shaped vessel under
water was in much more favourable circumstances for
obtaining high speed than any vessel on the surface of
the water, because it had been established theoretically
that a vessel of easy lines completely submarine met with
no resistance at all except the skin friction of the water,
no resistance, that was to say, such as that which arose
from the bow wave.

Mr. Anderson went on to say that he believed that if
Mr. Nordenfelt would apply a little more ingenuity and
perseverance to the perfecting of his boat, the result
would be the attainment of a very high speed under water,
and consequently a most formidable vessel   Mr. Nordenfelt himself said that it was absolutely proved that the
speed below for a given consumption of fuel for a given
boat must be greater than the speed above.   The fric-
tional resistance is less for a completely submerged body
than one travelling on the surface, because no waves are

created, and the water that is displaced in front closes in behind and helps to push the body forward. A boat moving on the surface throws out waves in front and on either side, and that means an absolute loss of energy , and for this reason a Whitehead torpedo travels faster under the water than on the surface. While this is true, theoretically and practically, the fact remains that in all recent submarine and submersible boats the surface speed is much greater than the speed submerged, this being due, of course, to the oil engines used on the surface having greater power than is attainable with the accumulators below water.

ARMAMENT.

The armament of the boats designed by Bushnell and Fulton was a case of explosive ; the armament of the *David*, that sank the *Housatonic*, was a spar-torpedo ; but the armament of all modern submarines is the automobile fish-torpedo. Mr. Holland in his earlier designs provided his boats with guns, but submarine cannon, firing heavy shells, have since been discarded.

In the earliest class of British submarines one torpedo expulsion tube is fitted at the extreme forward end of the vessel, opening outward 2 ft. below the light water-line, five Whitehead torpedoes, each 11 ft. 8 in long, being carried. But in later British and foreign boats the number of tubes has been increased. Our A, B, and C classes are immensely better than the original type.

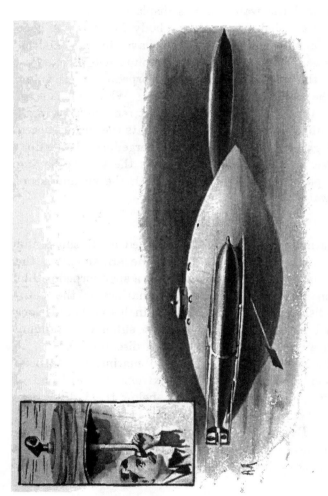

THE ARMAMENT AND THE PERISCOPE OF THE "GOUBET"

SAFETY AND HABITABILITY.

It may safely be said that no difficulty will be found in getting sailors to form the crew of a submarine boat in time of war. Great Britain, the United States, France, and other great naval Powers have only to call, and hundreds of brave fellows will volunteer, however great the odds against which they may have to fight. This being the case, our naval constructors must see to it that every precaution is taken to make the boats as safe and as habitable as possible.

Captain R. H. S Bacon, recently Inspecting Captain of Submarine Boats, made some remarks upon this question in the course of a discussion following a paper on " The Future of the Submarine Boat " at the Royal United Service Institution in June, 1904. He said :—

" I do not know whether the fact has ever struck any of you that one of the main considerations in the design of a submarine boat is a knowledge of the psychical conditions of the men. It is not merely a question of taking a man and putting him into a submarine. The man who designs a submarine boat that is going to be of any use has to study his crews, has to watch his officers, and has to watch his men ; he has to see the effect that a confined space has upon them, he has to watch the effect that submergence has on them, and one thing that comes out more than another is that you cannot put a man in a compartment that is too small. This is the death-blow to all little submarines—' Goubets,' and boats of that sort. This is largely because of the impossibility of getting men working under normal conditions in abnormally confined

spaces, and a man not under normal conditions is sure
. to be flurried and useless."

The accidents to which a submarine is subject are many.
The most serious is passing the safe limit of depth.   If
she descends beneath this limit the pressure will increase ;
her hull will be battered in ; she will diminish in volume ;
her downward course will be rapidly accentuated, and
there must inevitably follow the crushing in of the boat
and the death of the crew.

For every boat there is a limiting depth, beyond which
she must not go.   While it is quite possible to construct
a boat strong enough to resist the pressure at depths of
50 fathoms and over, it will not be necessary to go
deeper than 5 to 6 fathoms, or enough to clear the
keel of a big ship.   Still, it will be well to give the boat
a hull capable of resisting pressures greater than those
she will normally encounter.   By means of a hydrostatic
valve, or some similar arrangement, the submarine may
be kept from diving to too great depths.

Submarines possessing floatability have the power of
rising to the surface should any accident happen to the
motive power, steering gear, machinery, etc., and automatic arrangements are provided for working the horizontal rudders in order to keep the boat on an even keel.
Accident might, however, cause the boat to begin to sink,
and the advisability of the submarine carrying a false
bottom or detachable keel has been recognised, as this
could be dropped in an emergency, causing the vessel to
rise at once to the surface.   In the case of the French
boat *Lutin*, sunk near Bizerta, it appears, however, that
rust or damage caused the safety appliances to jam, so
that they could not be operated.

The vessel *Le Plongeur* carried a detachable boat, and Captain Hovgaard in his design also supplied such a boat. It was made to stand the same pressure as the submarine itself, and rested in a saddle-shaped packing, against which it was tightly pressed down by means of a number of clips. Inside the packing was a circular door in the boat, and a corresponding and smaller one in the ship, arranged in such a way that it was possible to get up into the boat, close the lower lid in the ship, and then the lid in the boat This done, all the handles of the clips were turned, and the water was to enter the space inside the packing, and if not, it might be made to do so through a small pipe leading from the outside to the space, and provided with a stopcock. The boat would now have a certain buoyancy, but would hang on in two main clips, placed one at each end of the detachable boat on mechanical connection with each other, so that they could only be let go both at the same time, thereby preventing jamming. When these clips were opened the boat would ascend to the surface ; communication with the vessel, if somebody should be left behind, might be kept up by telephonic connection.

M Goubet, M. Drzewiecki, and other inventors have provided their vessels with means for being propelled by the crew, working either oars or pedals, in the event of the machinery failing to act.

Respiration, or breathing, is a part of the life of all organisms, whether animal or vegetable. Air is taken into the lungs ; the oxygen is absorbed, while the carbonic acid is given back again to the atmosphere. The respiration of human beings or animals in closed chambers

to which the air is denied access is not possible beyond a
certain period.   The oxygen is sooner. or later, according
to the size of the chamber, used up, and the air becomes
so vitiated with the carbonic acid expelled by the lungs
that the vital functions of the body are arrested.

Many of the earlier submarine boats carried no reserve
of air, as the time that they were intended to remain
under water was not long ; but reference is made in old
writings to the " chymicall liquor " supposed to have
been used by Cornelius Drebbel to restore the purity of
the air in his under-water vessel.   What its composition
was we shall never know.

The air required for respiration in a submarine vessel
may be supplied in two ways.

1. By some chemical-method which purifies and re-
generates the vitiated air.

2. By compressed air or oxygen carried in special
reservoirs.   · ·

3. By pipes leading down from the surface to the submerged vessel, through which fresh air is drawn and the
foul air expelled.

4. By the return of the boat to the surface and the
taking in of a fresh supply of air.

Such substances as caustic soda, lime, bromide of mag-
nesium, etc., are capable of absorbing carbonic acid, and
have been used, but modern submarine vessels rely on
compressed-air compartments, in which, for breathing
and ventilation, air at 2000 pounds to the square inch is
stored.   In foreign boats the problem of air supply has
been solved, and boats have remained as long as sixteen
hours under water without the slightest strain.   Experi-

Cribb Southsea

THE NEW FLOATING DOCK FOR BRITISH SUBMARINES

ments have also been made with chemical substances of comparatively light weight, which would not only completely remove from vitiated air the carbonic acid, water vapour, and other non-respirable products, but would also automatically restore to it in exchange the quantity of oxygen which it lacked. In other words, the substance, when placed in contact with air vitiated by respiration, should completely regenerate it and restore to it its original qualities Such a chemical substance has been the subject of some communications to the Paris Academy of Sciences, in which it was mentioned that experiments were being made under the auspices of the Minister of Marine, and that these had proved that with three to four kilos of this new product it was possible for a man to live for twenty-four hours in a hermetically closed chamber. At present, however, submarine boats depend upon compressed air for respiration when submerged, and are likely to continue to do so.

VISION WHEN SUBMERGED.

When completely submerged the submarine boat is practically blind, and it is impossible to steer it by direct vision through the water However slow its course, the steersman would be unable to stop it before an obstacle which rose suddenly into the restricted circle of his aquatic vision, and he is therefore obliged to steer his course by means of bearings taken before descending.

At one time inventors believed that some light would come down through the water to help the steersman, but it is now acknowledged that once below the surface the boat is in'impenetrable darkness, though some have even proposed the use of a powerful electric projector which would emit a beam of light sufficient to light up a path fifty to sixty metres long in front of the submarine.

A submarine boat when navigating as an ordinary torpedo-boat on the surface or in the " awash " condition is steered from the cupola, or conning-tower, which is affixed to the top of the hull, and remains above the water when the hull is below. It used to be asserted that such a cupola would not only be of no use beneath the waves, but would also be a disturbing element in the equilibrium of the boat, reducing its speed, and for this reason the *Gymnote* and the *Gustave Zédé* were provided with tele-scopic domes capable of being pushed up or down at will The arrangement was very complicated, and did not give good results, so it was abandoned, and all modern sub-marines carry a fixed conning-tower on their deck platform.

When the submarine is submerged to a depth not greater than 10 to 12 feet such aids to vision as the optical tube and the periscope may be employed, but when the depth exceeds this limit the helmsman must rely on his compass, coming from time to time to the sur-face to verify and, if necessary, rectify his route.

The periscope (from the Greek περι, around, and σκοπειν, look) is an ingenious instrument by which ob-jects in a horizontal view may be seen through a vertical tube. It may be said to consist of a vertical tube with a lenticular total-reflection prism at the top by which horizontal rays are projected downward through the tube and brought to a focus, after which they are received by a lens, the principal focus of which coincides with that point. The vertical cylindrical beam thus formed is converted into a horizontal one again by a mirror inclined at 45° from the vertical axis of the tube, and is thus conveyed to an eyepiece through which, by turning the tube on its vertical axis with its attached prism, a view of all the supernatant objects around the vessel may be obtained. A screen or diaphragm, operated by a tangent screw, is used to cut off the view of the vertical plane in which the sun is. When used in a submarine boat, the top of the periscope rises above the surface as may be desired.

The optical tube with which the *Gustave Zédé* was at first provided before she carried a periscope consisted of a lens and a prism on the top of a tube, and the image of the surface was thrown on to a surface of paper ; and by the aid of the picture on the sheet of white paper the steersman could, under certain circumstances, tell approximately where he was going.

Considerable improvements have been introduced in the optical appliances of submarine boats since they were first introduced, and those who have had much experience are able to use the periscope with success and certainty. Much, however, necessarily depends upon the state of the atmosphere at the time, and poor results are attained in dark, cloudy, and rainy weather, or when the sea is rough. But the normal position of a submarine—or, at least, of a submersible boat—being at the surface, observations are taken when the boat is awash from the conning-tower, and the course can be steered by the compass, the boat coming to the surface from time to time to verify her position. The real skill of officers of submarine boats is displayed in the approach to an enemy unperceived, and the manner in which, by the periscope

H

and direct observation, the object is attained without the assailant being perceived.

A device for submarine vision, termed the cleptoscope, invented by Messrs. Russo and Laurenti, is reported to be used in the Italian submarines. In its original form the instrument was stated to give an exact view in a closed chamber of all that was to be seen round about a submarine to any one applying his eye to a small eye-piece. In its later form it gives the same image much enlarged, and visible to both eyes at once at some distance from the chamber. This, however, is but one type of the improved periscopic tube.

Finally, as an illustration of the disadvantages arising from the fact that the submarine is blind, the following story may be told, the accuracy of which cannot, however, be vouched for. An Italian submarine went out on one occasion for practice. All at once the crew found that they could neither go ahead nor astern, nor could they rise to the surface. They pumped out the spare water that was provided to give additional buoyancy, but with no effect. The heavy lead keel provided for an emergency was at last detached; still the boat refused to rise, and the crew gave themselves up for lost. The Port-guardship was riding in the anchorage at the time, and her captain heard a scraping and knocking at the bottom of his ship which could not be accounted for. It occurred to him at last to signal to the station on shore asking if the submarine boat was out for practice, and on being told she was, he shifted his anchorage, whereupon the submarine boat came to the surface with a rush like a cork, and the crew were rescued in a very exhausted condition.

SUBMARINE C 1 OF THE FOURTH BRITISH CLASS

Cribb, Southsea

The stern of the boat is entirely submerged, and extends beyond the edge of the picture to the right, the full length being about half as long again as the above-water part shown in the picture

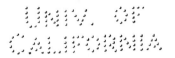

CHAPTER VI

THE ROMANCE OF UNDER-WATER WARFARE

"The torpedo has brought into the Navy a fresh zest, a new romance, and possibilities more daring than were ever existent before its adoption"

"For this cause I will make of your warfare a terrible thing,
    A thing impossible, vain ;
For a man shall set his hand to a handle and wither
    Invisible armies and fleets,
And a lonely man with a breath shall exterminate armies,
    With a whisper annihilate fleets ;
And the captain shall sit in his chamber and level a city,
    That far-off capital city.
Then the Tzar that dreameth in snow and broodeth in winter,
    That foilèd dreamer in frost,
And the Teuton Emperor then, and the Gaul and the Briton
    Shall cease from impossible war,
Discarding their glittering legions, armadas of iron
    As children's toys that are old.
As a man hath been brought, I will bring into judgment a nation ;
    Nor shall numbers be pleaded for sin.
And that people to whom I gave in commission the ocean,
    To use my waters for fight,
Let them look to the inward things, to the searching of spirit,
    And cease from boasting and noise.
Then nation shall cleave unto nation, and Babel shall fall .
    They shall speak in a common tongue
And the soul of the Gaul shall leap to the soul of the Briton
    Through all disguises and shows ;
And soul shall speak unto soul—I weary of tongues,
    I weary of babble and strife.
Lo ! I am the bonder and knitter together of spirits,
    I dispense with nations and shores."

STEPHEN PHILLIPS.

" A BLENDING of the heroic, the marvellous, the mysterious, and the imaginative in actions, manners, ideas, language, or literature ; tendency of mind to dwell upon or give expression to the heroic, the marvellous, the mysterious, or the imaginative."

Such is one of the definitions given in the " Century Dictionary " for the word " romance," and as in the following pages there will be much of " the heroic, the marvellous and the mysterious," there is every justification for using the term in connection with under-water warfare.

Some months since the writer was standing on the pier at Kyle of Loch Alsh, a tiny village in South-west Ross-shire, waiting for the boat going south to Oban.

The sky was leaden, and ever and again a squall swept over from Skye and blotted out the landscape for a time. Presently a little shiver of excitement ran through the group of tourists, fisher folk, and idlers gathered at the pier head.   All eyes were directed up Loch Alsh, and for a few minutes it was difficult to discover what it was that was attracting so much attention.

Gradually there came into sight the first of a little flotilla of torpedo-boats, making their way, in single column, line ahead, to the open sea.   Each was painted black from bow to stern, each bore a number in place of a name, and each crept along like a snake, surprised at finding itself observed, and anxious to escape from the haunts of men.   One by one they passed by, gathering speed as they went, and in a little while the last had disappeared into the mist and the rain, and nothing remained to show that they had passed save a few white patches of foam scattered over the sullen waters.

What were the thoughts uppermost in the minds of those who watched these tiny engines of destruction? Were they not of the next occasion on which Great Britain shall require her Navy to assume the offensive and " to take arms " against the foe that dares to threaten her proud supremacy?

Were they not of the fate of the crews of these vessels in the next great battle on the seas, and of the part they will be destined to play when the " Real Thing " comes?

The torpedo-boats and the destroyers of His Majesty's Navy are manned by brave and fearless officers and men, who take a keen interest in their work and who mean to show of what their ships are capable if ever they get the chance; while the torpedo lieutenant in a battleship, in spite of the good-humoured sneers of his brother-in-arms, the gunnery lieutenant, is not a whit less determined to inflict some injury with the weapon which is his especial care. The commander of a destroyer when he lies down at night in his " duffle suit " and endeavours to take his well-earned repose dreams of a naval action in which he plays a prominent part. It is a night attack, and the destroyers have orders to seek the enemy and torpedo him. As silently, and withal as speedily as possible, the mosquito fleet starts on its deadly mission. The pace is tremendous, and our commander, his nerves braced, his heart beating, and his mouth set, peers forth from the conning-tower into the darkness. His funnels are flaming slightly, but he dare not slacken speed, and all he can do is to pray Heaven that they do not betray him. Suddenly the foremost ship begins to signal. The quarry is discovered! Onward rush the destroyers, and out to meet

them come the destroyers of the enemy. The twelve-
pounders and the six-pounders are brought into play, and
the fight between the opposing forces waxes fierce. So
far our commander and his craft have escaped injury, and
the boat tears along, dodging its foes like a three-quarter
in Rugby football. He has set his heart on torpedoing a
mighty ironclad steaming ahead with her consorts at some
sixteen knots speed, and he means to get past the hostile
destroyers or die in the attempt Shells are bursting all
around, and his armoured conning-tower has been hit,
but so far luck has favoured him. Will the gods be kind
and allow him to accomplish his desire ? He is now
within torpedo range, and the moment has arrived for
the firing of the first torpedo. Out of its tube rushes the
Whitehead, plunges beneath the waves, and is seen no
more. A few anxious seconds, and then the commander
knows that it has missed its prey. Another must be fired ;
but the ironclad is unpleasantly near, and her quick-
firing guns are already discharging on him a heavy and
continuous fire.

The second torpedo is fired, and the destroyer waits
not another second, but makes away at topmost speed.
But " her mission is through." The sound of a mighty
explosion is heard, and the commander knows that he
has accounted for one of the battleships of the enemy.

The lieutenant of to-day thanks his stars for the opportunities that the torpedo has afforded him of assuming
the command of a torpedo-boat or a destroyer at an early
age, or of acting as torpedo lieutenant in a big ship. ·
There is no fear of his rusting or of his finding his life
uneventful while such posts as these are open to him ;

and there is also the chance of his acquiring great fame when the day of battle comes.

". . . They are young," says Mr. Rudyard Kipling, " on the destroyers,—the chattering black decks are no place for the middle-aged—they have learned how to handle 200 feet of shod death that cover a mile in two minutes, turn in their own length, and leap to racing speed almost before a man knows he has signalled the engine room. In these craft they risk the extreme perils of the sea and make experiments of a kind that would not read well in print. It would take much to astonish them when, at the completion of their command, they are shifted say to a racing cruiser. They have been within spitting distance of collision and bumping distance of the bottom , they have tested their craft in long-drawn channel jobs, not grudgingly or of necessity because they could not find harbour, but because they ' wanted to know, don't you know,' and in the embroilment have been very literally thrown together with their men. This makes for hardiness, coolness of head, and, above all, resource."

There is yet another dream that is dreamed by the younger of our young naval lieutenants, and this relates to an engagement in which the submarine boat plays a part.

Great Britain is at war with a rival Power ; hostilities have barely commenced, and one of the enemy's swiftest cruisers has been sent to gather information as to the probable movements of the British squadron. Her captain is noted for his daring and resource, and he has succeeded in obtaining news of a valuable character re-

specting the condition of our ships and their immediate
destination. Accompanied by two first-class torpedo-
boats, he has come, has seen, and is now making off to
join his fleet and to relate his news to the Admiral. It
is of the utmost impórtance that his message should not
be delivered ; the British fleet is not quite ready to strike,
and it does not wish the enemy to know this. Onward
steams the cruiser, the fastest vessel of her class in the
world. It is broad daylight, and she can be seen by our
own cruisers who, unhappily, are half a knot slower than
she is. British destroyers have attempted to torpedo her
as she steams quickly by, but her quick-firing guns and
her attendant torpedo craft have so far foiled their purpose, and the daylight is against them.

There is only one chance—the submarine flotilla.

It is lying off a port which the cruiser must soon pass
on her way down channel, and a wireless message, which
the cruiser is powerless to intercept, has been sent to the
commander of the " mother ship," a torpedo gunboat, to
send out his tiny fleet and endeavour to torpedo the
cruiser. The " catcher " has no chance herself against
the enemy's swift torpedo-boats, so she keeps in the back-
ground, ready to render assistance to her " ducklings "
should they happen to require it.

The cruiser and her attendants are sighted, and the order
to dive is at once given In a few moments there is
nothing to be seen of the five boats, and the look-out in
the cruiser is in blissful ignorance of his hidden foes.
Suddenly Submarine No 1 comes to the surface to take
bearings. She is observed by the look-out, the quick-
firers are immediately trained on her, and the torpedo-

boats, at full speed, rush to the attack. But she has disappeared before they can reach her, and no one has any idea which direction she has taken. The excitement is intense. The hearts of the cruiser's captain and crew beat fast, and eager eyes scan the face of the waters for any sign of the submarines, but there is nothing to be seen. All at once a lieutenant in the cruiser,

THE "GOUBET" OUT OF WATER

gazing down into the water, shouts to his captain. He has seen a submarine missile, but it is too late ! The torpedo strikes, an explosion ensues, and the cruiser's fate is sealed. Her satellites dart hither and thither like policemen in chase of a burglar, but their prey has eluded them, and is now making off to port. The commander of the submarine flotilla has done his work well. After coming momentarily to the surface he dived below. His comrades also had taken their bearings, and the

position of the cruiser, her speed, and her direction were
known. All five of the submarines discharged . their
torpedoes. Four missed, but one was more fortunate,
and was enough to encompass the destruction of the
enemy. After the explosion the commander thrust his
tiny periscope on the surface, and as a glance assured
him that the cruiser would float no more, he made off
with his boats to the shelter of port.

The torpedo-boats did not escape ; hunting for the
submarines, they forget to consider the possibility of an
attack on themselves, and it was only when they saw
four British destroyers at no great distance that they
sought refuge in flight. But they had delayed too long.
The twelve-pounders had something to say to them,
their own three-pounders were quickly silenced, and they
soon went to the bottom.

CHAPTER VII

THE MORAL INFLUENCE OF UNDER-WATER WARFARE

"I think that the enthusiasm with which, in some countries, the studies and the building of submarine boats have been accompanied is in great part due to the feeling implanted in human nature, by which danger appears the greater in proportion as it is more mysteriously and insidiously able to threaten the existence of its adversaries."
Rear-Admiral BETTOLO in *All the World's Fighting Ships* (1901).

IT was once said that the principal value of all methods of submarine warfare was analogous to that of the notice-board which tells the would-be burglar to " Beware of the dog."

In the face of a warning such as this the burglar is forced to take a rapid survey of the situation. In the first place, he cannot tell whether there really is any dog on the premises at all, and secondly, he has no means of discovering whether the animal, if there be one, is old, blind, or decrepit, and thus worthy of being disregarded. Which is his best plan ? to take his chance and trust to luck, or leave the place severely alone and look out for some other establishment where no such notice meets his eye ?

Some burglars might take one course and some another, according to their individual temperaments; but, at any rate, the warning serves this purpose—that it causes the would-be house-breaker to pause before he commits his crime, even if it does not act as a complete deterrent.

What the notice-board is to the burglar, the mine, the torpedo, or the submarine boat is to the naval officer, and in laying his plans he must take into consideration the possibility of being blown up by one or other of these methods of under-water attack. " The King's Navee " has no lack of brave men ready to risk their lives at a moment's notice, and a British officer, if told to accomplish any task, would as soon think of replying that there were mines, torpedo-boats, and submarines in the path of his advance as he would of going into action in a frock-coat and a silk hat.

He will undertake his task cheerfully and instantly, and he knows he can rely on the support of his crew ; but, at the same time, it is impossible both for captain and crew to disregard absolutely the unseen dangers that may lie in their way.

Though this will not prevent a British warship from going wherever it is bid, yet the knowledge that her company may at any moment be sent to the bottom by the explosion of a submarine mine or by the blow of a White-head torpedo must of necessity make them nervous, and will very likely have a bad influence on their powers of shooting straight. " The presence of mines," says a naval writer, " has a moral effect upon crews which does not altogether improve their shooting."

So great has been the recent improvement in the *matériel* of under-water warfare that we had no chance of gauging accurately its potential effect from a moral point of view until the Russo-Japanese war. Though

submarines were not employed by the belligerents, there
is ample evidence from the recent war, and also from
mimic battles, to show that the mine, the torpedo, and
the submarine will exercise great moral influence whenever
nations are plunged into naval hostilities.

There have been those who have declared that those
who handle such weapons will be far more subject to
moral, and indeed physical, effect than those against
whom they are directed ; and though there may be an
element of truth in this, it is certainly not true of the
British, the Japanese, or any other great and efficient
navy. Mines, indeed, in the war were almost as destructive to those who used them as to those against whom
they were directed.

It would be possible to quote many instances, both of
cases in which submarine defences have prevented the
carrying out of certain operations, and also of other cases
where they have been disregarded. Just as there have
been audacious burglaries in spite of " Beware of the
dog " notices, so there have been daring attacks in spite
of known submarine defences. There is always in warfare the possibility that the mine may fail to act at the
critical moment, that the torpedo may not succeed in
finding its mark, and that the submarine boat may miss
its prey.

The first occasion on which the moral influence of
modern under - water methods of warfare made itself
felt was during the American Civil War. The story
of Admiral Farragut's entrance into Mobile Bay, on
August 5th, 1864, is a well-known instance of a commander
advancing in spite of known dangers beneath the waves.

It has been admirably told in the life of the Admiral by Captain A. T. Mahan. The channel was known to be sown with mines, and one of his ships, the *Tecumseh*, had been sent to the bottom already by one of these unseen weapons. The Admiral reasoned thus : " The chances are that I shall lose some of my vessels by torpedoes or the guns of the enemy, but with some of my fleet afloat I shall eventually be successful. I cannot lose all I will attack regardless of consequences, and never turn back." As the *Hartford* passed the *Brooklyn* a warning cry came from the latter that there were torpedoes ahead.

" Damn the torpedoes ! " shouted the Admiral in the exaltation of his high purpose. " Four bells ! Captain Drayton, go ahead. Jouett, full speed ! " The *Hartford* and her consort crossed the line about 500 yards from Mobile Point, well to the westward of the buoy and of the spot where the *Tecumseh* had gone down. As they passed between the buoys the cases of the torpedoes were heard by many on board knocking against the copper of the bottom, and many of the primers snapped audibly, but no torpedo exploded.

The *Hartford* went safely through, the gates of Mobile Bay were forced, and as Farragut's flag cleared the obstructions his last and hardest battle was virtually won.

Mines had been plentifully sown by the Confederates, and across the deep water, 180 had been placed in a double line. The most effective were those made of laager beer kegs coated with pitch and fitted with a number of sensitive primers ; the others had tin or iron covers, but they corroded in the water and quickly became harmless. In addition, there were three electro-contact mines which were to be exploded from Fort Morgan. Had the mines been in an efficient state, Admiral Farragut and his fleet would assuredly have gone to the bottom. He took the risk—and won.

Turning now to the other side of the picture, it will be found that hidden enemies are always the most dreaded, and that the history of naval operations affords many examples of their moral influence hindering the carrying out of certain operations.

In the actions off Charleston, in the American Civil War, the mines and obstructions so influenced Admiral Dupont that he was content to maintain the blockade instead of risking his ships against them ; and his example is likely to be followed in future wars.

One of the clearest cases of the moral influence of sub-marine mines occurred during the Franco-Prussian War, when the French fleet were prevented from entering Prussian harbours simply through fear of submarine dangers. The naval campaign of 1870 consisted solely of the watching by a strong French squadron of North German ships which had taken refuge behind a reputed impassable barrier of subaqueous defences.

"The power of the French steamships," wrote Sir Cyprian Bridge, some years ago, "to stand in within practicable range of their heavy guns, and do enormous mischief to the rising naval establishment of the Bund, as it then was, was completely set at nought by the sub-aqueous defensive system which the weaker force had devised to redress the inequality between it and its rival. We shall do well to mark the results ; the stronger navy

I

did and could do practically nothing ; the smaller one pre-
served itself from injuries, and at the close of the war still
existed intact, as a nucleus for that splendid force, which
is now third amongst the navies of the world."

During the Franco-German war the French fleet was
kept off a port or harbour protected by dummy mines.
The story goes, that when the mines arrived the burgomaster was afraid to charge them, and laid them out
empty.   At the completion of the war, when the dummies
were taken up, the burgomaster was congratulated by
several consuls on the masterly way in which he had
performed his perilous task, no loss of life having been
caused.

There were so many instances of mines failing to
explode, or if exploding, doing no damage, that naval
officers might well have declared that the submarine mine
was nothing but a " military bugbear."   In 1863, during
the American-Civil War, the *New Ironsides* halted off
Fort Sumner, and just over a submarine mine containing
2000 lb. of powder, which failed to explode when fired
from the battery, as one of the wires had been accidentally severed by a waggon passing over it.   Instances of
the moral influences of the torpedo were afforded by the
Chino-Japanese and the Spanish-American wars...Al-
though the Chinese officers were quite unable to use the
torpedo with any effect, and evidently regarded the
weapon as of more potential danger to themselves than
to the enemy, the Japanese commanders on more than
one occasion decided against certain movements, owing
to a fear of the Chinese torpedo flotilla.

During the Spanish-American war the Americans

suffered severely from " torpedoitis," and were continually fancying they saw Spanish torpedo-boats, and firing on them, when in reality there were none present. As an American officer remarked, " whatever the actual shortcomings of a torpedo-boat flotilla, it must always act, at least, as an admirable antisoporific "· As to the Spaniards, they appeared to dread the mines they had themselves laid more than did the Americans.

The part played by submarine mines in the Russo-Japanese war was a revelation to many, and their moral influence will be greater in future wars than ever before.

One of the most amusing cases of the moral influences of torpedo warfare was related by Vice-Admiral · Sir Nowell Salmon at the Royal United Service Institution in 1892.

Sir Nowell was discussing the question of the value of the electric searchlight in battleships in warding off torpedo attack. He was inclined to think that he would rather not have it at all, for on any occasion that he had seen, whether it had been at a fixed station on shore or whether it had been a fixed station on board, making a quadrangle within which ships might lie, the torpedo station had always been the point of attack, and had always suffered · In one case, in which he put a squadron inside four ships to make a path of light round them, the ships showing the light were, of course, at once the point of attack, and were all attacked and sunk , one commander, indeed, said that he was sunk no less than seven times.

" I can remember a little incident in which I took part. It shows how very curiously the electric light may act

in some cases. The squadron inside the rectangle of
light was in total darkness, and my boat, in which I was
inspecting the preparations, happened to get within the
beam of one of the ships showing the light. Just as this
happened I saw a boat inshore of me. I thought she was
one of the attacking boats steaming up inshore. Of
course, I set to work to cut her off, as I was commanding
the defending squadron. I steamed as hard as ever I
could. I got my muskets ready, and so on. Still she
went past me, going inshore as I thought ; and it was not
until I recognised my own shadow shaking its fist at the
engineer for not clapping on more steam that I found
I was chasing the shadow of my own boat thrown on the
cliff. In a very few seconds I should have been hard and
fast ashore."

"The real strength of the destroyer," one writer has
said, " consists not so much in what she can do against
large ships—certainly not in what she ever has done so
far—but in the fear entertained by her adversaries of the
harm she is held to be capable of doing. Her menace is
tremendous, and really paralysing to some minds." This
probably applies much more to submarines than to
destroyers.

CHAPTER VIII

THE SUBMARINE IN ACTION

ONCE, and only once, has a submarine boat succeeded in inflicting any damage on an enemy in actual warfare. This was during the American Civil War, when one of the Confederate *Davids* succeeded in blowing up the Federal frigate *Housatonic*, and in annihilating itself at the same time. Before this event under-water vessels had attempted to destroy hostile craft, but with no success. In 1776 Bushnell's diving torpedo-boat made an attack on the English frigate *Eagle*, and in 1777 on the English man-of-war *Cerberus* and other vessels. Although it failed to inflict any injury on a single vessel, three of the crew of a prize schooner astern of the *Cerberus*, hauling one of Bushnell's drifting torpedoes on board, were killed by the explosion.

In 1801 Fulton attempted to destroy one of the English Channel Fleet off Boulogne by means of his drifting torpedoes, but owing to the ship altering her position at the moment of setting the torpedo adrift, the attack failed. In 1804-5 Fulton, who had now joined the British forces, attacked some of the French ships, but the torpedoes exploded harmlessly. From the death of Fulton to the commencement of the American Civil War numerous inventive minds built or projected submarine craft of all shapes and sizes, but none of these ever participated in an actual engagement.

The exploits of the diving torpedo-boats known by the generic name of *David*, during the contest between the Federals and the Confederates, are fully described in a later chapter, and there is therefore no need to dwell further on this period in the history of under-water warfare. Since then no submarine boat has ever been taken into battle, nor have any of these boats played any part in the actual operations of warfare; although during the Spanish-American war Spain might, perhaps, have used the *Peral*, and the United States the *Holland*. Again, in the Russo-Japanese war, if submarines had been present, there can be no doubt that they would have affected the course of the operations. After the actions it was asserted that submarines had actually been employed; but this was not the case, for neither the Russians nor the Japanese had any such boats fit for service at the seat of war, and each was well informed as to the situation of the other.

In mimic warfare, however, submarines have played their part, and although no very definite conclusions respecting their possible value in time of war may be drawn from their performances in peace manœuvres, still these episodes are full of interest, and leave no doubt as to the value of these craft.

It may be of interest to note that the first of these occasions was in September, 1900, during the manœuvres of the U.S. North Atlantic Squadron off Newport, Rhode Island, when the *Holland* made an attack upon the fleet by herself, without convoy, at a distance of seven miles out from the mouth of the harbour, and, with her own crew alone in her, torpedoed the flagship of the squadron, the *Kearsarge*, commanded by Captain Wm. M. Folger. Lieut. Caldwell, who commanded the *Holland* on this occasion, wrote regarding the incident :—

"The *Holland* was not seen by any vessel of the block-ading fleet or torpedo-boats, although she was within torpedo range of three of the former and several of the latter. I consider the attack was a success because the

THE SUBMARINE IN ACTION

Holland could in all probability have torpedoed three blockading vessels without being discovered."

It must be added that Admiral O'Neil, who had but a poor opinion of the value of submarines in war, wrote at the time as follows :—

"On 25 September, 1900, during some manœuvres of the North Atlantic Fleet off Newport, Rhode Island, the *Holland*, on a very fine evening and under exceptionally favourable circumstances, steamed seven miles as a sur-face boat only outside Newport harbour, and, like the torpedo-boat *Porter*, claims to have put the battleship

Kearsarge out of action, which was not allowed by the umpire, as it was decided that the *Kearsarge* had already been put out of action by the torpedo-boat *Dahlgren.*"

From 1898 onwards French under-water vessels have often engaged in mimic warfare, and many glowing accounts have been published of their wonderful performances. Often, it may be true, the attacks have been made in peculiarly favourable conditions, but they have been conducted for the purpose of training officers and men, and, as has been shown in an earlier chapter, a notable degree of proficiency has been attained ; and the highest French authorities are firm believers in the potency of the submarine arm of naval warfare.

Submarine attacks have become a portion of the routine of training in all navies that possess boats of the class, and are just as much a part of the regular work of these navies as are the operations of torpedo-boats or other classes of vessels. This is the truest confirmation of their value, and gives the soundest confidence in their future. The day has gone by in which the sensational journalist made capital of the working of submarine boats. This has now become a commonplace of operations, and submarines going out of harbour or returning are a frequent sight at naval ports at home and abroad. Yet a few years ago a submarine attack was a subject of big headlines in the papers and on newspaper bills.

Thus when Englishmen took up their morning papers on 5 July, 1901, there. met the gaze such headings as " Submarine's great feat " ; " How the *Gustave Zédé* torpedoed a big battleship " ; " New Naval Warfare " ; " French Navy the most powerful in the world."

Excited journalists filled columns in describing what had occurred, and one of the correspondents on that occasion made some remarks that will bear quoting now.

"After every deduction has been made," he said, "there is no disputing the fact that the submarine has proved its tremendous possibilities in warfare. In consequence of this success of the *Gustave Zédé* the French are suffering from a bad attack of naval fever. Some would call it ' tête montée.' ' Where is Britain's naval supremacy now ? ' is a question which was often asked to-day. ' C'est magnifique ! ' say the papers, describing France's submarine fleet. ' By reason of her submarine division the navy of France is the most dread and powerful in the world.' "

That episode is now ancient history. It has been repeated over and over again, in other circumstances and with other ships, and assuredly will be repeated many times more. It would not do to exaggerate the lessons of such episodes If battleships never placed themselves in positions where submarine and submersible boats could attack them with advantage, there would be no proper opportunities for the higher training of officers and men of the submarine service. In a previous chapter it was shown what successes have been attained by French boats in recent manœuvres, and how high is the value set upon them, not as replacing battleships, but as complementary to them, by Admiral Fournier. In this country like exercises are performed, but we say little about them, and the successes or failures of the submarine in action are not known to the public at large.

CHAPTER IX

THE ANTIDOTE TO SUBMARINES

THE great problems that arise from the introduction of submarines have not yet been solved. There is yet no knowledge as to how the submarine herself shall best be attacked, nor does there seem as yet to be any certainty as to the right methods of protecting the hulls of vessels from the consequences of the explosions of torpedoes and mines.

Mr. John P. Holland, discussing the first of these matters in an article which he contributed to the *North American Review* for December, 1900, wrote as follows :—

" When the first submarine torpedo-boat goes into action she will bring us face to face with the most puzzling problem ever met in warfare. She will present the unique spectacle, when used in attack, of a weapon against which there is no defence. You can pit sword against sword, rifle against rifle, cannon against cannon, ironclad against ironclad ; you can send torpedo-boat destroyers against torpedo-boats, and destroyers against destroyers, but you can send nothing against the submarine boat, not even itself. You cannot fight submarines with submarines. The fanciful descriptions of the submarine battle of the future have one fatal defect. You cannot see under water. Hence you cannot fight under water. Hence you cannot defend yourself against an attack under water except by running away. If you cannot run away you are doomed. Wharves, shipping at anchor, the buildings in seaport towns, cannot run away, therefore the sending of a submarine against them means their inevitable destruction. No ; as nearly as the human mind can discern now, the submarine is indeed a ' sea-devil ' against which no means that we possess at present can prevail. It is no use for the defence to mine, for the submarine would countermine, and torpedo-nets would be of no use, for it would blow a hole through them, and any attempt to discover the position of the boat when below the surface is about as promising a pursuit as dredging with a butterfly-net for a half-dollar that had been thrown into New York Bay."

It is true that in the present state of the science of submarine warfare it is impossible to fight submarines with submarines, and it is recognised that the best chance of destroying an under-water vessel is when it comes to the surface to take a momentary glance at the position of its victim before launching its torpedo.

When a means of distinguishing objects beneath the waves has been evolved, then it will be time enough to discuss the possibility of constructing a submarine boat destroyer which shall itself go beneath the surface and seek out the submarine to deal it its deathblow.

Every advance in military and naval science that tends to strengthen the attack has been met by some invention or device calculated to enable the defence to withstand it.

In the early days men went into battle wearing heavy armour, but nowadays, although bullet-proof cuirasses and bullet-proof shields have been suggested, the foot soldier carries no protection on his person, but relies instead upon entrenchments and fortifications.

It may be remembered that when the hostilities in

South Africa commenced, certain experts declared that the new lyddite shells would annihilate the Boers in a very short space of time. The capabilities of the enemy for defending himself had been under-estimated by these gentlemen, and the terrible slaughter which was predicted at Paardeberg did not occur, owing to the wonderful entrenchments beneath which the Boers and their families sheltered.

Any system of entrenchment is, of course, impossible upon the high seas, and therefore men-of-war have to carry armour plate to protect their sides from the effects of shell and shot.

But no sooner had metallic armour been applied to the sides of war vessels than the manufacturers set to work to increase the size and destructive capacity of the shot, and for years past a duel has been in progress between the projectile and the plate ; each improvement in the one has led to an improvement in the other, and all the resources of science have been requisitioned to render the projectile more deadly and the plate more impervious to its attack and lighter than before.

The advent of the torpedo as an effective weapon of attack brought about the " torpedo-boat," which was met first by the " torpedo-catcher," and then by the " torpedo-boat destroyer " ; while as protection against the torpedo itself, nets and crinolines have been devised for the purpose of foiling the objects of the attack. A net-cutter on the bows of the torpedo has, however, made its appearance, and some consider it unlikely that nets would be of much protection to a ship, even when stationary, though this requires to be proved.

The destructive effects of explosive shells have been met by the shipbuilders by the subdivision of the air space of a warship into water-tight compartments, and the desire of the enemy's gunners to inflict injury upon the boilers, the engines, or the propellers, has led imaginative inventors to endeavour to devise types of warlike craft that shall be almost entirely destitute of armour, but constructed on such a principle—both as to hull and machinery—that can be raked fore and aft and shot through in all directions without becoming either water-logged or deprived of motive power.*

So far as we are aware, the only nation that has seriously taken up the question of an antidote to submarines is Great Britain. At present the submarine boat, owing to its slow speed and narrow range of action, is more suited for defence than attack, though as it is year by year improving it may soon become a valuable attacking weapon. France long preferred to build sea-going torpedo-boats, and Great Britain destroyers; and in the same way, while France was rapidly constructing a flotilla of submarines, Great Britain, while beginning to build submarines, devoted attention to the best method of meeting under-water attack.

The means of attack against submarines at present are :—

1. By quick-firing guns.

2. By firing shells full of high explosive, which, bursting in the water near the boat, will beat it in.

3. By firing explosives at the end of a spar.

* See *Twentieth Century Inventions*, by G. Sutherland, 1901.

When running awash, the submarine presents a very small target ; the hull is 3 to 5 feet below the surface, which would deflect all projectiles from machine-guns ; and the armoured conning-tower, which is alone visible, would be a difficult object to hit.

After running awash for some distance the submarine will submerge herself, but, in spite of periscope and optical tube, she will most probably have to come to the surface once or twice to take a short, sharp look round before firing her torpedo. This is the moment when the attack must be made upon the diving vessel, and the idea is to destroy her either by firing a shell from a gun, or an out-rigger torpedo from a swiftly moving vessel. In so much as it is difficult to make a shell burst with certainty at the right instant, the second method is the one that seems most to commend itself to the authorities.

The Lords of the Admiralty, in the course of their visit to Portsmouth in June, 1901, witnessed the working of a method of destroying submarines that had been devised by the *Vernon's* staff. The trials took place at a considerable distance from shore, and were confidential, and therefore no official account of what took place has appeared. Still, from various sources it was possible to piece together a " story," the moral of which (according to some writers) seems to have been that a satisfactory method of destroying the enemy's submarine boats had been found, and that thenceforth the British fleet had nothing to fear from the attacks of these " marine devils."

In the present state of the science, it was said a submarine attacking a ship was bound to come to the surface to take bearings, or else to betray her presence by optic tube or periscope ; and, with the new invention that had been evolved in the *Vernon*, the sighting of a submarine entailed her almost certain destruction. Sighting her was said to be now practically certain, though it was not to the public benefit that the means which would be employed should be stated, as the principle had other and varied uses.

The experiments were made with the destroyer *Starfish*. On the starboard side certain plates had been strengthened, and above there was a crutch upon which worked a spar or outrigger torpedo. A spar-torpedo is really a movable observation mine. In the present instance it consisted of a stout pole some 42 feet in length, at the end of which was an explosive charge of 32 lb. of wet gun-cotton, explodable by an electric current by the crew in the boat. Normally this boom stows inboard and forward, but on going into action it is slung out well forward and immersed in the water at the proper moment. This immersion carries the boom end downward and aft, and it is exploded directly the submarine is passed. The idea was that the speed of the destroyer would carry her past the centre of the explosion before the full effects could reach her. Her strengthened plates would add to her safety, and it was thought that, in any case, destroyers were too light and " cork-light " to be seriously affected

As for the submarine below the waves, the men of the *Vernon* made out a pitiable case for her. She would experience the full force of the terrific concussion. Within from 50 feet to 100 feet or more of the centre of

explosion, according to the charge employed, the sides
of the submarine would be compressed sufficiently to
cause fatal leaks, while even at a greater distance stability would be destroyed.

At the Portsmouth experiment the "dummy" submarine consisted of a barrel sunk some 10 feet below the
surface of the water to represent a submerged boat.
This was attacked and destroyed by the torpedo-boat

EXIT SUBMARINE

destroyer *Starfish* in the following way. When within
striking distance of the barrel, the boom was dropped and
the gun-cotton exploded by electrical contact. The
officers who carried out the experiment are reported to
have said that any submarine within an area of 60 feet
of the outrigger boom when the explosion occurred must
infallibly have been annihilated by the bursting of the
charge, and that if a submarine came up to within a

thousand yards of a boom - fitted destroyer, it would certainly be done for.

It was stated that the single experiment carried out at Portsmouth was not enough to indicate exactly the best position for the boom, and that the first boats to be fitted would probably vary somewhat between having it on the quarter or right aft The additional weight of the boom was slight ; in the case of the *Starfish*, the destroyer experimentally fitted, the weight had been more. than compensated for by fitting her with aluminium instead of the usual torpedo tubes.

To say that if a submarine rises anywhere near a destroyer armed with a spar her destruction will be absolutely certain is probably going too far. To. blow up a stationary barrel was not a very difficult task.;. but it must not be forgotten that if the destroyer sights. the submarine, the submarine will also sight the destroyer, and may endeavour to launch a torpedo at.the destroyer before the latter can explode her weapon This, however, would be a questionable procedure, for a destroyer would not make an easy mark, and the commander of a submarine boat would be careful not to discharge his precious torpedoes at a doubtful or unsatisfactory object. A submarine, having sighted a destroyer, can of course dive and make off in a direction which the latter could not foretell, and there would seem to be a good chance of her escaping.

The method of attacking submarines by means of spar-torpedoes is now discredited, and the system would not be tried in ordinary circumstances. Another suggestion seeming to possess greater possibilities is that destroyers

K

should be equipped with small torpedoes costing comparatively little, and adapted expressly for discharging at submarine boats.

Submarines will probably act in conjunction with torpedo-boats and destroyers, and the object of these vessels will be to ward off the attacks of hostile torpedo-boats and destroyers.

It has been said that in action the moral effect of the submarine would probably outweigh its practical effect, and it is now urged that the moral influence of an antidote to submarines will be very great.

" The risks of ordinary submarine work," said a writer, " are not so great as many people imagine ; and they can, in a great measure, be overcome by practice. But the deadly spar will quite alter this. The men in the submarine cannot acquire familiarity with this in peace ; not till war will it operate. Then, whenever they are rising, they will know that a destroyer *may* be within reach, and that, if so, absolute annihilation is *certain*, and annihilation in a particularly horrible form." *

(These remarks would apply with equal justice to the moral effect of the possibility of the hulls of submarine boats being struck by small torpedoes.)

* "Our preparations for attacking submarines with spar torpedoes fitted to torpedo-boats or destroyers are exciting the ridicule of those foreign nations who from experience know what submarines are like. We claim that our specially-rigged spar-torpedo can reach a submarine at a depth of 10 feet below the surface ; but why a submarine should run at 10 instead of 30 or 40 feet does not appear. The truth seems to be that if the submarine can be reached at all by the spar-torpedo, she could, at least in the majority of cases, be reached much more expeditiously and certainly by means of the gun."—W. LAIRD CLOWES, at the Institution of Naval Architects, 1902.

" Excitement may sustain them ; they may figure it out that their chances of life and death are on a par with those of the soldier in a frontal attack, but it is, at least, doubtful. It is difficult to make the analogy ; and, moreover, there is the chill of the water to consider. Nerves and courage both suffer from cold, and the interior of a submarine has always the chill of a tomb (!). Inside it men sit, and may not move without endangering the craft's stability. It will need a high courage thus to sit absolutely without means of knowing whether a painful annihilation is coming in a few minutes ; it will certainly render it difficult to take careful observations— and careful observations are a vital necessity. And the Frenchman, of all races of men, seems least fitted to be calm under such circumstances. It must further be remembered that if a destroyer is within a thousand yards she will be easily able to steam up and destroy the boat, for a thousand yards a minute is now destroyer speed. The boat, on the other hand, cannot, save under favourable circumstances, see a distance of a thousand yards, certainly not in a hasty rise and plunge again. She might just distinguish a big ship, but that is about all. On the verge of a frightful death it will take a very cool man even to see that."

The French appear to have considered the possibility of some " antidote," for the submersible *Narval* has a double hull, and in the space between the two sea-water is allowed to circulate freely. Whether this device would enable the boat to resist the force of an explosion is a question which could only be satisfactorily decided in actual warfare. The type has not been repeated. Meanwhile the bomb-proof hull will certainly receive attention.

The periscope and the optical tube have not done away with the necessity for the submarine to come to the surface to correct her course and take her bearings, but there are those who claim that even if the necessity were removed, the whereabouts of the submarine would be revealed by tell-tale foam and bubbles.

Several inventors have devoted attention to the electric steering of torpedoes after they have been discharged, and some consider that wircless torpedoes would be an efficient antidote to submarine boats. That such weapons can be produced there is little doubt, but that they will be sufficient to drive submarines from the seas appears extremely doubtful—at any rate, just at present.

The possibility of a battleship or a cruiser being able to inform herself of the advance of a submarine vessel must be considered. Water is an excellent conductor of sound, and a microphone or some similar apparatus could be arranged to give notice of the approach of an invisible ship, even when it was some distance away. The ironclad could then surround herself with her torpedo nets or steam away, leaving the submarine powerless to overtake her. The new arrangements in use for submarine sound signalling, between ships and shore stations, seem to point in the direction indicated.

The French very naturally watched with intense interest the attitude of the British Navy towards submarine boats, and the experiments that were carried out by the officers of the *Vernon*, with a view to discovering the most effective method of destroying under-water craft, were carefully followed. M. Lockroy, however, suggested that it would only be possible to fight against submarines when the steering of balloons had been made possible, the black form of the vessel, he said, being very easily distinguished in the water from a certain height.

PART II

CHAPTER X

ALTHOUGH no mention of a submarine vessel having been actually constructed can be found earlier than the seventeenth century, and although the torpedo and the mine were not invented till still later, the art of submarine warfare and subaqueous exploration dates back to a very much earlier period.

The earliest form of under-water attack was carried out by divers long before explosive compounds were invented, and the old writers have strange stories to tell of fierce fights beneath the waves.

"The first divers learned their art," says John Beckmann, in his *History of Inventions and Discoveries*, by early and adventurous experience, in trying to continue under water as long as possible without breathing, and, indeed, it must be allowed that some of them carried it to very great perfection. This art, however, excites little surprise, for, like running, throwing, and other bodily dexterities, it requires only practice; but it is certain that those nations called by us uncultivated and savage excel in it the Europeans who through refinement and luxury have become more delicate and less fit for such laborious exercises."

In early times divers were employed for peaceful as well as for hostile purposes. They were kept in ships to assist in raising anchors and to recover goods thrown overboard in times of danger, and by the laws of the Rhodians they were allowed a share of the wreck, proportional to the depth at which they had gone in search of it. "The pearls of the Greek and Roman ladies," writes Beckmann, "were fished up by divers at the great hazard of their lives, and by the like means are procured at present those which are purchased as ornaments by our fair."

In the operations of war divers were used for many purposes. Beckmann tells us that when Alexander was besieging Tyre divers swam off from the city under water to a great distance, and with long hooks tore to pieces the mole with which the besiegers were endeavouring to block up the harbour.

We learn from Herodotus (viii. 8) that when the fleet of Xerxes was advancing to the invasion of Greece "there was in the force one Skyllias, a Skionaian, the best diver of his time, who in the shipwreck off Pilion had saved many things for the Persians, and had also obtained many things himself." This diver deserted to the Greeks, and gave them the benefit of his skill as well as of recent intelligence concerning their enemy. He was the means of destroying a number of the Persian ships by a curious kind of submarine attack. Accompanied by his daughter Kyane, whom he had instructed in his art, he dived during a storm and "cast off" the

cables from the anchors which held the vessels, the result
being that they were driven on shore and wrecked.

·Thucydides (iv. 26) gives an instance of a case of
divers being employed as subaqueous auxiliaries during
the siege of Syracuse

" The besieged had driven piles into the water before
their old docks, that their vessels might be in safety behind them and the Athenians be unable to stand in
amongst them and do any damage to the shipping."
The latter endeavoured to remove this species of nautical
entrenchment, and for this purpose they constructed a
raft on which were turrets and parapets to cover the men
who embarked on it. It was towed up to a line of piles
and used as a kind of covering battery for the crews of
boats who removed the piles, which had been " sawed off
close to the bottom by divers." A serious obstruction
was offered by some piles driven in till their heads were
below the surface of the water, in the hope that the besieging ships might run upon them. But the divers, by
persevering efforts, succeeded in sawing them through,
thus enabling the besiegers to remove them.

The Chronicles of the early Middle Ages supply instances of the employment of divers in naval warfare.
The Baltic, we read, was so infested with pirates that a
Swedish force was sent against them. The Swedish
admiral, observing that the pirate vessels lay at anchor
in a certain bay, sent in at night men from his own fleet
to dive beneath them and make holes in their bottoms.
The following day he engaged them. In the action the
leaks made by the subaqueous assailants during the night
proved so serious that the piratical crews had to turn

their attention chiefly to stopping them and to baling out their vessels. The number available to fight their enemy was in consequence so reduced that the Swedes gained a complete victory, and the power of the pirates was annihilated.

Again, at the siege of Malta by the Turks in the sixteenth century some furious under-water fighting occurred. The Maltese were excellent divers, and the Knights took advantage of their skill to assist in the erection of a barricade across the mouth of one of the creeks which indent the shores of the Grand Harbour. This obstruction the Turkish besiegers endeavoured to remove, and accordingly they made upon it a series of determined attacks. The divers left their work to drive them off, and a terrible and weird struggle ensued, frequently below the surface of the water, which finally ended in the repulse of the infidel assailants.

One must accept *cum grano salis* the stories told by writers regarding the time that divers were able to continue under water. Beckmann said that the divers of Astrakhan employed in the fishery there could remain for seven minutes under water. The divers in Holland seem to have been very expert, for an observer, during the time they were under water, was obliged to breathe at least ten times. "Those who collect pearl-shells in the East Indies can remain under water a quarter of an hour, though some are of opinion that it is possible to continue longer ; and Mersenne mentions a diver, named John Barrinus, who could dive under water for six hours." Beckmann evidently found it a little difficult to swallow this, so he adds, "How far this may be true I shall leave others to judge."

An account of a Sicilian diver, Nicolo Pesce, given by Kircher, is yet more marvellous than any of those just cited. So great was his skill that he carried letters for the king from Sicily to Calabria. The story goes that the king offered him a gold cup if he would explore the terrible Gulf of Charybdis. He remained for three-quarters of an hour amidst the foaming abyss, and on his return described all the horrors of the place to the astonished monarch, who requested him to dive once more to further examine the gulf. For some time he hesitated, but upon the promise of a still larger cup and a purse of gold he was tempted to plunge again, with the melancholy result that he never came to the surface.

A history of the art and practice of diving, although it would present many points of interest, is foreign to our subject, and attention must be confined to the question of submarine warfare.

Some writers on this subject, whilst making such statements as "the confinement of gunpowder in water-tight cases and its submarine explosion for the destruction of floating and other bodies is almost as old as villainous saltpetre itself," or "the ancients understood the manufacture of subaqueous explosives, or, at least, combustibles," do not trouble to give any particular instances. A French writer is reported to have collected accounts of the use of such devices against ships below the water line, but a diligent search has failed to reveal the name of the author.

"The fact that some under-water explosive compound," said Admiral Sir Cyprian Bridge in an article he contributed to *Fraser's Magazine* many years ago,

" had been known in ancient times was not lost sight of in the stirring intellectual revolution of the Renaissance, which, amongst other legacies, bequeathed to mankind the outlines of the modern art of war. It is not surprising, therefore, that we should meet with the use of such an agent in the wars of the sixteenth century. The most celebrated instance of its employment was by the Italian Giannibelli (*sic*) at Antioch during the siege of the city by the Prince of Parma."

Perhaps the Admiral was referring to what Lieutenant Sleeman says is the earliest record of the employment of a torpedo (i.e., a case of explosive possessing the power of aggression). In 1585 an Italian engineer named Zambelli invented a floating mine, and succeeded in destroying a bridge built over the Scheldt by the Prince of Parma. Zambelli's mine consisted of a flat boat filled with gunpowder arranged in it so as to secure the maximum effectiveness, and provided with a long sulphur metal rope and clockwork for its ignition.

A few years before this feat (in 1578) an Englishman, by name William Bourne, published a book entitled *Inventions or Devices*. He suggested in his seventeenth article, " How for to sink a ship that hath laid you aboard without shooting of ordnance." William Bourne is in some books said to have actually invented a plunging apparatus for use in warfare, but no circumstantial account of such a vessel is extant.

The Marquis of Worcester, in his *Century of Inventions* (1663), describes, in section 9, " An engine, portable in one's pocket, which may be carried and fastened on the inside of the greatest ship, *tanquam aliud agens*, and at any appointed minute, though a week after, either by day or night, it shall irrecoverably sink that ship." The smallness of the engine suggests some explosive missile connected with clockwork as the only means to insure its being compact and operating on a precise day at a stated point of time. Section 10 is as follows : " A way from a mile off to dive and fasten a like engine to any ship so as it may punctually work the same effect either for time or execution."

In 1596 John Napier of Merchiston wrote a statement of four " Secret Inventions," concluding with the re- mark : " These inventions, besides devices of *sailing under the water* with divers other devices and stratagems for burning of the enemies, by the grace of God, and work of expert craftsmen, I hope to perform."

Pepys, in his *Diary*, under date 14 March, 1662, says : " In the afternoon came the German Doctor Knuffler, to discourse with us about his engine to blow up ships. We doubted not the matter of fact, it being tried in Crom- well's time, but the safety of carrying them in ships; but he do tell us, that when he comes to tell the King his secret, (for none but the Kings, successively, and their heirs must know it,) it will appear to be of no danger at all."

The foregoing extracts show that the possibility of a practical method of submarine attack was beginning to take shape in the minds of philosophers and inventive geniuses. " Fire and powder ships," " machines," " in- fernals," " catamarans," and similar devices for accom- plishing the destruction of an enemy were known at this time, and it is not strange that the idea of making the explosion take place *beneath* the water should have suggested itself.

CHAPTER XI

WHO invented the first boat which was capable of being propelled beneath the water ? Opinions differ as to the correct answer to this question. David Bushnell's boat (*circa* 1773) is the first of which we have any definite record, but William Bourne (1580), Magnus Pegelius (1605), and Cornelius van Drebbel (1620) have all been credited with having constructed under-water vessels. In the previous chapter it has been shown that the earliest form of submarine attack was carried out by divers. The prototype of the submarine boat was undoubtedly the diving bell, the history of which contrivance, although presenting many points of interest, it will be impossible to relate here.

According to some writers, to William Bourne, the English mathematician, belongs the credit (in 1580) of operating the first submarine boat as such, in contradistinction to a diving-bell ; but there is nothing to show that Bourne did more than discuss the question, as did also Magnus Pegelius, although the latter is reported to have built a small submarine vessel in the year 1605.

The Dictionary of National Biography credits Cornelius Drebbel, who was born in 1572, in the town of Alkmaar, in Holland, and who died in London in 1634, with the invention of a submarine boat "which was **Drebbel's** navigable without the use of artificial light, **reputed** from Westminster to Greenwich." We have **Submarine.** spent some time in endeavouring to verify this assertion, but the references to the boat are vague and unsatisfactory. However, as Drebbel is by some accounted the "Father of Submarine Navigation," it seems scarcely fitting to dismiss him without further thought.

In that curious old volume entitled *New Experiments Physico-mechanical touching the Spring of the Air and its Effects*, by the "Honourable Robert Boyle, Esq.," mention is made of Drebbel's boat, and it may be interesting to transcribe the passage. It occurs on p. 188 of the second edition, published at Oxford in 1662.

"But yet on occasion of this opinion of Paracelsus, perhaps it will not be impertinent if before I proceed, I acquaint your lordship with a Conceit of that deservedly Famous Mechanician and Chymist, *Cornelius Drebell*, who among other strange things that he performed, is affirmed (by more than a few credible Persons) to have contrived for the late learned King *James*, a vessel to go under Water; of which tryal was made in the *Thames* with admirable success, the vessel carrying twelve Rowers besides Passengers; one of which is yet alive, and related to an excellent Mathematician that informed me of it. Now that for which I mention this story is, That having had the curiosity and opportunity to make particular Enquiries among the relations of *Drebell*, and especially of an ingenious Physitian that marryed his daughter, concerning the grounds upon which he conceived it feasible to make men unaccustomed to continue so long under Water without suffocation, or (as the lately mention'd Person that went in the Vessel affirms) without inconvenience, I was answered that *Drebell* conceived, that 'tis not the whole body of the air but

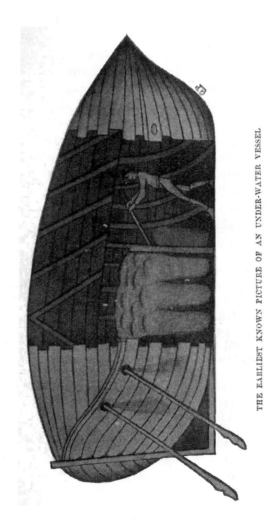

THE EARLIEST KNOWN PICTURE OF AN UNDER-WATER VESSEL

a certain Quintessence (as Chymists speake) or spirituous part of it that makes it fit for respiration, which being spent the remaining grosser body, or carcase (if I may so call it) of the Air, is unable to cherish the vital flame residing in the heart : so that (for ought I could gather) besides the Mechanicall contrivance of his vessel he had a Chymicall liquor, which he accounted the chief secret of his Submarine Navigation. For when from time to time he perceived that the finer and purer part of the Air was consumed or over-clogged by the respiration, and steames of those that went in his ship, he would, by unstopping a vessel full of the liquor speedily restore to the troubled air such a proportion of vital parts as would make it again for a good while fit for Respiration. Whether by dissipating or precipitating the grosser exhalations, or by some other intelligible way, I must not now stay to examine, contenting myself to add, that having had the opportunity to do some service to those of his Relations, that were most intimate with him, and having made it my business to learn what the strange liquor might be, they constantly affirmed that *Drebell* would never disclose the Liquor unto any, nor so much as tell the matter whereof he made it, to above one Person, who himself assured me what it was."

It is much to be wished that fuller accounts were extant respecting Drebbel's boat and the methods he employed to enable his passengers to breathe under water. W. B. Rye, in one of the notes to his work, *England as Seen by Foreigners* (1865, p. 232), gives a carefully compiled account of Drebbel's inventions, and quotes from a Dutch Chronicle of Alkmaar, by C. van der Wonde (1645), a passage relating to his submarine boat.

" He built a ship in which one could row and navigate under water from Westminster to Greenwich, the distance of two Dutch miles ; even five or six miles, or as far as one pleased. In this boat a person could see under the surface

L

of the water and without candle-light, as much as he needed
to read in the Bible or any other book. Not long ago this
remarkable ship was yet to be seen lying in the Thames or
London river."

As to what Drebbel's " Chymicall Liquor " really was
there is no chance of discovering. Professor W. P.
Bradley has pointed out that the name " Quintessence of
Air " is very suggestive of oxygen. The life-giving com-
ponent of air (not discovered until a century and a half
after Drebbel's time) is volumetrically the " quintessence," the fifth part of air. " Is it possible," he asks,
" that Drebbel had discovered some liquid which easily
disengaged the then unknown oxygen gas, and thus was
able to restore to vitiated air that principle of which
respiration deprives it ? Undoubtedly not. It is much
more likely that he possessed a solution capable of absorbing the carbonic acid gas which is produced by
respiration, and that the name given it was entirely
fanciful and without special significance. But even if
Drebbel's claim was a piece of pure quackery with no
substantial basis at all, it is nevertheless not without
interest, for it shows, as we might have anticipated, that
the problem of ventilation, one of the most important
with which the inventors of submarines have to deal, was
at least appreciated by Drebbel the pioneer."

A writer of the period, one Harsdoffer, tells how
Drebbel was led to the construction of his boat :—

" One day when walking along the banks of the Thames
Drebbel noticed some sailors dragging behind their barques
baskets full of fish ; he saw that the barques were weighed
down in the water, but that they rose a little when the baskets

allowed the ropes which held them to slacken a little. The idea occurred to him that a ship could be held under the water by a somewhat similar method and could be propelled by oars and poles. Some time afterwards he constructed two little boats of this nature, but of different sizes, which were tightly closed with thick skin, and King James himself journeyed in one of them on the Thames. There were on this occasion twelve rowers besides the passengers, and the vessel during several hours was kept at a depth of twelve to fifteen feet below the surface."

This royal excursion under water terminated, we read, "fort hereusement."

The Abbé de Hautefeuille, in a brochure which appeared in 1680, entitled "Manière de respirer sous l'Eau," writes thus :—

"Drebbel's secret was probably the machine which I had imagined consisting of a bellows with two valves and two tubes resting on the surface of the water, the one bringing down air and the other sending it back. By speaking of a volatile essence which restored the nitrous parts consumed by respiration Drebbel evidently wished to disguise his invention and prevent others from finding out its real nature."

Ben Jonson, in his comedy *The Staple of News*, first acted by His Majesty's servants in 1625, has a hit at certain inventions of the time, and amongst these is the boat of Master Drebbel. Thomas, Act III, Scene 1, says :

> "They write here one Cornelius' son
> Hath made the Hollanders an invisible eel
> To swim the tavel at Dunkirk and sink all
> The shipping there.
> *Pennyboy, junior.* But how is't done ?
> *Grabal.* I'll shew you, sir,
> It is an automa. runs under water
> With a snug nose, and has a nimble tail

Made like an auger, with which tail she wriggles
Betwixt the costs of a ship and sinks it straight.
P., jun. Whence have you this news ?
Fitton. From a right hand I assure you.
The eel-boats here, that lie before Queen-hythe
Came out of Holland.
P., jun. A most brave device
To murder their flat bottoms."

That Ben Jonson should class the submarine boat of
Drebbel with such a proposal as that of bringing an
army over seas in cork shoes—

" All his horse
Are shod with cork, all fourscore pieces of ordnance
Mounted upon cork carriages, with bladders
Instead of wheels, to run the passage over
At a spring tide ; "

and with the discovery of perpetual motion—

" By an ale-wife in St. Katherine's
At the sign of the Dancing Bear "—

gives one an idea of how the world in general viewed
Drebbel's invention. And yet the inventor found favour
in the eyes of James I, who bestowed money upon him,
gave him a lodging in Eltham Palace, took a great interest in his experiments, and, when his life was in danger
at Prague, owing to a revolution, succeeded in obtaining
his release by personal intercession.

In return for his Majesty's favour, Cornelius invented
an " ingenious machine " for producing perpetual motion,
which became one of the wonderful sights of the day.
According to a description in the *Biographie Universelle*,
it consisted of a globe of glass in which, by means of the
four elements, Drebbel imitated perpetual motion. In

the space of twenty-four hours one could behold the course of the sun, the planets, and the stars. By means of this marvellous globe he showed " the cause of cold, of the ebb and flow of the sea, of storms, of thunder, of rain, of the wind, *enfin tout le mécanisme de la nature.*"

In the diary of Lewis Frederick, Prince of Wurtemberg, under date Tuesday, 1 May, 1610, occurs the passage : " His Excellency went to Elham Park to see the perpetual motion ; the inventor's name was Cornelius Trebel, a native of Alkmaar, a very fair and handsome man, and of very gentle manners, altogether different from such-like characters ; we also saw there Virginals, which played of themselves."

Undoubtedly Drebbel was ahead of his time, but one cannot credit him with all the wonders he is reported to have achieved. Some of his biographers state that he invented a telescope, a microscope, and a thermometer ; an incubator for hatching fowls ; an instrument for showing pictures or portraits of people not present at the time ; and a method of producing at will the most extreme cold. Drebbel was evidently highly thought of at the Courts of James I, Rudolph II, and Ferdinand II, but this was perhaps due more to his being " a very fair and handsome man of very gentle manners " than to his scientific attainments.

One of his biographers refers to him thus : " Cornelius van Drebbel, ein Charlatan," and others have dubbed him alchemist, empiric, magician, and professor of the Black Art.

Mr. Rye's estimate is perhaps the truer :—

"But however extravagant and improbable some of the following descriptions may appear, yet, allowing as we ought to do for the crude state of physical science and the credulity of the times in which he lived, as well as the then prevailing tendency to clothe scientific investigation and experiment with an air of mystery, Cornelius Drebbel is entitled, we think, to hold a respectable position among the ingenious inventors and mechanicians of the early part of the seventeenth century."

Bishop Wilkins on Submarine Navigation Drebbel's boat attracted the attention of the Right Reverend John Wilkins, whose mathematical and philosophical works were published in London in the year 1708.

John Wilkins was a remarkable man, considerably in advance of his day in scientific speculation. As few people nowadays read his books, a brief extract from his *Mathematical Magick : or the Wonders that may be Perform'd by Mechanical Geometry*, may be read with interest and amusement.

The book is divided into two parts, the first entitled "Archimedes, or Mechanical Powers," the second, "Doedalus, or Mechanical Motions."

Chapter V of Part 2 deals with "the possibility of framing an Ark for Submarine Navigation: the Difficulties and Consequences of such a Contrivance."

"It will not be altogether impertinent," says the author, "with the Discourse of these gradient *Automata* to mention what Mersennus doth so pleasantly and largely descant upon concerning the making of a ship wherein men may safely swim under the water. That such a Contrivance is feasible, and may be effected, is beyond all question, because it hath been already experimented here in *England* by *Cornelius*

Dreble ; but how to improve it unto Publick Use and Advantage, so as to be serviceable for remote Voyages, the carrying of any considerable Number of Men, with Provisions and Commodities, would be of such excellent Use, as may deserve some further enquiry."

The difficulties are divided into three heads :—

1. " The letting-out or receiving in anything as there shall be occasion without the admission of Water. If it hath not such a convenience these kind of Voyages must needs be very dangerous and uncomfortable both by Reason of many noisome and offensive Things which should be thrust out, and many other needful Things which should be received in. Now herein will consist the Difficulty, for to contrive the opening of the vessel so that anything may be put in or out, and yet the Water not rush into it with much Violence as it doth usually in the leak of a Ship."

The learned Doctor's remedy is as follows :

" Let there," he says, " be certain leather bags made of several bignesses, long and open at both ends, and answerable to these let there be divers windows made in open spaces in the frame of the ship round the sides, to which one end of these bags might be fixed, the other end coming within the ship. The bag being thus fastened and tied close about towards the window, then any thing that is to be sent out might be safely put into that end within the ship : this being again close shut, and the other end loosened, the thing may be safely sent out without the admission of any water."

In taking anything in, it was to be first received into that part of the bag towards the window, which being close tied down at the other end may then be safely opened.

" It is easy to conceive, how by such means as these a Person may be sent out or received in, as there shall be occasion ; how the water which will perhaps by Degrees leak into several parts may be emptied out again, with divers other like advantages. Tho' if there should be a leak at the bottom of the vessel, yet very little Water would get in, because the Air would get out."

The fate of the unhappy person thrust out of the vessel by means of the leather bags is too dreadful to contemplate, and the sailors called upon to man a modern war submarine may congratulate themselves that this con-

A CONCERT IN A SUBMARINE (1855)
The *Diable Marin* of W. Bauer

venient contrivance imagined by the ingenious prelate has not come into use. As to the taking in of things into the boat, one does not quite gather how they would get into the bag, or how the bag would be first untied and then tied again by those inside the vessel.

The second difficulty in such an Ark is

" the Motion or fixing of it according to occasion : the directing of it to several places as the Voyage shall be designed, without which it would be very useless, if it were to remain only in one Place, and were to remove only blindfold, without any certain Direction : And the Contrivance of this may seem very difficult because these submarine Navigators will want the usual advantages of Wind and Tide for Motion, and the sight of the Heavens for direction."

The progressive motion of the boat would be effected by the help of several oars made to contract and dilate like the fins of a fish, the holes through which they passed into the ship being tied about with the aforementioned leather bags.

" It will not be convenient, perhaps, that the motion in these Voyages should be very swift because of these Observations and Discoveries to be made at the Bottom of the Sea, which in a little space may abundantly recompense the, slowness of the Progress."

Dr. Wilkins had grasped the fact that if the ark were so ballasted as to be equal weight with the like magnitude of water, it would then be easily movable in any part of it.

As for the ascent and descent of the craft, this was to be accomplished by

" some great Weight at the Bottom of the Ship (being Part of its Ballast), which by some Cord within may be loosened from it. If this Weight is let loose so will the Ship ascend from it (if need be) to the very Surface of the Water ; and again as it is pulled close to the Ship, so will it descend."

The idea of taking in water-ballast for sinking the ark does not seem to have occurred to the author.

" For directing the course of the vessel the Mariner's Needle would be employed, but the patent difficulty of all is this, How the Air may be supplied for Respiration, How constant Fires may be kept in for light and the Dressing of Food, how those Vicissitudes of Rarefaction and Condensation may be maintained."

While our author will not go so far as to say that a man may by custom, "which in other things doth produce such strange incredible effects," be enabled to live in the open water as do the fishes, yet he thinks that long use and custom may strengthen men against many such inconveniences of this kind which to inexperienced persons may prove very hazardous : thus it will not perhaps be so necessary to have the air for breathing so "pure and desecated" as is required for others.

The difficulty of respiration under water may be met in several ways.

"The submarine ark should be of such a large capacity that as the air is corrupted in one part so it may be purified and renewed in the other : if the mere refrigeration of the air would fit it for breathing, this might be somewhat helped with bellows, which would cool it by motion : it is not altogether improbable," says the doctor, " that the lamps and fires in the middle of it like the reflected beams in the first region rarefy the air and the circumambient coldness towards the sides of the vessel like the second region, cooling and condensing of it would work such a Vicissitude and change of air as might fit it for all its proper uses."

Finally, if none of these conjectures will help, the author mentions that there is in France one Barrières, a diver, who hath found out the art whereby a man might easily continue under water for six hours together.

" Whereas Ten Cubical Feet of Air will not serve another Diver to breathe in for Half an Hour, he by the help of a Cavity not above one or two Foot at most will have Breath enough for six hours and a Lanthorne scarce above the usual size to keep a candle burning as long as a Man please. Which (if it be true and were commonly known) might be sufficient help against the greatest difficulty."

Dr. Wilkins makes no mention of the "Chymicall Liquor" which Drebbel is reported to have discovered for the purifying of the air inside the boat when under water, and it is probable that he attached little value to the accounts of this remarkable substance.

Having so far dealt with the difficulties of submarine navigation and their remedies, the author proceeds to discuss the many advantages and conveniences of such a contrivance.

First of all, says he—" 'Tis private ; a Man may thus go to any Coast of the World invisibly without being discovered or prevented in his journey."

Certainly this would be a convenience to the criminal fleeing from justice, to a deposed ruler wishing to escape from his conquerors, and to others desirous of effacing themselves for a time.

Secondly—" 'Tis safe from the Uncertainty of Tides and the Violence of Tempests, which do never move the Sea above Five or Six paces deep, from Pirates and Robbers which do so infest other Voyages. From Ice and great Frosts, which do so much endanger the Passages towards the Poles."

Could Bishop Wilkins but have perused Mr. John Holland's article in the *North American Review* for December, 1900, in which proposals for a submarine passenger service across the Channel are put forward, he would have been gratified to find the inventor of a practical under-water vessel of the same opinion as himself regarding the "advantages and conveniences" of travelling beneath rather than on the waves.

The late M. Goubet also imagined a submarine cross-Channel service.

Thirdly—" It may be of very great advantage against a Navy of Enemies, who by this means may be undermined in the Water and blown up."

Sixty-seven years after these words were written David Bushnell launched his submarine boat, which carried a torpedo charged with 130 lb. of gunpowder, to be affixed to the side of the vessel to be blown up. In 1864 the *David*, owned by the Confederates, blew up the *Housatonic*, and though this is the only occasion on which a submarine has done any damage to the foe in an actual encounter, it is more than likely that in the next great naval war under-water vessels may " be of very great advantage against a Navy of Enemies."

Fourthly—" It may be of special use for the Relief of any Place ·that is besieged by Water to convey unto them Invisible Supplies ; and so likewise for the Surprizal of any Place that is accessible by Water."

Fifthly—" It may be of unspeakable Benefit for Submarine Experiments and Discoveries, as—The several Proportions of Swiftness betwixt the ascent of a Bladder, Cork, or any other light Substance, in comparison to the descent of Stones or Lead. The deep Caverns and Subterranean Passages where the Sea Water, in the course of its circulation, doth vest itself into other Places and the like. The Nature and Kinds of Fishes, the several Arts of Catching them, by alluring them with Lights, by placing divers nets about the sides of this Vessel, shooting the greater sort of them with Guns, which might be put out of the ship by the help of such Bags as were mentioned before, with divers the like Artifices and Treacheries, which may be more successfully practised by such who live so familiarly together. These fish may serve not only for food but for Fewel likewise, in respect of that oil which may be extracted from them ; the Way of Dressing Meat by Lamps being in many Respects the most convenient for such a Voyage. The many fresh springs that may probably be met with at the Bottom of the Sea, will serve for the Supply of Drink and other Occasions."

Dr. Wilkins is, however, convinced that, above all, his Ark will be most valuable in the discovery of submarine treasures—

" not only in regard of what hath been drowned by Wrecks, but the several precious Things that grow there ; as Pearl, Coral Mines ; with innumerable other Things of great Value which may be much more easily found out and fetch'd up by the help of this than by any of the usual ways of the Urinators."

For the better fulfilment of this purpose, the author suggests that there should be some lesser cabins tied about the Great Ark at various distances, where several persons as scouts might be lodged for the taking of observations according as the Admiral should direct them. Dr. Wilkin's prediction has been realised, and in Mr. Simon Lake's *Argonaut* there exists a machine which is bound to play an important part in " the discovery of Submarine Treasure."

In the penultimate paragraph of the chapter on the submarine ark Dr Wilkins waxes enthusiastic over the immense possibilities latent in such a contrivance.

" All kinds of Arts and Manufactures may be exercised in this Vessel. The Observations made by it might be written and (if need be) Printed here likewise. Several Colonies may there inhabit, having their Children born, and bred up, without the knowledge of land, who could not chuse but be amazed with Strange Conceits upon the Discovery of this Upper World."

In conclusion, the author writes :—

" I am not able to judge what other Advantages there may be suggested, or whether Experiment would fully answer these Notional Conjectures. But, however, because the Invention did unto me seem ingenious and new, being not impertinent to the present Enquiry, therefore I thought it might be worth the mentioning."

Mersenne " Mersennus," to whom the learned Bishop refers, was a monk of the order of the " Minims," who lived from 1588–1648, and was the chief friend and literary agent of Descartes. He gave in his writings some attention to submarine navigation. He proposed that the shell of a boat which he projected, but never built, should be of copper or some other metal, and that in shape it should resemble a fish, and in order to avoid its turning round both ends should be pointed.

In time of war the boat would destroy the keels of the enemy's ships. At the port-holes were placed big cannon. An arrangement of packing with a plug valve prevented the introduction of water. At the moment of firing the guns were brought close to the openings and the plug-valve was raised ; after the shot had been discharged the plug fell automatically back to its place. In order to replenish the air pneumatic machines and ventilators would be used ; for steering, the compass would act as well beneath the waves as on the surface ; for lighting, phosphorescent bodies would be used. The boat was to have wheels, and was to be moved by means of oars. Mersenne was the first to affirm that even the most violent tempests could not be a source of danger to the submarine vessel, as the disturbance was felt but a little distance below the surface.

Another monk of the same order, Father Fournier, about the year 1640, gave to the world his ideas on the problem of navigating beneath the water.

In the year 1653 a Frenchman, whose name we have been unable to discover, is said to have built and operated a submarine boat at Rotterdam. It was 72 feet long,

RACING THE "CAMPANIA"
Apostoloff's Proposed Submarine

12 feet high, and 8 feet broad. It was traversed down its entire length by a system of very solid girders, whose extremities, projecting beneath the bottom, were covered with iron. Ordinarily the boat was not meant to be submerged lower than the "awash" condition, but the part above the water was made to slope with the idea of turning aside the projectiles aimed at it. In the centre of the boat was a kind of paddle wheel, but the inventor was careful to keep many details secret regarding its propulsion and its method of attack. For some little

time he showed his invention for a small pecuniary re-
muneration, but it failed to attract the notice of those in
authority.

In the *Annual Register* of the year 1774, at page 245,
there appears an authentic account of a late unfortunate
transaction with respect to a diving machine at Plymouth.
This relates to the death of a Mr. Day who lost his life in
a boat of his own construction in Plymouth Sound.

Day　　It appears that Mr. Day, " the sole projector of the scheme, and as matters have
turned out, the unhappy sacrifice to his own ingenuity,"
planned a method of sinking a vessel under water with
a man in it, who should live there for a certain time, and
then by his own means only bring himself up to the
surface. He tried his project in the Broads near Yar-
mouth, fitting a Norfolk market-boat for his purpose.
and succeeded in sinking himself thirty feet under water,
where he continued during the space of twenty-four
hours. Elated with this success, he then wanted to avail
himself of his invention. He conversed with his friends,
perfectly convinced that he had brought his undertaking
to a certainty ; but how to reap the advantage of it was
the difficulty that remained.

That this vessel might serve some useful purpose,
whether peaceful or warlike, does not seem to have occurred to Mr. Day, who was content seemingly to construct a diving boat capable of sinking and rising again
to the surface, without furnishing it with any method of
propulsion. A friend of the inventor suggested that if
he acquainted the sporting gentlemen with the discovery

and the certainty of the performance, considerable " betts " would take place as soon as the project should be mentioned in Company. Struck by this happy idea, Mr. Day looked into the " Sporting Kalendar," and finding therein the name of Blake decided that it was to this gentleman that he ought to address himself. Accordingly, in November, 1773, Mr. Blake received the following letter :—

" SIR,—I have found out an affair by which many thousands may be won. It is of a paradoxical nature, but can be performed with case ; therefore, sir, if you chuse to be informed of it, and give me £100 for every £1000 you shall win by it, I will very readily wait upon you, and inform you of it. I am, myself, but a poor mechanic and not able to make anything of it without your assistance.

" Yours, &c.,
" J. DAY."

Mr. Blake naturally had no conception of Mr. Day's design, nor was he sure that the letter was serious. He wrote, however, to the inventor, and appointed an interview, when the latter announced his project. He declared " that he could sink a ship one hundred yards deep in the sea with himself in it, and remain therein for the space of twenty-four hours, without communication with anything above ; and at the expiration of the time rise up again in the vessel."

Mr. Blake was not a little staggered at this dare-devil proposal, but agreed to advance money for the construction of a model. This having proved satisfactory, Mr. Blake advanced a further sum for the building of a practicable vessel. This, it would appear, had a false

M

bottom, " standing on feet like a butcher's block, which
contained the ballast ; and by the person in the vessel
unscrewing some pins, he was to rise to the surface leaving
the false bottom behind."

The boat was at length built, and in the presence of
Mr. Blake a trial descent was made. The day fixed for
the test which was to decide the bet arrived, but Mr.
Blake reduced the depth of water from one hundred yards
to one hundred feet, and the time from twenty-four to
twelve hours.

" The vessel was towed to the place agreed upon ; Mr.
Day provided himself with whatever he thought necessary,
went into the vessel, let the water into her, and with great
composure retired to the room constructed for him and shut
up the valve. The ship went gradually down to twenty-two
fathom water at 2 o'clock on Tuesday, June 28 (1774), in
the afternoon, being to return at 2 o'clock the next morning.
He had three buoys as messengers which he could send to
the surface at option to announce his situation below ; but
none appearing, Mr. Blake, who was near at hand in a barge,
began to entertain some suspicions. He kept a strict look-
out, and at the time appointed, neither the buoys nor the
vessel coming up, he applied to the *Orpheus* frigate, which lay
just off the barge, for assistance. The captain with the most
ready benevolence supplied them with everything in his
power to seek for the ship. Mr. Blake in this alarming situation was not content with the help of the *Orpheus* only ; he
made immediate application to Lord Sandwich (who happened
to be at Plymouth) for further relief. His Lordship with
great humanity ordered a number of hands from the dock-
yard, who went with the utmost alacrity and tried every
effort to regain the ship, but unhappily without effect."

According to Admiral Hichborn (U.S.N.), writing a
few years ago, J. Day had the distinction of being the

only known victim of the dangers of submarine navigation. This distinction depended upon the supposition
that reports of submarine accidents were much more reliable two hundred and forty years ago than they had
been for the last forty years, during which period there
had been *authentic* newspaper reports of the loss of
eighty-two lives in attempting submarine navigation in
the United States. " Fifty of these lives were not lost
at all, and the other thirty-two, though lost in a boat
designed to operate as a submarine, were all lost when,
and apparently because, she was not so operating." This
referred to the *David*, which in the American Civil War
destroyed four crews of eight men each.

Mr. Charles Babbage, in his article on the Diving Bell
in the *Encyclopædia Metropolitana*, describes Day's
under-water boat. He writes :—

" Having purchased a sloop of 50 tons, it was prepared by
building an air-tight chamber in the middle 12 feet long,
9 feet broad, and 8 feet deep, and capable of containing 75
hogsheads of air. Considerable pains were taken to make
this as strong and as secure as possible. In the middle of
the top of this chamber was a square hole, a scuttle just
sufficiently large to admit a man ; it was bevelled outwards,
in order that the valve which was to close the chamber might
be driven in more tightly. Screws were applied to this valve,
in order to screw it home, and it, as well as the scuttle, was
lined with flannel. On the decks of the vessel three buoys of
different colours, white, red, and black, were fixed by plugs
in such a manner that they were to be disengaged by driving
another plug from the inside of the chamber. These were
designed as signals to indicate the state of health of the
adventurer during his stay under water. The white was to
denote his being very well, the red indifferent, and the black

his being very ill. The ballast of 20 tons, by which the vessel was to be sunk, and by disengaging of which it was to be raised again, was fixed to four iron rods passing through tubes into the chamber. The vessel was ballasted internally with 10 tons, which with the twenty suspended from her would, it was imagined, cause her to sink when full of water. Thus perished a man whose intrepidity resulted from his ignorance of the dangers he encountered, and who fell a victim to his obstinate confidence in the success of a plan concerning which his knowledge was totally insufficient to enable him to judge. The depth of water in which the vessel sank was 22 fathoms ; the pressure of more than four atmospheres thus produced in all probability crushed in the sides of the chamber soon after it reached the bottom."

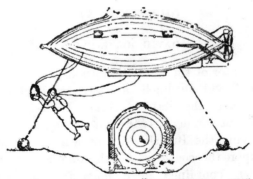

THE "INTELLIGENT WHALE" OF HALSTEAD. (1892)

CHAPTER XII

DAVID BUSHNELL

THE originator of the modern method of submarine warfare was David Bushnell, a native of Saybrook (now Westbrook), in the State of Maine, U.S.A., who in the latter part of the eighteenth century conceived the idea of destroying the British ships of war which were employed upon the coasts of North America by exploding gunpowder, contained in a magazine, beneath their bottoms. In order the better to fix the charge to the ships, Bushnell built in 1775 the first practical submarine boat, and the first of which any detailed account is extant.

In a letter written in October, 1789, to Thomas Jefferson, the Minister Plenipotentiary of the United States at Paris, David Bushnell gives a very interesting description of his vessel and its achievements. This deserves to be printed here in full in view of the many quite remarkable devices (considering the period) which the inventor originated.

" The external shape of the submarine vessel bore some resemblance to two upper tortoise shells of equal size, joined together, the place of entrance into the vessel being represented by the opening made by the swell of the shells at the head of the animal. The inside was capable of containing the operator and air sufficient to support him thirty minutes without receiving fresh air. At the bottom, opposite to the entrance, was fixed a quantity of lead for ballast. At one edge, which was directly before the operator, who sat upright, was an oar for rowing forward or backward. At the other edge was a rudder for steering. An aperture at the bottom, with its valve, was designed to admit water for the purpose of descending, and two brass forcing pumps served to eject the water within when necessary for ascending. At the top there was likewise an oar for ascending or descending, or continuing at any particular depth. A water gauge or barometer determined the depth of descent, a compass directed the course, and a ventilator within supplied the vessel with fresh air when on the surface.

" The entrance into the vessel was elliptical, and so small as barely to admit a person. This entrance was surrounded with a broad elliptical iron band, the lower edge of which was let into the wood, of which the body of the vessel was made, in such a manner as to give its utmost support to the body of the vessel against the pressure of the water. Above the upper edge of this iron band there was a brass crown or cover, resembling a hat with its crown and brim, which shut watertight upon the iron band ; the crown was hung to the iron band with hinges so as to turn over sidewise when opened. To make it perfectly secure when shut it might be screwed down upon the band by the operator or by a person without.

" There were in the brass crown three round doors, one directly in front and one on each side, large enough to put the hand through. When open they admitted fresh air. Their shutters were ground perfectly tight into their places with emery, hung with hinges, and secured in their places when shut. There were likewise several small glass windows in the crown for looking through, and for admitting light in the day-time, with covers to secure them. There were two air-pipes in the crown. A ventilator within drew fresh air through one of the air-pipes and discharged it into the lower part of the vessel ; the fresh air introduced by the ventilator expelled the impure light air through the other air-pipe. Both air-pipes were so constructed that they shut themselves whenever the water rose near their tops, so that no water could enter through them, and opened themselves immediately after they rose above the water.

" The vessel was chiefly ballasted with lead fixed to its bottom ; when this was not sufficient a quantity was placed within, more or less according to the weight of the operator ; its ballast made it so stiff that there was no danger of over-setting. The vessel, with all its appendages and the operator, was of sufficient weight to settle it very low in the water. About 200 lb. of lead at the bottom for ballast could be let down 40 or 50 feet below the vessel ; this enabled the operator to rise instantly to the surface of the water in case of accident.

" When the operator would descend he placed his foot upon the top of a brass valve, depressing it, by which he opened a large aperture in the bottom of the vessel, through which the water entered at his pleasure ; when he had admitted a suffi-cient quantity he descended very gradually ; if he admitted too much he ejected as much as was necessary to obtain an equilibrium by the two brass forcing pumps which were placed at each hand. Whenever the vessel leaked or he would ascend to the surface he also made use of these forcing pumps. When the skilful operator had obtained an equilibrium he could row upward or downward, or continue at any particular depth, with an oar placed near the top of the vessel, formed upon the principle of the screw, the axis of the oar entering the vessel ; by turning the oar one way he raised the vessel, by turning it the other way he depressed it.

"A glass tube, 18 inches long and 1 inch in diameter, standing upright, its upper end closed, and its lower end, which was open, screwed into a brass pipe, through which the external water had a passage into the glass tube, served as a water-gauge or barometer. There was a piece of cork with phosphorus on it put into the water-gauge. When the vessel descended the water rose into the water-gauge, condensing the air within, and bearing the cork with its phosphorus on its surface. By the light of the phosphorus the ascent of the water in the gauge was rendered visible, and the depth of the vessel under water ascertained by a graduated line.

"An oar, formed upon the principle of the screw, was fixed in the fore part of the vessel ; its axis entered the vessel, and being turned one way, rowed the vessel forward, but being turned the other way rowed it backward ; it was made to be turned by the hand or foot.

"A rudder, hung to the hinder part of the vessel, commanded it with the greatest ease. The rudder was made very elastic, and might be used for rowing forward. Its tiller was within the vessel, at the operator's right hand, fixed at a right angle on an iron rod which passed through the side of the vessel ; the rod had a crank on its outside end which commanded the rudder by means of a rod extending from the end of the crank to a kind of tiller fixed upon the left hand of the rudder. Raising and depressing the first-mentioned tiller turned the rudder as the same required. A compass marked with phosphorus directed the course, both above and under the water, and a line and lead sounded the depth when necessary.

"The internal shape of the vessel, in every possible section of it, verged towards an ellipsis, as near as the design would allow, but every horizontal section, although elliptical, yet as near to a circle as could be admitted. The body of the vessel was made exceedingly strong, and to strengthen it as much as

possible a firm piece of wood was framed, parallel to the con-
jugate diameter, to prevent the sides from yielding to the
great pressure of the incumbent water in a deep immersion.
This piece of wood was also a seat for the operator.

" Every opening was well secured. The pumps had two sets
of valves. The aperture at the bottom for admitting water
was covered with a plate perforated full of holes to receive the
water and prevent anything from choking the passage or
stopping the valve from shutting. The brass valve might like-

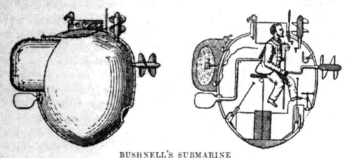

BUSHNELL'S SUBMARINE

wise be forced into its place with a screw if necessary. The
air-pipes had a kind of hollow sphere fixed round the top of
each to secure the air-pipe valves from injury ; these hollow
spheres were perforated full of holes for the passage of the air
through the pipes. Within the air-pipes were shutters to
secure them should any accident happen to the pipes or the
valves on their tops.

" Wherever the external apparatus passed through the body
of the vessel the joints were round and formed by brass pipes,
which were driven into the wood of the vessel, the holes
through the pipes were very exactly made, and the iron rods
which passed through them were turned in a lathe to fit
them ; the joints were also kept full of oil to prevent rust
and leaking. Particular attention was given to bring every
part necessary for performing the operations, both within and
without the vessel, before the operator, and as conveniently

as could be devised, so that everything might be found in the dark except the water-gauge and the compass, which were visible by the light of the phosphorus, and nothing required the operator to turn to the right hand or to the left to perform anything necessary."

Description of a Magazine and its Appendages designed to be conveyed by the Submarine Vessel to the bottom of a Ship.

" In the fore part of the brim of the crown of the submarine vessel was a socket, and an iron tube passing through the socket; the tube stood upright, and could slide up and down in the socket 6 inches. At the top of the tube was a wood screw (A), fixed by means of a rod, which passed through the tube, and screwed the wood screw fast upon the top of the tube; by pushing the wood screw up against the bottom of the ship and turning it at the same time it would enter the planks; driving would also answer the same purpose. When the wood screw was firmly fixed it could be cast off by unscrewing the rod, which fastened it upon the top of the tube.

" Behind the submarine vessel was a place above the rudder for carrying a large powder magazine. This was made of two pieces of oak timber, large enough when hollowed out to contain 150 lb. of powder, with the apparatus used in firing it, and was secured in its place by a screw turned by the operator. A strong piece of rope extended from the magazine to the wood screw (A) above mentioned, and was fastened to both. When the wood screw was fixed, and to be cast off from its tube, the magazine was to be cast off likewise by unscrewing it, leaving it hanging to the wood screw; it was lighter than the water, that it might rise up against the object to which the wood screw and itself were fastened.

" Within the magazine was an apparatus constructed to run any proposed length of time under twelve hours; when it had run out its time it unpinioned a strong lock resembling a gunlock, which gave fire to the powder. This apparatus was so pinioned that it could not possibly move till, by casting off the magazine from the vessel, it was set in motion.

" The skilful operator could swim so low on the surface of
the water as to approach very near a ship in the night without
fear of being discovered, and might, if he chose, approach the
stem or stern above water with very little danger. He could
sink very quickly, keep at any depth he pleased, and row a
great distance in any direction he desired without coming to
the surface, and when he rose to the surface he could soon
obtain a fresh supply of air. If necessary he might descend
again and pursue his course."

*Experiments made to prove the Nature and Use of a
Submarine Vessel.*

" The first experiment I made was with about two ounces
of gunpowder, which I exploded 4 feet under water, to prove
to some of the first personages in Connecticut that powder
would take fire under water.

" The second experiment was made with 2 lb. of powder
enclosed in a wooden bottle and fixed under a hogshead, with
a 2-inch oak plank between the hogshead and the powder.
The hogshead was loaded with stones as deep as it could
swim ; a wooden pipe descending through the lower head of
the hogshead and through the plank into the powder contained
in the bottle, was primed with powder. A match put to the
priming exploded the powder, which produced a very great
effect, rending the plank into pieces, demolishing the hogshead,
and casting the stones and the ruins of the hogshead, with a
body of water, many feet into the air, to the astonishment of
the spectators. This experiment was likewise made for the
satisfaction of the gentlemen above mentioned.

" I afterwards made many experiments of a similar nature,
some of them with large quantities of powder ; they produced
very violent explosions, much more than sufficient for any
purpose I had in view.

" In the first essays with the submarine vessel I took care
to prove its strength to sustain the great pressure of the incumbent water when sunk deep before I trusted any person
to descend much below the surface, and I never suffered any

person to go under water without having a strong piece of rigging made fast to it, until I found him well acquainted with the operations necessary for his safety. After that I made him descend and continue at particular depths, without rising or sinking, row by the compass, approach a vessel, go under her, and fix the wood screw mentioned in No. 2, and marked A, into her bottom; &c., until I thought him sufficiently expert to put my design into execution.

" I found, agreeably to my expectations, that it required many trials to make a person of common ingenuity a skilful operator. The first I employed was very ingenious, and made himself master of the business, but was taken sick in the campaign of 1776 at New York before he had an opportunity to make use of his skill, and never recovered his health sufficiently afterwards.

" After various attempts to find an operator to my wish, I sent one who appeared more expert than the rest from New York to a 50-gun ship lying not far from Governor's Island. He went under the ship and attempted to fix the wooden screw into her bottom, but struck, as he supposes, a bar of iron which passes from the rudder hinge, and is spiked under the ship's quarter. Had he moved a few inches, which he might have done without rowing, I have no doubt but he would have found wood where he might have fixed the screw, or if the ship were sheathed with copper he might easily have pierced it ; but not being well skilled in the management of the vessel, in attempting to move to another place he lost the ship. After seeking her in vain for some time, he rowed some distance and rose to the surface of the water, but found daylight had advanced so far that he durst not renew the attempt. He says that he could easily have fastened the magazine under the stem of the ship above water, as he rowed up to the stern and touched it before he descended. Had he fastened it there the explosion of 150 lb. of powder (the quantity contained in the magazine) must have been fatal to the ship. In his return from the ship to New York he passed near Governor's Island, and thought he was discovered by the enemy on the island.

Being in haste to avoid the danger he feared, he cast off the magazine, as he imagined it retarded him in the swell, which was very considerable. After the magazine had been cast off one hour, the time the internal apparatus was set to run, it blew up with great violence.

"Afterwards there were two attempts made in Hudson's River, above the city, but they effected nothing. One of them was by the aforementioned person. In going towards the ship he lost sight of her, and went a great distance beyond her. When he at length found her the tide ran so strong that, as he descended under water for the ship's bottom, it swept him away. Soon after this the enemy went up the river and pursued the boat which had the submarine vessel on board, and sunk it with their shot. Though I afterwards recovered the vessel, I found it impossible at that time to prosecute the design any farther. I had been in a bad state of health from the beginning of my undertaking, and was now very unwell ; the situation of public affairs was such that I despaired of obtaining the public attention and the assistance necessary. I was unable to support myself and the persons I must have employed had I proceeded. Besides, I found it absolutely necessary that the operators should acquire more skill in the management of the vessel before I could expect success, which would have taken up some time, and made no small additional expense. I therefore gave over the pursuit for that time, and waited for a more favourable opportunity, which never arrived.

"In the year 1777 I made an attempt from a whale-boat against the *Cerberus* frigate, then lying at anchor between Connecticut River and New London, by drawing a machine against her side by means of a line. The machine was loaded with powder, to be exploded by a gunlock, which was to be unpinioned by an apparatus to be turned by being brought alongside of the frigate. This machine fell in with a schooner at anchor astern of the frigate, and concealed from my sight. By some means or other it was fired, and demolished the schooner and three men, and blew the only one left alive overboard, who was taken up very much hurt.

" After this I fixed several kegs under water, charged with powder, to explode upon touching anything as they floated along with the tide. I set them afloat in the Delaware, above the English shipping at Philadelphia, in December, 1777. I was unacquainted with the river, and obliged to depend upon a gentleman very imperfectly acquainted with that part of it, as I afterwards found. We went as near the shipping as we durst venture ; I believe the darkness of the night greatly

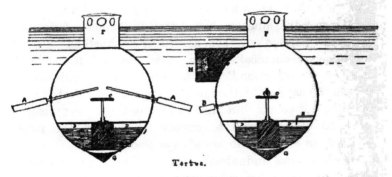

Tortue.

BUSHNELL'S SUBMARINE

A A. Oars   B. Rudder.   C. Seat.   D. Immersion tank.   E. Pipe.   F. Conning tower.
G. Safety weight.   H. Torpedo.

deceived him, as it did me. We set them adrift to fall with the ebb upon the shipping. Had we been within sixty rods I believe they must have fallen in with them immediately, as I designed ; but, as I afterwards found, they were set adrift much too far distant, and did not arrive until, after being detained some time by frost, they advanced in the daytime in a dispersed situation, and under great disadvantages. One of them blew up a boat with several persons in it who imprudently handled it too freely, and thus gave the British that alarm which brought on the battle of the kegs.

" The above vessel, magazine, &c., were projected in the year 1771, but not completed until the year 1775."

The above account appears in the fourth volume of the Transactions of the American Philosophical Society, and also in the fourth volume of Nicholson's *Journal of Natural Philosophy* (1801).

Disappointed in the failure of his submarine boat to accomplish the things of which he felt sure it was capable, Bushnell went to France, and finally settled in Georgia, where he lived under the pseudonym of Dr. Bush until the year 1826, when he died at the ripe age of ninety.

General Washington, in a letter to Thomas Jefferson, dated 26 September, 1775, described Bushnell as "a man of great mechanical powers, fertile in inventions, and master of execution." With regard to the submarine vessel, he says : "I thought, and still think, that it was an effort of genius, but that too many things were necessary to be combined to expect much from the issue against an enemy who are always upon guard."

Bushnell was undoubtedly the first inventor who combined in his design submarine navigation and torpedo warfare, and his invention, crude though it was, was the embryo of the modern diving torpedo-boat. The principles on which it was built may be traced in almost all the later submarine craft, and the improvements that have taken place have been mostly due to the general progress of engineering ; the "oar placed near the top of the vessel" may be compared with Mr. Nordenfelt's vertical screws.

CHAPTER XIII

FULTON'S SUBMARINE BOATS

"What will become of navies, and where will sailors be found to man ships of war, when it is a physical certainty that they may at any moment be blown into the air by means of diving-boats, against which no human foresight can guard them?"—M. St. Aubin (in 1802).

ROBERT FULTON was born in 1765 in Little Britain, Pennsylvania, and died at New York on 24 February, 1815. In the year 1796 Fulton went to Paris, residing at the house of Joel Barlow, then resident minister for the United States, for seven years. While in Paris two projects occupied a large portion of his time. The first was a carcass, or box, filled with combustibles, which was to be propelled under water and made to explode beneath the bottom of a vessel.

The second was a submarine boat. In 1797 Fulton submitted his vessel to the approval of the Government of the Directory, promising to furnish them with an agent by which they could dispose of their enemies, particularly British, in all parts of the world. A Commission appointed to examine his ideas reported favourably on them, but the Minister of the Marine would have nothing to do with them. Fulton then made a model of his submarine, which met with the approval of another Commission, but again the Minister of Marine was obdurate. Fulton now tried the Dutch Government, but they did not look with any favour on the new methods of under-water warfare.

Three years later (in 1800) Fulton approached Napoleon, who appeared to think well of his schemes, for he appointed La Place, Mouge, and Volney to examine them, and also gave him 10,000 francs to carry out experiments.

In May, 1801, Fulton built his first submarine boat, the *Nautilus*. She made her first trial on the Seine opposite the Invalides. Fulton and one sailor formed the crew, and, with nothing but a candle to light the interior, they remained submerged twenty minutes. On coming to the surface, they found that the current had carried them some considerable distance down the river, so again sinking beneath the surface Fulton steered his vessel to the point of departure. On 3 July, 1801, Fulton embarked with three companions on board his " plunging boat " in the harbour of Brest ; the four men descended in the *Nautilus* a depth of 23 feet, which seemed to be the greatest depth the boat would stand. They remained below in total darkness for one hour. At subsequent descents Fulton tried to employ candles, but found they destroyed the vitality of the air. Bull's-eyes were then inserted in the top of the boat, and these alleviated, to a certain extent, the prevailing gloom.

Once Fulton, with three persons, is said to have stayed for six hours at a depth of 5 feet by the aid of a copper globe of 1 cubic foot capacity " containing 200 atmospheres " ; on another occasion he sailed out of the harbour, then quite suddenly lowered his mast, and disappeared from view, showing how quickly he could submerge his craft.

N

The *Nautilus* was a cigar-shaped boat about 7 feet in diameter. The hull was of copper, but supported by iron ribs. It had one mast, a mainsail, and a jib, which moved her at the rate of 2 miles an hour on the surface, and were stowed in two minutes when preparing to dive. Under the water the vessel was moved by the exertions of two men, the "propelling engine" consisting of a wheel rotated by a hand-winch, at the rate of 2½ miles an hour. A third man steered from a small conning-tower, while Fulton governed the position of the boat by regulating the machine which kept her balanced and determined her depth below the surface. She was 21 ft. 4 in. long, and was furnished with a keel under the whole length of the hull.

Having proved that man could exist for some time beneath the surface in a vessel and could steer it, Fulton made experiments with a torpedo, or case of explosive. On the first occasion he blew a small ship to fragments with 20 lb. of powder.

As he had shown his ability to blow up old hulks in French waters, Fulton proposed to build a large submarine vessel, but failed to obtain official support, partly because those in authority considered that submarine explosions were not legal warfare. One of these writes that "this type of warfare carries with it the objection that those who undertake it and those against whom it is made, will all be lost. This cannot be called a gallant death."

Fulton asked a reward for each vessel he destroyed, the reimbursement of the price of his ship (40,000 francs), and, lastly, a patent giving himself and his crew the quality of belligerents, so that if they were captured they would not be hanged as pirates.

That submarine warfare was considered by some "immoral" at the time is evident from the statement of Admiral Pléville le Pelley, the Minister of Marine. "It seems impossible to give a Commission for belligerency to men who employ such a method of destroying the fleet of the enemy."

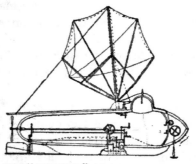

THE "NAUTILUS" OF ROBERT FULTON

As Fulton was equally unsuccessful in his effort to interest Napoleon in steam navigation, the disappointed inventor crossed the Channel in order to discover whether the English would show themselves any readier to grasp new ideas, and would prove capable of foreseeing the possibilities of his inventions.

It was in May, 1804, that Fulton came to England, and from some accounts it would appear that the English Government, alarmed at Fulton's plans, invited him, at the suggestion of Earl Stanhope, to lay his ideas before them. The inventor explained to the naval authorities that his system rendered above-water fleets unnecessary,

but they did not at all relish the idea of fighting beneath
the waves.

Mr. Pitt, however, then Prime Minister, was very much
taken with the American and his torpedoes, and appointed a Commission to watch certain experiments.
The Commission consisted of Mr. Pitt, Lords Mulgrave,
Melville, and Castlereagh, Sir Joseph Banks, Mr. Caven-
dish, Admiral Sir Home Popham (the only naval man in
the Commission), Major Congreve, and Sir John Rennie.

Although Mr. Pitt and some few others were disposed
to look with favour on Fulton's devices, the Commission
as a whole were of the same opinion as Admiral Earl St.
Vincent, who remarked that it was foolish for Pitt to
encourage " that gimcrack, for so he was laying the foundation for doing away with the Navy, on which depended
the strength and prestige of Great Britain."

Thus Fulton's plans were declared to be impracticable
by the Commission. Mr. Pitt still refused to relinquish
his faith in Fulton, and on 15 October, 1805, he caused
an experiment to be made on an old Danish brig, which
was blown to pieces by 170 lb. of powder. Even this
wonderful result failed to appeal to those in authority,
for while they recognised that torpedoes and submarine
boats might prove useful to weaker nations, and might
be used with effect by them, they declared that such
weapons of warfare could have no place in the naval
equipment of the Mistress of the Seas. It is said that
Fulton was offered a large sum of money to suppress his
inventions, but this is doubtful. Full details of Fulton's
boat and various confidential reports are amongst the
Admiralty papers in the Record Office.

In the year 1806 Fulton returned to New York and made overtures to the United States Government. Receiving some encouragement, he succeeded, after many unsuccessful efforts, in blowing up a vessel which had been prepared for the purpose. Admiral Porter in 1878 wrote : " A midshipman nowadays at our Torpedo School at Newport would consider himself disgraced if he failed to destroy a ship of the line in ten minutes with less explosive powder, especially if the ship lay at anchor and gave him every opportunity to operate upon her." The Admiral seems to forget that Fulton was a pioneer, and laboured under every possible disadvantage in prosecuting his work.

In 1810 Congress appropriated 5000 dollars to assist Fulton in developing his ideas. After many trials, most of which were failures, the United States brig *Argus* was prepared for Fulton's final experiment. By order of Commodore Rodgers, the vessel had been so protected with spars and netting reaching to the bottom as to be practically unassailable, and the attempt to blow her up by a submarine torpedo was unsuccessful, as Fulton himself acknowledged, though he could not refrain from adding that " a system then in its infancy, which compelled a hostile vessel to guard herself by such extraordinary means, could not fail of becoming a most important mode of warfare."

Could Fulton have foreseen the manner in which his crude devices were to develop into the Whitehead torpedo and submarine boat of to-day he would have had something to cheer him in his hours of depression.

After the failure of the *Argus* experiment, Fulton de-

voted his attention to steam navigation, and was more
successful in this line than in his efforts to introduce
torpedo warfare, though he considered the latter a matter
of greater moment than the former.

In a letter to Joel Barlow, dated New York, 22 August,
1807, Fulton says, after describing his celebrated steam
voyage up the Hudson :—

" However, I will not admit that it (steam navigation) is
half so important as the torpedo system of defence or attack,
for out of this will grow the liberty of the seas—an object of
infinite importance to the welfare of America and every
civilised country. But thousands of witnesses have now seen
the steamboat in rapid movement and they believe ; but they
have not seen a ship of war destroyed by a torpedo, and they
do not believe. We cannot expect people in general to have
knowledge of physics or power to reason from cause to effect,
but in case we have war and the enemy's ships come into
our waters, if the Government will give me reasonable means
of action, I will soon convince the world that we have surer
and cheaper modes of defence than they are aware of."

Referring to the failure of Fulton to induce the various
Powers to adopt his submarine boat and torpedo, Admiral
Porter said (in 1878) that naval men seventy years ago,
whether in this country or abroad, saw no prospect in
the success of Fulton's scheme but the destruction of the
service which was then their pride and glory, and it was
hardly to be wondered at that all plans to destroy ships
by other means than the legitimate eighteen-pounder
were looked upon with disfavour. So the torpedo slept,
but in time it reappeared invested with such deadly
attributes that no nation could afford to disregard its
claims as the most destructive implement of naval war-

fare yet devised. During the "Second War of Independence" (1812–1814) some unsuccessful attacks were made by a diving vessel on British men-of-war, and this is generally understood to have been one of Fulton's vessels.

The following extract is from a work published by James Kelly in 1818 :—

"About this time—that is the summer of 1813—some infamous and insidious attempts were publicly encouraged for the destruction of the British men-of-war upon the coasts of America by torpedoes and other explosive machinery, as will appear from the following extract from the American newspapers.

"'A gentleman at Norwich, U.S., has invented a diving boat, which by means of paddles he can propel under water at the rate of three miles an hour, and ascend and descend at pleasure. He has been three times under the bottom of the *Ramillies* off New London. In the first attempt, after remaining under some time, he came to the top of the water like the porpoise for air, and as luck would have it, came up but a few feet from the stern of the *Ramillies*.

"'He was observed by a sentinel on deck, who sang out "Boat ahoy!" immediately on hearing which the boat descended without making a reply. Seeing this an alarm gun was fired on board the ship and all hands called to quarters, the cable cut and the ship got under weigh with all possible despatch, expecting to be blown up by a torpedo.

"'In the third attempt he came up directly under the *Ramillies*, and fastened himself and his boat to her keel, where he remained half an hour and succeeded in perforating a hole through her copper, but while engaged in screwing a torpedo to her bottom the screw broke and defeated his object for that time. So great is the alarm and fear on board the *Ramillies* of some such stratagem being played upon them that Commodore Hardy has withdrawn his force from before New London, and keeps his ships under weigh all the time instead of lying at anchor as formerly.' "

This " dishonourable attempt," evidently made under the sanction of the American executive, induced Sir Thomas Hardy to address letters to the public authorities of New London and to the Government of the States of Connecticut on the subject. In these Sir Thomas Hardy states that " he is fully apprised of the efforts to destroy the *Ramillies*, and that he shall do all in his power to defeat them, but he thinks it right to notify publicly that since the attempt he had ordered on board from fifty to a hundred American prisoners of war, who in the event of the efforts to destroy the ship by torpedoes or other infernal inventions being successful, would share the fate of himself and his crew. That in future, whenever a vessel was taken, the crew would be kept on board until it has been ascertained that no snare was laid for the destruction of British seamen, and that the regulations would be observed when a vessel was boarded and abandoned by her crew."

Sir Thomas adds that his example would be followed by all the commanders of his squadron.

These representations had some effect on the American public, for on the contents of the letter being known a public meeting was held, and as many of the citizens had relations and friends prisoners of war on board the British squadron, it was determined to present a remonstrance to the American executive against the further employment of torpedoes in the ordinary course of warfare.

Admiral Porter says that these submarine attacks were mostly unauthorised by the U.S. Government and disapproved by the Navy, "who preferred the more chivalric method of sinking vessels with eighteen and twenty-four pounders, or mowing down their crews with grape and canister."

It is almost certain that the submarine craft that attacked the *Ramillies* as she lay off New London was one of Fulton's boats..

In the year 1814 Fulton constructed the *Mute*, a huge submarine capable of holding a hundred men, and deriving its name from the silent engine that propelled it. The *Mute* was 80 ft. 6 in. long, 21 ft. wide, and 14 ft. deep. It was armoured on the top with iron sheets, beneath which was a wood lining almost a foot in thickness. Before the trials could be completed Fulton died, and thus the story of this ardent inventor's notions concerning submarine warfare comes to a close.

In 1810 Fulton published at New York a book, *Torpedo War and Submarine Explosions*, in which he gives an account of the various devices he had contrived for blowing up ships, piers, etc,' and of the actual experiments he had made. He seems to have elaborated his submarine boat after his torpedo had been invented, and his idea was that an under-water vessel would be useful in discharging torpedoes. His method of attack was to float the torpedo down to the object to be attacked, and to guide and even explode it by means of lines. He seemed not to have thought of the use of the spar-torpedo as it has been known in recent times.

CHAPTER XIV

SUBMARINES DURING THE AMERICAN CIVIL WAR

FROM the death of Robert Fulton down to the commencement of the American Civil War no very startling developments in under-water warfare are to be chronicled. During the Schleswig-Holstein War of 1848–50 the modern subaqueous explosive mine first came into use in actual warfare, and mines were also employed during the Crimean War ; in 1859 by the Austrians at the time of the threatened attack on Venice by the French ; and by the Chinese in 1857–8 to defend the streams in the neighbourhood of Canton.

The mine and the torpedo both played their part in the American Civil War, and since then both these weapons have been adopted as valuable factors of offence and defence by all the great Powers. When the Southern Confederacy seceded from the United States in 1861, one of the first steps of its naval department was to form a torpedo section to protect approaches to places liable to attack by the Northern fleet. It was during the war that the idea was applied of taking the mine to the hostile ship by means of a boat, for the mine, besides being immovable, was liable to be picked up or cut adrift by the enemy. A charge of powder was placed at the end of a long pole carried in the bows of the boat ; when darkness

186

came on the boat crept up to the enemy, the pole and charge were run under water until in contact with the hull of the enemy, and the explosive was then ignited by means of electricity. Thus came into being the " spar " or " outrigger " torpedo, a weapon which found a place in the armament of the British torpedo-boat. The Confederates affixed the spar-torpedo to at least one ironclad ship and many small steam vessels, and much damage was inflicted on the enemy by its employment.

It must be remembered that automobile or fish torpedoes had not been invented at this time, and that the only under-water weapons used on both sides were fixed mines and spar-torpedoes.

It was in order to use the spar-torpedo to the greatest advantage that the diving torpedo-boat was employed, and in this chapter we shall have to deal with a very famous incident in the history of submarine navigation, namely, the sinking of the Federal frigate *Housatonic* by a submarine boat manned by the Confederates and armed with a spar-torpedo.

Early in the war the Federal or Northern Government entered into negotiations with a Frenchman, whose name we have been unable to discover, to build and operate a submarine boat against the Confederate or Southern vessels. In particular the North desired to blow up the Confederate *Merrimac* in Norfolk Harbour. It has been stated that $10,000 were to be paid for the boat when finished, and $5000 for each successful attack with her. The boat was apparently constructed at the Navy Yard at Washington, and paid for by the Federals, but before they could learn the art of navigating the vessel the

Frenchman, taking his gains with him, left the country.
Whether the boat would have proved of much value is
to be doubted, and the probability is that the inventor
would have been as unsuccessful as were the Federals in
working the craft.

Admiral Hichborn terms it " an absurd arrangement
of duckfoot, hand-worked paddles in an age when the
screw propeller was in common use."

It was 35 feet long and 6 feet in diameter, and was
built up of steel plates. Immersion was obtained by the
admission of water, and the mode of propulsion on the
surface or below the water was by eight pairs of oars or
paddles which opened and shut like the leaves of a book,
and were worked by sixteen men placed half on the port
and half on the starboard. The maximum speed was
2½ knots on the surface. Fresh air was produced by two
machines—one consisted of a bellows passing air over
a chamber of lime, the other produced oxygen. The
armament was a spar - torpedo. According to one
account, it was towed round by a steamboat to Port
Royal, and foundered in a storm of wind off Cape
Hatteras.

· Early in 1863 the Confederates cut down a gunboat
at Charleston and converted it into a half-submerged
torpedo-boat. It does not appear to have done any
mischief, but Mr. H. W. Wilson, in his *Ironclads in Action*,
says that it may have been the vessel which on the night
of 19 April, 1864, approached the *Wabash*. The Northern
vessel was at anchor when something was seen near her
in the water, and challenged. She slipped her cable and
went ahead, opening a heavy fire upon the strange craft,

after which it disappeared, whether as the result of a shot or not is uncertain.

On the night of 5 October, 1863, an attack was made upon the United States ironclad *New Ironsides*, of 3,486 tons, carrying twenty guns, at anchor in the midst of the blockading squadron off Charleston, by a submarine vessel owned by the Confederates. This boat was built by Theodore Stoney at Charleston, and was called the *David*, a name given by the Southerns to some subsequent under-water craft in memory of the fight between the lad David and the giant Goliath.

This first *David* was 54 feet long, and at her widest section 6 feet in diameter. She was cigar-shaped, and was propelled by a screw driven by steam power. When in action she lay almost flush with the water, her funnel and steering chamber alone projecting above the surface. (Another report says that she was so far submerged that only about 10 feet in length of the hull was visible 2 feet above the water) Her armament consisted of a single spar-torpedo with a 60-lb. charge of gunpowder, which was folded alongside when not in use, and only run out on an iron bar to a distance of 10 feet for the actual attack, ignition being effected by an acid fuse rendered active by a collision nearly end on. Her maximum speed was 7 knots an hour.

. " With a crew of volunteers Lieut. Glassell took her out, and, a little after nine in the evening, the *Ironsides* watch saw her approaching. She looked to them like a plank, since all that could be seen was the coaming of her hatchway. Several officers were on deck, and the *David* was at once hailed. Her only answer was a volley of musketry, which mortally wounded

one Federal officer. An instant later the ironclad received a
violent blow from the explosion of a torpedo containing 60 lb
of powder, which threw up a column of water, shook the ship
severely, and broke one man's leg on board her. After the
smoke and spray had cleared away the *Ironsides* was found
to be uninjured and the boat had disappeared. Her crew
jumped overboard at the moment of firing the torpedo, and
Glassell, as he swam about, hailed a Northern coal schooner,
on board which he was taken, whilst a second man escaped to
the *Ironsides*. The engineer of the *David*, however, after the
explosion swam back to the boat, to which he found the pilot
clinging for dear life, as he was unable to swim. Helping
him on board, he discovered that the *David* could yet float,
though the explosion had put out the fires, and together the
two took her back to Charleston."

In a paper on " Offensive Torpedo Warfare," read
before the Royal United Service Institution in 1871,
Commander W. Dawson, R N , writes of the attack as
follows :—

" Observe the elements of failure. A charge destructive
enough if exploded in actual contact, but innocuous to a
strongly built ship by the accidental interposition of seven or
eight feet of water, yet held near enough to the operating
vessel to place her in immediate danger, either from the direct
action of the explosion upon her thin sides, or from her being
swamped by the falling columns of water, self-acting fuses, so
arranged as to necessitate the most exposed direction of
attack, viz., the enemy's broadside ; an acid composition
sluggish enough in its action to allow time for the boat to
rebound after collision, the few feet required to render the
explosion harmless, and last, not least, a commander and
crew, who, having never fired their weapon before, were in
greater terror of their own torpedo than the enemy would
have been. Can we wonder that the conductor of this enter-
prise jumped overboard before the explosion, that his little

vessel had her fires extinguished and was nearly swamped, and that the *New Ironsides*, though severely injured, was not compelled to return into port ?   The crew, deserted by their commander, relighted the fires, and brought the boat safely into harbour."

The first attempts of the Confederates with their submarine boat having proved a failure, the Federal officers on the outside blockade grew somewhat careless, and the final result of the Confederates' efforts was that one of the fine new vessels of the Federal fleet, the *Housatonic*,

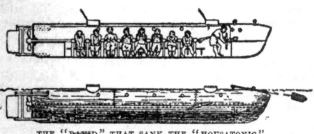

THE "DAVID" THAT SANK THE "HOUSATONIC"

Hundley

1,264 tons, and carrying 13 guns, was destroyed in Charleston harbour on the night of 17 February, 1864.

The *David*, that accomplished this feat, unique in the annals of submarine warfare, had been built at Mobile by Messrs. McClintock and Howgate, and brought overland to Charleston.   She had lateral fins by which she could be raised and submerged, and ballast tanks to lighten her and enable her to rise to the surface, though these, we read, uniformly refused to act.   She carried no reserve of air, and hence she well deserved the name "peripatetic coffin."   She was about 60 feet long, and elliptical in transverse section.   Her crew consisted of nine men, eight of whom propelled the vessel by operating cranks on the screw shaft, while the ninth acted as pilot.

It was originally designed to make the attack by passing under the keel of a ship towing a contact torpedo, having a small reserve buoyancy. Under favourable conditions the torpedo would be drawn under water when the vessel descended, strike the bottom of the ship, and explode on contact.

During her first cruise under the orders of Lieut. Payne (or Paine ?) an enemy's vessel passed close to her without noticing her ; the swell raised by her paddles sank the *David*, and Payne alone of all the crew saved himself. When the boat was recovered from the bottom Lieut. Payne persuaded eight sailors to embark with him ; a squall of wind caused the boat to fill with water, Lieut. Payne and two bluejackets alone escaping by leaping out of her as she went down. No sooner was the boat recovered from the bottom than her gallant commander offered to try again. A new crew volunteered, and all went well for a time. But one night, off Fort Sumter, she capsized, and only four (of whom Lieut. Payne was one) escaped.

A third time she was raised, and the next essay was made in the Cooper River, under the lead of Mr. Aunley, one of the men who had constructed the boat. Alas ! She sank for the fourth time, having caught her nose in the bottom, and all hands were drowned. Once more she was recovered, only to foul the cable of a schooner at anchor in the harbour, and to sink for a fifth time.

Up to this time five crews of eight each had volunteered for service in the ill-starred *David*, and of these forty men no less than thirty-five had perished. The brave Southern sailors, instead of fighting shy of the submarine, were as ready as ever to face death again. The *David* was recovered, and Lieut. Dixon, with Captain Carlson, both officers in the Confederate army, volunteered with five others to take her out against the Northern fleet. The Federal corvette *Housatonic* lay outside the bar in Charleston harbour, and it was on this vessel that, on the evening of 17 February, 1864, the attack was made, an attack which is thus vividly described by Admiral David Porter, U.S. Navy, in his book, *The Naval History of the Civil War :*—

" At about 8.45 p.m. the officer of the deck on board the unfortunate vessel discovered something about 100 yards away, moving along the water. It came directly towards the ship, and within two minutes of the time it was first sighted was alongside. The cable was slipped, the engines backed, and all hands called to quarters. But it was too late—the torpedo struck the *Housatonic* just forward of the mainmast, on the starboard side, in a line with the magazine. The man who steered her knew where the vulnerable spots of the steamer were, and he did his work well. When the explosion took place the ship trembled all over as if by the shock of an earthquake, and seemed to be lifted out of the water, and then sank stern-foremost, heeling to port as she went down. Her captain, Pickering, was stunned and somewhat bruised by the concussion, and the order of the day was ' *Sauve qui peut.*' A boat was despatched to the *Canandaigua*, not far off, and that vessel at once responded to the request for help, and succeeded in rescuing the greater part of the crew. Strange to say, the *David* was not seen after the explosion, and was supposed to have slipped away in the confusion ; but when the *Housatonic* was inspected by divers, the torpedo-boat was

o

found sticking in the hole she had made, and all her crew
were dead in her. It was a reckless adventure these men had
engaged in, and one in which they could scarcely have hoped
to succeed. They had tried it once before inside the harbour,
and some of the crew had been blown overboard. How could
they hope to succeed on the outside, where the sea might be
rough, when the speed of the *David* was not over five knots,
and when they might be driven out to sea! Reckless as it
might be, it was the most sublime patriotism, and showed the
length to which men could be urged on behalf of a cause for
which they were willing to give up their lives and all they
held most dear."

THE SINKING OF THE "HOUSATONIC"

It was by deeds such as these that North and South
are to-day united as they never were before.

The *David*, that finally succeeded in sinking the
Housatonic, proved so costly an experiment in human
lives because she was not worked as a submarine, but
as a low-freeboard surface torpedo-boat, a purpose for
which she was never designed, and for which, as we have
seen, she proved dangerous and inefficient. As some one
has observed, she was intended for submerging at pleasure—her own pleasure, however, not that of her crew.

During the attack on the *Housatonic*, on 17 February, the vessel did not run under water. The crew submerged it to the hatch coaming and left the cover open, against the protest of Mr. Howgate, who despatched it on its mission. The attack was made by a spar torpedo, and the wave thrown up by its explosion when it struck the *Housatonic* entered the open hatchway and swamped the vessel. Most accounts of the feat of the *David* state that *all* the crew were drowned. From the following extract it would seem that the gallant captain survived the attack :—

"I remember on one occasion during the war," wrote Hobart Pacha in an article, "The Torpedo Scare," appearing in *Blackwood's Magazine* for June, 1885, "when I was at Charleston, meeting in a coffee-room at that place a young naval officer (a Southerner) with whom I got into conversation. He told me that that night he was going to sink a Northern man-of-war which was blockading the port, and invited me to see him off. I accompanied him down to his cigar-boat, as he called it, and found that she was a vessel about forty feet long, shaped like a cigar, on the bow of which was placed a torpedo. On his stepping on board with his crew of four men his boat was immersed till nothing but a small piece of funnel was visible. He moved off into the darkness at no great speed—say at about five miles an hour. The next evening, on visiting the coffee-house, I found my friend sitting quietly smoking his pipe. He told me that he had succeeded in making a hole in the frigate which he had attacked, which vessel could, in fact, be seen lying in shallow water some seven miles off, careened over to repair damages. But he said that, on the concussion made by firing the torpedo, the water had rushed in through the hatches of his boat, and she had sunk to the bottom. All his men were drowned. He said he didn't know how he escaped himself, but he fancied that he came up through the hatches, as he found himself floating about, and swam on shore. This affair was officially reported by the American blockading squadron, corroborating the fact of the injury done to the frigate, and stating that the torpedo-boat was got up with four dead bodies in her hold. Here is one system which might be utilised in naval warfare if perfected, and I am given to understand that a submarine torpedo-boat is already invented by Mr. Nordenfelt."

After the sinking of the *Housatonic* the Federals again turned their attention to submarine warfare, and in October, 1864, some trials were made on the Hudson with a boat named the *Stromboli*, constructed at Fairhaven from the designs of an engineer, one Wood. It was not, properly speaking, either a submarine or a diving boat, but by letting in a certain quantity of water into the reservoirs it could be brought flush with the surface, leaving only the conning-tower, the chimney, and the ventilator above the waves. A steam engine propelled the *Stromboli* at a speed of ten miles an hour, while a spar-torpedo formed the armament. On 16 November, 1864, the *Stromboli* was under the command of John Lay, and was ordered to proceed to Hampton Roads to attack the Confederate cruisers. It appears to have arrived on 6 December, but its subsequent doings are not to be discovered.

Another semi-submarine which figured in the American Civil War was the *Sputyen Duyvil*, built by Messrs. Mallory and Co., from the plans of Messrs William Wood and John Lay. She was made of wood, and her dimensions were: length, 74 feet; beam, 20 feet; draught, 7½ feet. On going into action she could be immersed to a depth of 9 feet in order to put her armoured side below water ; she was to fight with her deck, which was placed with 3-in. armour, flush with the water. Amidships, and standing about 3 feet above the deck, was a pilot house from which the boat could be steered. The *Sputyen Duyvil* was attached to James River's squadron during the year 1865, but there is no evidence that she was ever brought into use ; her torpedoes were fired on contact, and were worked through a hollow iron boom projecting from the bow, and having inside it a rod to which the torpedo was to be attached.

THE " SPUTYEN DUYVIL."

CHAPTER XV

THE WHITEHEAD TORPEDO—"THE MOST WONDERFUL MACHINE IN THE WORLD"

"When you have been shown lovingly over a torpedo by an artificer skilled in the working of its tricky bowels, torpedoes have a meaning and a reality for you to the end of your days."—RUDYARD KIPLING.

"The next great naval war will bestow upon the torpedo and its users a halo of romance which will eclipse entirely that surrounding the gun and the ram."

"The arts of ship-builders and steel-workers stand for nothing when a Whitehead torpedo succeeds in striking a ship's bottom and tears and rents it with the explosion of 200 lb. of gun-cotton In the hands of ignorant or careless people the Whitehead is nearly as dangerous to its friends as to its foes, but in the hands of skilful and resolute men it is the most terrible engine of warfare which the world has ever seen."—Lieut. G. E. ARMSTRONG, in *Torpedoes and Torpedo Vessels.*

"The spar-torpedo is the dagger which a determined man plunges into the body of an enemy who does not protect himself with a coat of mail ; the Whitehead torpedo is the bullet which, easy to discharge from afar, kills the enemy in its path."—Lieut D. ARNAULT.

ALTHOUGH twenty-five Federal vessels are known to have been sunk and destroyed, and nine others more or less injured by various kinds of torpedoes during the great war of secession, the many objections to the employment of the spar-torpedo were only too evident. The necessarily close proximity of the craft attacking and the ship attacked resulted in some cases in the destruction of the former as well as the latter, and inventive minds therefore set to work to devise a submarine weapon which could be discharged at the enemy from a distance. The result was the automobile fish-torpedo, an instrument of warfare which is to be found in every navy, and the sole armament of the modern submarine boat.

In a history of under-water warfare a description of the Whitehead torpedo, which is in reality a crewless submarine boat, must find a place, but a word may be said beforehand respecting the difference between the " Mine " and " Torpedo."

The mine is a stationary or drifting charge of explosive contained in a case moored beneath the surface of the water. The torpedo is a case of explosive, which by some means or other is provided with the power of aggression, either on or below the surface. The mine awaits the enemy, in fine, whilst the torpedo goes to seek him. Into the details of Submarine Mining it is not proposed to enter here.

Torpedoes are divided into two classes—(1) Uncontrollable ; (2) controllable. Class 1 comprises Projectile, Rocket, Drifting, and Automobile torpedoes ; the last-named are now practically the only kind of uncontrollable torpedo employed. In nearly all navies the " Whitehead " is the type adopted ; the German uses the " Schwartzkopff," which differs only from the former in that it is made of phosphor-bronze instead of steel. Controllable torpedoes comprise Spar, Towing, Dirigible, Locomotive, and Automobile. Great Britain has adopted the Brennan locomotive torpedo for coast defence only, and she recently retained the spar-torpedo, though it is doubtful if this would ever be used in a naval engagement again.

The Whitehead Torpedo ⸻Somewhere about the year 1860 an officer of the Austrian Marine Artillery devised plans for the construction of a surface screw boat or fire-ship, to be propelled either by a steam or hot-air engine, or by clockwork, to be steered from the shore by means of long tiller ropes, and to carry in its fore part a large charge of gun-cotton, the explosion of which was effected by means of a pistol in communication with a movable blade at the bow, and with one vertical and two horizontal spars, so that if any of these arrangements came into contact with the object aimed at the pistol was fired and the charge exploded.* On the death of this officer, which took place before he had time to put his ideas into practice, the pen drawings came into the possession of Captain Lupuis, an officer of the Austrian navy. During the sixties Captain Lupuis carried out a series of experiments with a view of discovering a means of propelling a floating torpedo along the surface of the water, and directing it by means of ropes and guiding lines. The forward end of the torpedo was to be charged with explosive, and on coming in contact with a vessel it would be exploded by the automatic firing of a pistol. The motive power was to be either steam or clockwork. The Austrian Government, before whom he laid his plans, told him that they could not consider them until he discovered some reliable form of motor and a better method of steering. In the year 1864 Captain Lupuis sought the advice and assistance of Mr. Whitehead, at the time

---

* A picture of this—the original idea for a locomotive torpedo—appears in the twenty-ninth volume of the Journal of the Royal United Service Institution.

manager to an engine manufacturing company at Fiume, and the result was that the latter invented the famous locomotive torpedo that bears his name.

The first Whitehead fish-torpedo was produced in 1866, but it was a very much less terrible engine of destruction than the torpedo is to-day   It was built of steel, was 14 inches in diameter, 16 inches at the fins, and weighed 300 lb.   Its explosive charge was 18 lb. of dynamite.   The motive power was compressed air charged to a pressure of about 700 lb. to the square inch, and the air chamber was made of ordinary boiler plates.   The speed was only 6 knots for a short distance.   Mr. Whitehead's design was a great improvement on Captain Lupuis's.   It ran beneath the waves, it was independent of outside aid when once started, and its motive power was superior both to steam and clockwork.   Still, it was by no means a perfectly reliable weapon, and its great fault was that it failed to keep a uniform depth in the water.

By 1868 Mr. Whitehead had invented the " Balance " Chamber, which has since proved a very effective means of controlling the depth of the torpedo.   In 1868 a committee of Austrian naval officers experimented with two Whiteheads whose dimensions were as follows :—

	Small. ft. in.	Large ft in
Length	11 7	14 1
Maximum diameter	0 14	0 16
	lb.	lb
Weight	346	650
Charge (gun-cotton)	40	60

The trials were carried out at Fiume ; the Austrian gunboat *Genese* was handed over to Mr. Whitehead to fit with a bow ejecting tube, and the target consisted of the yacht *Fantasie*. The result was the adoption of the Whitehead by the Austrian Government in 1868.

Although the Austrian Government purchased the secret of the Whitehead torpedo, they were unable to secure the exclusive right of manufacture. On the invitation of the British Admiralty, Mr. Whitehead came to England in 1870, bringing with him two torpedoes and a submerged tube.

The first two English torpedoes were of two sizes, and of the following dimensions :—

	Length. ft. in.	Max diam. in.	Charge.
No. 1. Large size	14 0	16	67 lb. gun-cotton.
No. 2. Small size	13 10½	14	18 lb. dynamite.

The trials were carried out on board the *Oberon*, an old paddle-wheel sloop. Over 100 runs were made, and the average speed obtained was 8·5 knots for a distance of 200 yards, and 7·5 knots for 600 yards. The balance chamber proved capable of keeping the torpedo at the required depth, although at times it behaved in an erratic fashion. After the trials the committee of investigation reported that in their opinion " any maritime nation failing to provide itself with submarine locomotive torpedoes would be neglecting a great source of power both for offence and defence." Acting on this verdict, the English Government, in April, 1871, purchased the secret and right of manufacture of the Whitehead torpedo for £15,000.

Naturally certain conservative officers, incapable of recognising the possibility of improvement in the weapons of naval warfare, sneered at the torpedo ; but their scorn had little effect, and in a short time all the great navies of the world had adopted the Whitehead or some similar form of fish-torpedo.   One instance will be sufficient to show that naval men failed in many cases to realise the potential value of this instrument of destruction.

Commander W. Dawson, R.N , in a paper read before the Royal United Service Institution, commenting on the drawbacks of the Whitehead, remarked that he did not attach much value to self-contained powers of locomotion in submarine projectiles, and said that he believed that progress must be looked for in modification of the outrigger and the towing torpedoes, which were free from complicated mechanism, simple in their application, and, above all, safe to the operators and to friendly vessels.

In 1876 Mr. Whitehead produced an improved torpedo. It had a diameter of only 14 inches, a speed of 18 knots for a distance of 600 yards, and a charge of 26 lb. of gun-cotton   It was fitted for the first time with the "servo-motor," which, as Lieut. Armstrong remarks, makes the steering almost as perfect as if a mannikin helmsman were steering the torpedo from the inside.   In 1884 it was still further improved.   The speed was raised to .24 knots, and the explosive charge was increased.   In 1889 the speed was again raised to 29 knots for 1000 yards, and the charge was 200 lb. of gun-cotton.

The Whitehead torpedoes carried in His Majesty's ships to-day are of two dimensions :—

	Diameter in.	Speed kts.	Range yds	Charge.
A .. .	18	32	600	200 lb. gun-cotton
B ..	14	30	600	80 ,, ,,

Several different patterns of Whitehead torpedoes are turned out at the various factories, but they all resemble each other in their main characteristics.

The "baby," as the seaman calls it, is a cigar-shaped object made of steel or of phosphor-bronze. It is divided into compartments, and in the foremost of these is placed in war time the explosive charge. At the head is the end of a pointed rod penetrating the explosive, and when the torpedo comes into contact with a solid object, the point

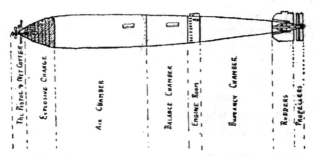

MARK IX., R.G.F., FOURTEEN INCH WHITEHEAD TORPEDO

of the rod is driven in against a detonator which explodes the charge and tears a hole in the ship's bottom. Abaft the explosive chamber comes the air chamber; herein is stored the compressed air which acts as the motive power of the torpedo. Behind this is the balance chamber, where all the automatic steering apparatus is fixed. Abaft this are the engines; these are worked by the compressed air from the air chamber and revolve a shaft, on to the end of which are two screw propellers working in opposite directions. Farthest aft of all is another hollow air compartment termed the buoyancy chamber. There are four rudders — two vertical for steering from right to left, and two horizontal for maintaining the proper depth.

One might be forgiven for thinking that the narrower the fore part of the torpedo the faster would be its speed ; a study of fishes shows, however, that this is not Nature's principle, and the Whitehead is therefore thicker at the fore than at the tail ; technically, it has " a full entrance with a very fine run." The Whitehead is divided into eight sections, containing :—

1. The firing arrangement.
2. The explosive chamber.
3. The air chamber.
4. The " balance " chamber.
5. The engine chamber.
6. The buoyancy chamber.
7. The bevel wheel chamber.
8. The horizontal and vertical rudders and propellers.

1 AND 2. THE FIRING ARRANGEMENT AND EXPLOSIVE CHAMBER

At the head of the Whitehead is the end of a pointed steel rod which penetrates the chamber containing the explosive. When the torpedo's nose comes into contact with a ship's side, or in fact any rigid object, the point of this rod is driven in against a detonator cap inserted in the centre of the charge : the immediate result is an explosion sufficient to tear a large hole in the ship's hull. The detonator is fulminate of mercury, which, when ignited by a sudden blow, expands to about 2500 times its own size. The sudden expansion gives such a severe blow to the gun-cotton around it that it at once explodes. Special precautions have to be taken to prevent the torpedo from damaging the ship from which it is fired : it might happen through carelessness that a lieutenant would fire one with the port closed, and so three checks are provided. The rod is so arranged that it cannot go back until a small " collar " with propeller fans on it has revolved off. When the torpedo enters the water the fans begin to turn, and when it has run some 30 yards the collar is worked off. Even then the charge will not explode unless the blow to the rod is severe enough to shear off a little copper pin standing in the way. Lastly, there is a third precaution in the shape of a safety-pin which holds the collar fixed until it is withdrawn at the last moment as the torpedo is launched into the tube.

It happened in the Russo-Turkish war that a Russian lieutenant in command of a torpedo-boat forgot to haul out the " safety pin," and the consequence was that, though the torpedo reached the target, it failed to explode. From what has been said it will be understood that torpedo warfare is not quite so simple as it looks. In time of peace the torpedo is not fitted with its war head, and so for daily purposes a steel dummy head is used, while there is an arrangement that causes it to rise to the surface on completion of its run. To facilitate its recovery, a " Holme's light " is carried on to the head. This consists of an arrow-headed tin canister pierced with tubes and full of phosphide of calcium, which on contact with the water gives out both a strong light and a strong smell.

3. The Air Chamber.

This contains the motive power of the torpedo, and it comes just behind the explosive chamber. The air is compressed into the compartment by means of air-compressing pumps fitted on board ship, and the latest types are tested to a pressure of 1700 lb. to the square inch.

4. The Balance Chamber.

Next the air chamber comes the balance, or secret chamber, although the secret is now universally known. Here is contained the mechanism for automatically transmitting to the horizontal rudders the movements necessary for keeping the torpedo at a uniform and prearranged depth below the surface during its run. It consists of a hydrostatic valve and a pendulum, whose combined movements are transmitted to an air cylinder called a "servo-motor," placed in the engine-room. The hydrostatic valve is kept in its place by a spring that is forced in by the pressure of the water when the torpedo goes below a certain depth to which the valve has previously been adjusted. If the pressure be less than that of the set depth the opposite action takes place. This valve is connected with the servo-motor, which in its turn acts on the horizontal rudders. The pendulum consists of a heavy iron weight curved to correspond with the circular section of the torpedo, and suspended by the pivoted steel rods or arms. It swings in a fore-and-aft direction, and is connected by rods to the rudder for a certain distance after the discharge of the torpedo. A controlling gear is provided which keeps the rudders fixed. It will thus be seen that by the combined actions of the hydrostatic valve and the pendulum the Whitehead, after leaving the tube, is brought to the proper depth very rapidly, and is held at this depth throughout her run. Both these devices are necessary, as the torpedo has a great tendency to run down an inclined plane at great speed, and this requires to be checked. In addition, the balance chamber contains various valves (the stop valve, the charging valve, the starting valve, the delay action valve, and the reducing valve) through which the air passes on its way to the engines from the air chamber.

5. THE ENGINE CHAMBER.

Inside the engine-room are the propelling engines and the servo-motor. The engines are of the single-acting three-cylinder Brotherhood type. The compressed air, after leaving the air reservoir, passes through the main pipe to the pressure-reducing valve. In the latest pattern 18-inch Whitehead the indicated horse-power is 56. The torpedo is started by means of a trigger which projects a little beyond the casing of the torpedo, and which automatically opens the starting valve when the torpedo is fired ; the trigger just before leaving the tube is caught by a catch in the tube which draws it back when the catch releases itself.

THE SERVO-MOTOR.

This ingenious apparatus was called into existence owing to the fact that the mechanism of the balance chamber was unable, through its feeble power, to work the horizontal rudders of the faster Whiteheads direct. The servo-motor is, then, the air engine from which is derived the power to move the diving rudders. It is only about four inches long, but so great is its power that with only half-an-ounce pressure on the slide valve the piston is capable of lifting 180 lb. It consists of a cylinder, a piston, and a cylindrical slide valve. Its balance mechanism acts on the slide valve of the servo-motor, and this acts on the piston, and the motion of the piston is transmitted to the diving rudders by means of a rod and a system of levers.

6. THE BUOYANCY CHAMBER.

Abaft the engine-room is the buoyancy chamber, which gives the necessary buoyancy to the torpedo · to guard against the collapse of the chamber flat steel rings are fitted into it for support. In the " tail," the rearmost compartments of the torpedo, are carried the bevel wheel mechanism, the vertical and horizontal rudders and the propellers, and the counter mechanism for adjusting the length of run.

THE GYROSCOPE.

From the foregoing description of the many devices employed to enable the Whitehead to accomplish the tasks for which it is intended, it might be thought that everything that science could imagine has been done to ensure its efficiency. There still, however, remained one

great drawback to the efficiency of the torpedo, and this
was its deflection from right to left, which was often so
serious as to prevent it from striking the object at which
it was aimed.   The hydrostatic valve and the pendulum
were sufficient to keep the torpedo at the required depth
without diverging from its true vertical course, but it
was apt to swerve from its course in a right or left direction, either by reason of the blow it received on striking
the water, by dents on its shell, by air leakage, or other
causes.   An error of only one degree in its course means
a lateral error of nearly 50 feet at 800 yards, and it was
in order to prevent the deflection of the Whitehead out
of the line of fire that the principle of the gyroscope has
been applied to the torpedo.   In addition to her pair of
ordinary vertical rudders, which may be set to any angle
up to 20 degrees by means of a clamping screw, the
torpedo carries a pair of movable vertical rudders placed
in recesses in the vertical fins and controlled by the
gyroscope through a servo-motor.   The ordinary vertical
rudders are usually discarded if the latter are carried.

The working of the gyroscope, as applied to the Whitehead torpedo, may now be described.   In the centre of
the lower part of the buoyancy chamber is placed a small
heavy-rimmed fly-wheel or gyroscope about $1\frac{3}{4}$ lb. in
weight, carefully suspended on gymbals (like a ship's
compass) in a vertical position, and transverse to the
axis of the torpedo.   The apparatus is " set " by winding
up a strong spring, and the action of firing the torpedo
from the tube releases the spring and causes the gyroscope to spin round at a rate of about 2200 revolutions
a minute.   The use of the gyroscope is based on the fact

P

that if a wheel be set spinning on its axis with any considerable velocity, it will always tend to revolve in the same plane to which it is set spinning. The gyroscope works a servo-motor, which in its turn works a pair of movable vertical rudders, and the slightest deviation from the direction in which the torpedo was originally fired causes the gyroscope to move the rudders and bring back the torpedo to its predetermined course. Thanks to the hydrostatic valve, the pendulum, and the gyroscope, the Whitehead torpedo is almost certain to hit the object at which it is aimed. In peace manœuvres the Whitehead has often been run absolutely dead straight, with no divergence either up or down, or from right to left, to a distance of 2000 yards. In 1890 the range of the Whitehead (Mark X R.L.) was officially placed at 800 yards, so the value of the gyroscope is quite evident.

Torpedoes are fired in four ways—

1. By submerged tubes.
2. By above-water tubes.
3. By revolving tubes.
4. By boat's "dropping gear."

The torpedo is blown out of the tube either by compressed air suddenly injected into the rear end, or by an impulse charge of a few ounces of powder, usually cordite. The air pressure varies from 300 to 600 lb. to the square inch, and the powder charge from 4 oz. to 6½ oz. Submerged tubes are, of course, tubes below the water-line, and all the most recent ships are fitted with these, as their advantages over above-water tubes are universally recognised. After the Chino-Japanese war

THE FIRING OF A WHITEHEAD TORPEDO

all governments, when demanding designs for new war-ships, made it almost a *sine qua non* that the torpedoes should be discharged from below water. In firing torpedoes from above-water tubes the torpedo is liable to be hit by the enemy, and it is generally considered that if the tube be hit by even a small projectile it must inevitably explode ; the submerged tube affords protection both to the men and the weapon, while the torpedo is less deflected on entering the water. The weight of the submerged tube is some seven tons, two tons more than an above-water one. In order to avoid any possibility of the Whitehead inflicting injury on the vessel firing it, and in order that it may be as little deflected as possible, a guiding bar is run out of the tube by means of pneumatic power when the torpedo has been placed in it. The guiding bar holds and guides the torpedo until quite clear of the ship, when by means of a secret apparatus it releases the torpedo at the end simultaneously ; without this arrangement the torpedo would be enormously deflected towards the stern directly it began to leave the tube, and would probably strike the ship from which it had just been fired.

Revolving tubes are carried either singly or in pairs on board torpedo-boats and destroyers, and the torpedoes are fired from them by powder impulse only. "Dropping gear" is only used in second-class torpedo-boats and picket boats. It consists of a pair of clip tongs suspended from pivoted davits ; the tongs being opened, the torpedo falls into the water, the engines are set in motion, and it speeds off to do its deadly work. The torpedoes for the British Admiralty are made at the Royal Gun

Factory, by Messrs. Greenwood and Batley, of Leeds, and by the Whitehead factory at Portland. The Whitehead Company has another factory at Fiume, whence it supplies almost all the Great Powers with torpedoes.* The torpedo is discharged by an officer in the conning-tower ; by the aid of a torpedo director he makes the necessary adjustments, and fires the torpedo by pressing an electric key, thus completing a circuit connected with the firing apparatus in the tube.

A BRITISH DESTROYER

* In December, 1906, Messrs. Armstrong, Whitworth, showed at Weymouth that a torpedo fitted with a "heater" would travel double the distance at a given speed and the same expenditure of air that it would without "heater." If the torpedo be run for the same distance with a "heater" as a torpedo without "heater," the 100 per cent gain would be realised by increasing the speed, and at a range of 2000 yards this increase is from 26 knots to 33·5 knots. At a further experiment a speed of 35·3 knots was obtained for a distance of 2000 yards. It was decided to proceed at once with the designs of a new torpedo, specially constructed to use hot air.

CHAPTER XVI

THE NORDENFELT SUBMARINES

ABOUT the year 1878 a gentleman in holy orders, Mr. Garrett by name, designed a submarine boat, which was built by Messrs. Cochrane, of Liverpool. It was 45 feet long, of the shape of two cones, with a central cylindrical portion. This vessel, to which the name of *Resurgam* was given, was tried in the Birkenhead Float in 1879. It descended by means of pistons, which varied the displacement of the boat by being drawn in and pushed out, as well as by central rudders which steered it up and down. Compressed-air tanks were provided, and chemicals were stored to purify the air after use.

Soon after a larger boat was constructed, in which steam replaced manual labour as the motive power; when about to sink the chimney was removed and an air-tight stopper fitted on the opening to the up-take; the furnace mouths were similarly closed by doors, like those of a gas retort, and the boat sank. Power was supplied on Lamm's system by the hot water in the boiler. After a number of experiments she was finally lost off the Welsh coast.

The attention of Mr. Thorsten Nordenfelt (the inventor of the gun which bears his name) was directed to Mr. Garrett's design, and the result was that he decided to build a submarine vessel himself. He acknowledged that the negative experience gained during the trials of the Garrett boat had been of advantage to him in avoiding the faults which made that boat unsuccessful.

"Norden- Mr. Nordenfelt's first submarine boat was felt I" built at Stockholm, and was tried in the Sound of Landskrova, in Sweden, in September, 1885, in the presence of delegates from most of the leading governments.

Its dimensions and details were as follows :—

Length 64 ft., beam 9 ft. (over sponsons 12 ft.), draught 11 ft., displacement 60 tons ; speed on measured mile 9 knots ; distance travelled without re-coaling 150 miles ; depth to which safe descent was possible, about 50 ft. Engines, surface condensing compound type, with two cylinders and cranks at 90° ; at pressure of 100 lb. to square inch, indicating 100 h.p. Boiler of ordinary marine return tube type, having one furnace, and about 200 square feet of heating surface ; two hot-water cisterns, rhomboidal in body with spherical ends. The boilers and cisterns contained about eight tons of water. Both boilers and cisterns were made for a working pressure of 150 lb. to square inch. One fish-torpedo, 14 feet long, was carried outside on the bow and discharged mechanically. The sinking apparatus consisted of two vertical propellers driven by a 6-h.p. double-cylinder engine, and placed in sponsons on each side of the boat. The revolution of these caused the boat to descend horizontally when its buoyancy had been sufficiently diminished. There was one cold-water tank in the centre of the boat, holding about four tons of water, for regulating buoyancy. This tank was used as coal bunker when doing long surface runs. In the stern was a four-bladed propeller 5 feet in diameter, and the rudder for port and starboard steering was placed aft of this propeller.

In the bow on either side were balanced rudders on one and

the same axle, always maintained in the horizontal position. The crew consisted of three men, and when the boat was closed up there was sufficient air to supply three men for six hours without causing discomfort, and this was not supplemented by any storage of compressed air or restorative chemicals. The depth below the surface at which the boat travelled could be varied in two ways—either by varying the speed of the vertical propellers, or by reducing the speed of the engines driving them by an automatic valve controlling the steam supply. On the surface the boat was driven by working the boiler in the usual manner, and the temperature of the water in the cisterns was kept up to a degree corresponding to a steam pressure of 150 lb. When it was desired to descend, the ashpit and fire door were closed, as also the funnel inside the boat, and the vertical propellers were started. For sub-surface travelling there was available, as propelling power, the steam given off by the heated water (about eight tons), and this was found sufficient for a distance of 14 knots ; on one occasion, when the boat was opened up, there was still over 20 lb. pressure in the boiler.

"Norden- Mr. Nordenfelt recognised that for the defelt II" fence of open coasts and for operations where it might be necessary to keep the sea for days together, without being able to seek the shelter of inlets or the mouths of rivers, other and larger proportions than those of his first 64-foot boat would be desirable.

He accordingly constructed a boat on such larger lines, the details of which are as follows :—

Length 100 ft., beam 12 ft., displacement 160 tons ; speed on measured mile 12 knots ; distance travelled without recoaling 900 miles , depth to which descent could safely be made, about 50 ft. Engines, surface condensing compound type, with two cylinders, and cranks at 90°, and at a pressure of 100 lb. of steam, indicating 250 h.p. Boiler, of the

ordinary marine return tube type, having two furnaces ; about
750 square feet of heating surface.   Hot-water cistern, rhomboidal in body with spherical ends.   Both boiler and cistern
made for a working pressure of 150 lb. per square inch.
Armament, two fish-torpedoes, 14 feet long, carried outside
on the bow and discharged mechanically.   Two Nordenfelt
quick-firing machine guns consisting of 1-inch calibre.   Sinking apparatus, two *vertical* propellers, driven by two engines,
each indicating 6 h.p. ;   these propellers were placed in the
fore and aft line.   This was an improvement on the earlier
boat, whose screws were fitted in side sponsons.   The mere
arrest of these propellers sufficed to bring the boat to the surface, as it had a reserve buoyancy.   Bow fins, whose action
was both automatic and controllable, maintained the boat
in the horizontal position.   The main propeller was placed
abaft the rudder.   Two main cold-water cisterns placed at
each end, and containing 15 tons of water each, also one in
centre of boat for regulating buoyancy containing 7 tons ;
coal bunkers on the side of boiler ;   8 tons of coal carried at
the side of hot-water cistern and in middle of boat.   Crew,
three men in a watch ;   two watches carried.   With coal in
the bunkers only this boat could keep the sea for five days
or more.   No attempt was made to purify the air when submerged.   When descending, the boat was perfectly horizontal,
and was invariably kept so when moving under water by
means of the bow rudders operated by a plumb weight.

Nordenfelt II had two distinct conditions of existence
as a torpedo craft—that of a surface boat and a submarine one.   The sinking operations were as follows :
the furnaces were hermetically closed, upon which combustion was soon brought to an end.   The piece of funnel
connecting the boiler with the outward portion was then
removed and the doors placed in position.   Whilst these
changes were being effected water was allowed to run

into the ballast tanks to reduce the buoyancy to its proper limit, and this arrived at, nothing remained but to close up the conning-tower and to set in motion the vertically acting screws to place the boat quite out of sight.

In a paper which he read before the Royal United Service Institution, on 5 February, 1886, Major-General Sir Andrew Clarke in the chair, Mr. Nordenfelt, after mentioning previous under-water vessels, gave his views as to the reason of their failure.

" First of all," he said, " they were always built too small and too weak. The longest was 45 feet, and their small dimensions and weak plates made them useless in bad weather and dangerous for submersion ; the small air space available forced the crew to use chemical means to obtain pure air. Secondly, they were never made for firing a fish-torpedo ; consequently they had to endeavour to fix a mine to the bottom of a vessel, a feat which Mr. Nordenfelt considered impracticable, owing to the risk of contact with the vessel, which, especially if she were pitching or moving, might easily destroy the boat. Thirdly, in all the early boats the mines were charged with only black powder, the effect of which was less destructive than that of the gun-cotton or dynamite in the fish-torpedoes. The effect of the explosion, again, against a wooden ship was nothing like as serious as against the thin bottom plates of an ironclad. Fourthly, all the boats hitherto in use were propelled by hand power ; this gave too much hard work to the crew, who could not take the boat any distance on the surface previous to the actual attack, and made it quite impossible for it to face any rough weather. In the Nordenfelt boat the use of steam diminished the number of men, and they had so little to do when below the surface that the temperature, lower than in modern stokeholes, was no detriment. Fifthly, all previous boats had most unreliable means of descending and ascending. The descent by steering

downwards in the American boats of the Civil War period
was quite as dangerous as the attempts before and after that
time to lower and raise the boats, and to keep them steady
at any desired depth, by means of increasing and decreasing
the weight of the boats by more or less water-ballast or by
altering their displacement."

None of these boats used the principle which Mr.
Nordenfelt applied to pull his boat down by mechanical
means, while relying upon its always retained buoyancy

'NORDENFELT II" RUNNING AWASH

for rising ; so that if the mechanical apparatus failed, the
boat rose at once to the surface. Again, they did not
have the tendency to steadiness given by the two forces
of constant pulling down by the vertical screws, acting
all the time, whether still or moving, against the pulling
upwards caused by the buoyancy.

Mr. Nordenfelt considered it most dangerous to rely
upon a detachable weight in case of emergency, as the
apparatus for detaching it would be always liable to fail.
He confessed that he could not imagine how the longitudinal instability of a submerged boat could possibly
have been satisfactorily controlled by any of the means
applied to the previous boats. Even Goubet's system of

moving water or weights fore and aft inside the boat must act more slowly and cause more diving and oscillation than his rudders, which always remained in the horizontal, and thus controlled the slightest tendency of the boat to get out of the longitudinally horizontal position. He considered it absolutely essential to keep the boat horizontal when moving, as he believed that any inclination downwards with the impetus of a heavy boat would almost to a certainty carry the boat below its safe depth before it could be effectually counteracted by shifting weights.

The reason which led Mr. Nordenfelt to construct his submarine boats was the almost insuperable difficulty in carrying the Whitehead and Schwarzkopf fish-torpedoes with any degree of certainty up to the short distance at which they could be considered infallibly effective. It seemed to him that a much greater chance would be given for carrying the torpedoes within striking distance if, instead of trying to rush the distance by many boats, all the time exposed to the destructive fire from machine guns, he could carry the torpedo secretly up to this distance without the probability of being seen at all, and without any probability of being struck by the enemy's shot, even if seen.

The tactics to be adopted by his submarines in action were thus laid down by Mr. Nordenfelt. Out of sight of the enemy the vessel ran on the surface with its cupola and about three feet of its turtle back out of water, but by forced draught, blowing out its smoke under the surface. When she arrived within such distance of the enemy that she might be discovered, she descended into the water so far that the cupola alone appeared above the waves ; this was done by taking in water into the cold-water tanks sufficient to reduce the floatability to what the horizontal screws were capable of overpowering. The " reduced floatability " was never done away with, but the descent from the " awash " position was effected by starting the vertical screws, thus overcoming mechanically the buoyancy of the boat, which was pulled down to a less or greater depth depending upon the speed given to the screws.

The three main points in Mr. Nordenfelt's system on which he laid special stress were these :—

1. That by using water as the means of storing up energy he was in possession of a reservoir which could never get out of order, and which could be replaced at any hour in any part of the world, and without any extraneous assistance from shore or other ships. The reason of all others which at once decided him to adopt the hot-water system was the enormous factor of safety obtained by his being able to blow out, by steam pressure without the use of machinery, large weights of water, which would lighten the boat and counteract any leak likely to occur. Mr. Nordenfelt had little faith in electricity as a motive power, which is not surprising considering the accumulators then in use.

2. The submerging the boat by mechanical means. Mr. Nordenfelt was convinced that previous attempts had proved unsuccessful, mainly because either they depended upon varying the displacement of the boat by taking in water to submerge her and to regulate the depth at which they desired to operate, or they de-

scended by steering downwards. His objection to the first-named method of descending, by taking in water and thus increasing the specific gravity of the boat, was that practically there was no difference in the specific gravity of water on the surface or at 50 feet depth ; thus when the boat had lost its buoyancy at the surface it had also no buoyancy at any given depth, and the risk was thus very great of suddenly descending beyond a safe depth.

"NORDENFELT II" AT CONSTANTINOPLE

3. The horizontal position Mr. Nordenfelt believed to be a *sine qua non* for a submarine boat.

When Mr. Nordenfelt built his boats electric accumulators were very much inferior to those of to-day. No designer of an under-water vessel would think nowadays of using the steam given off by heated water for under-water propulsion. As to his theory that a submarine boat must always descend on an even keel, this has since proved to be entirely erroneous ; the modern diving torpedo-boat goes down at an angle, and is brought to the horizontal position at the required depth either automatically or by hand-worked mechanism.

During her trials *Nordenfelt I* hardly did herself justice, but nevertheless, in the beginning of 1886, she was bought by the Greek Government, and in April, 1886, trials took place in the Bay of Salamis, when Mr Nordenfelt's agent carried out the various conditions imposed

Shortly after the first boat had been bought by Greece, Turkey ordered two submarine boats (*Nordenfelt II* and *III*) from the inventor. Both boats were sent to Turkey in sections, but only one was assembled and tested. In 1887 it underwent trials at Constantinople, which were witnessed by the Sultan himself, who expressed himself highly satisfied with the performance of the boat.

"**Norden-** Mr. Nordenfelt's fourth vessel was built by **felt IV**" the Naval Construction Company at Barrow, the machinery being supplied by Messrs. Plenty and Sons, Newbury.

The principal dimensions were :—

Length 125 ft ; diameter 12 ft. ; displacement fully immersed, 245 tons ; in light surface condition, 160 tons. The engines turning the main propeller were especially designed for using steam at varying pressures, and indicated 1000 h p. when working with steam at a pressure of 150 lb. At that power her estimated speed was 15 knots. Submerged, her speed was 5 knots. Fourteen auxiliary engines were carried for driving, air circulating, and feed pumps for steering and sinking. In the middle was the entrance to the stokehole through a scuttle 4 feet in diameter. Fore and aft of this scuttle were two funnels, and about 30 feet from the stem and stern of the boat were the conning-towers, 2 feet high and of the same diameter. They were of 1-inch steel, and were considered perfectly impervious to any shot which in warfare would ever be directed against them. In the forward tower were placed at the hands of a commander means of controlling every motion of the vessel. The boat was divided into five compartments: (1) The torpedo-chamber containing two tubes; (2) quarters for four officers; (3) the boiler-room; (4) the engine-room; (5) the men's quarters, cooking galley, stoves, etc. The crew consisted of nine men all told; 35 tons of cold water were carried in the tanks; and 27 tons of hot water in the boilers. These latter were expected to store sufficient heat for a run of 20 miles under water. The coal bunkers held stores of coal which, at a speed of 8 to 9 knots, could drive the boat a distance of 1000 miles. Should it be necessary to transport her to a greater distance, her water tanks could be filled with coal, enabling her to steam 2500 miles. Two vertical propellers, one forward and one aft, kept the vessel submerged and overcame the retained force of buoyancy (500 lb.). The boat was lighted by candles; without any special provision of air it contained enough for a crew of nine men for about six hours.

Nordenfelt IV made her passage from Barrow-in-Furness to Southampton through some heavy seas, and during the voyage she was tested by her commander in every wind and every condition of wave and sea, and she proved that she was capable of being manœuvred in any weather, however bad.

On 26 May, 1887, she underwent her first examination before a body of critics, composed for the most part of skilled, experienced scientific officers of both branches of the service. She was first run with nothing above water save the two conning-towers and a few inches of her back, at the rate of about 6 miles an hour. The time occupied by the trial in the awash condition was 1½ hour, and at the end of the time a sufficiency of steam was stored up in the boilers to drive her a distance of about 24 miles. On the pumps being put in motion,

Q

some twenty tons of water were pumped out in eight
minutes. The funnels were then fixed, the fires relighted, and the *Nordenfelt* was soon making 15 knots
on the surface.

. On 19 December, 1887, a semi-official trial of the
Nordenfelt took place, when she manœuvred successfully
both on the surface and submerged, but no attempt was
made to fire the torpedoes. ·

"The neutral tint she was painted," wrote the special
correspondent of the *Engineer*, "rendered her almost
invisible at the distance of even a few hundred yards,
while as a target she presented nothing to attack save
the two conning-towers and a few inches of her turtle
back, and as these were of great strength; and rendered
still more invulnerable by their shape, it is all but certain
that no gun carried in any other torpedo-boat would
ever do her the slightest injury, while she at the same
time possesses the enormous advantage of being able to
attack without smoke, or fire, or noise. Indeed, given
these advantages of a minimum of target and a total
absence of noise and smoke, we fail to see what more
could be desired in any vessel of war."

. In a leading article in the issue of. 23 December, 1887,
the *Engineer* said : "We may—we hope we shall—have
quite a little fleet of *Nordenfelts* when Christmas comes
round again. When once Columbus had shown the way
to America, the water was freely traversed."

The correspondent of the *Army and Navy Gazette* said
that the *Nordenfelt* had a great and assured future before
it, that with a gun or two on her turtle back, and working
as an above-water torpedo-boat, she certainly possessed

many advantages over the ordinary first-class torpedo-boat, and that her powers of submerging should make her the more valuable rcaft, the cost being the same: " It is not likely or advisable that a number of such boats should be at once built, but the country which can give £100,000 for a Brennan torpedo would do well to further, in every possible manner, trials and experiments with a boat so simple, yet possessing such possibilities in the future."

It will be very naturally wondered why, in spite of these favourable opinions, the *Nordenfelt* was so soon for-gotten. The answer may be found in some recent issues of the *Engineer*. This journal published, during the years 1886–1888, all the information that was suffered to leak out concerning the experiments with the Norden-felt boats. In 1901, by the courtesy of Mr. P. W. D'Alton (Chief Engineer to the Central London Railway), who was associated with Mr. Garrett and Mr. Nordenfelt, it was enabled to state much more than had hitherto been made public.

Taking first the Turkish boat, it was easily proved that as a boat working near the surface, but not wholly sub-merged, she was fast, manageable, and a very dangerous foe because of the difficulty of finding her, and the very small mark which she offered.

As a submarine boat she was entirely a failure.

" She had the fault of all submarine boats, viz., a total lack of longitudinal stability. All submarines are practically devoid of weight when under water. The *Nordenfelt*, for example, weighed by a couple of hundredweights less than nothing when submerged, and had to be kept down by screw propellers

provided for the purpose The Turkish boat was submerged
by admitting water to tanks aided by horizontal propellers,
and raised by blowing the ballast out again and reversing the
propellers. Nothing could be imagined more unstable than
this Turkish boat. .The moment she left the horizontal position the water in her boiler and the tanks surged forwards and
backwards and increased the angle of inclination. She was
perpetually working up and down like a scale beam, and no
human vigilance could keep her on an even keel for half a
minute at a time. Once, and we believe only once, she fired
a torpedo, with the result that she as nearly as possible stood
up vertically on her tail and proceeded to plunge to the bottom
stern first. On another occasion all hands were nearly lost.
Mr. Garrett was in the little conning-tower. The boat was
being slowly submerged—an operation of the utmost delicacy
—before a committee of Ottoman officers, when a boat came
alongside without warning. Her wash sent a considerable
quantity of water down the conning-tower, the lid of which
was not closed, and the submarine boat instantly began to
sink like a stone. Fortunately Mr. Garrett got the lid closed
just in time, and Mr. Lawrie, the engineer, without waiting
for orders, blew some water ballast out. It was an exceedingly narrow escape. In spite of these difficulties, the Ottoman officers were so impressed that the Turkish Government
bought the boat. It goes without saying that it was only
with the greatest difficulty the price was extracted from the
Sultan's treasury. But no use whatever has been made of
her, and she lies rotting away in Constantinople, unless,
indeed, she has found her way piecemeal to the marine-store
dealers. A paramount difficulty in the way of utilising her
was that no engineers could be got to serve in her. If men
were appointed they promptly deserted. Indeed, it may be
taken as certain that not one man in five hundred is fit to
take charge of any submarine boat."

The *Engineer* was not less severe on *Nordenfelt IV*.

"To all intents and purposes the *Nordenfelt* was a total failure as a submarine boat. She began badly. As soon as she was launched from the stocks at Barrow it was seen that a mistake had been made in calculating weight, as she was down by the stern, drawing 9 feet aft and about 4 feet 6 inches forward. This would have been partially rectified by her torpedoes, but she never had one on board. Extra ballast had to be put in forward, and it was always held, rightly or wrongly, that this made it all the more difficult to keep her on an even keel when submerged. The extra weight carried militated greatly against her speed as a surface boat. Another mistake was that the water-ballast tanks were too large, or perhaps it would be more correct to say that they were not sufficiently subdivided. When she was in just the proper condition to be manœuvred by her horizontal propellers the ballast tanks were only about three quarters full, and the water being left free surges backwards and forwards in them. It must not be forgotten, however, that ample tank capacity was necessary because the quantity of ballast needed depended on the number of tons of coal and stores on board. Sub-division would, however, have prevented the surging of the ballast water. If, for example, the boat was moving forward or on an even keel at, say, two knots, if a greaser walked forward a couple of feet in his engine-room, her head would go down a little. Then the water surged forward in the tank, and she would proceed to plunge, unless checked, and in shallow water would touch the bottom, as she did on the Mother Bank in the Solent, or if in deep water she would run· down until the pressure of water collapsed her hull. No one who has not been down in a submarine can realise their extraordinary crankiness. The *Nordenfelt* was always rising or falling, and required the greatest care in handling."

PART III

APPENDIX I

BRITISH SUBMARINES

"It has been said that the submarine is the weapon of the weaker power; now it is recognised that it adds strength to the stronger."

PROBABLY the first occasion in recent years on which mention was made of submarine boats in Parliament was subsequent to the trial of the *Nautilus*, a diving boat invented by Messrs. Campbell and Ash, during a trial in which several exalted personages nearly lost their lives. Lord George Hamilton described the incident in the House of Commons, and created some amusement by his relation, and there is no reason to believe that the submarine was looked upon by members other than as an erratic toy to whose mercy no wise man would entrust his person.

Mr. Nordenfelt built his several submarine boats, one bought by the Turkish and another by the Greek Government, but though in several quarters the advisability of the Admiralty purchasing one or more Nordenfelt boats was suggested, nothing came of it at the time.

Mr. Edmund Robertson, K.C., dealing in the *Nineteenth Century*, of May, 1900, with the question of submarine boats, remarked that five or six years before he wrote he knew the opinion of the technical advisers of the Admiralty, and that they did not see their way to recommend the Admiralty or the Government to make any provision for submarine vessels of war.

After that time, however, very few weeks passed but some

231

writer took up the cudgels on behalf of the submarine, and urged the Admiralty to consider the advisability of constructing boats.

The keen interest taken in France in under-water warfare was reflected to a certain extent in this country, and on 9 February, 1899, Mr. Charles McLaren addressed a question to the First Lord of the Admiralty, in which he referred to the " extraordinary value " assigned by the French minister to the new vessels, and asked " whether the British Admiralty attached any importance to these experiments, or had any intention of adding any such vessels to the British Navy ? " Viscount Goschen's answer was : " It would be inexpedient at this stage for me to express the opinion of the Admiralty as to the reported performances of the new submarine boats. With reference to any action which the Board of Admiralty may take, I am not at present prepared to make any statement."

The position of the Admiralty in the early part of 1900 may be ascertained from an answer given by Viscount Goschen to a question put by Captain Norton on 6 April. " Close attention has been given by the Admiralty to the subject of submarine boats. The submarine boat, even if the practical difficulties attending its use can be overcome, would seem so far as the immediate future is concerned to be eventually a weapon for maritime Powers on the defensive, and it is natural that those nations which anticipate holding that position should endeavour to develop it. The question of the best way of meeting its attack is receiving much consideration, and it is in this direction that practical suggestions should be valuable. It seems certain that the reply to this weapon must be looked for in other directions than in building submarine boats ourselves, for it is clear that one submarine boat cannot fight another." In the debate on the Ship-building vote the First Lord made a further statement. " The importance of submarine boats had been pointed out, and it had been said that it was their duty to make experiments. The nations which were likely to have the greatest use for these boats might gain from their experiments more than others. He did not propose to make publicly any declaration as to these boats. Of course, he did not wish to encourage or discourage other nations, but he must ask the Committee to excuse him going into the question."

In the same debate Mr. Arnold-Forster, who a few months later was appointed Parliamentary and Financial Secretary to the Admiralty, made some remarks on this " somewhat cryptic utterance," as Mr. Robertson called it. " If in the matter of submarine boats the First Lord of the Admiralty had said that in the opinion of the engineering advisers of the Admiralty to design and work a submarine boat was so remote of accomplishment that there was no reasonable probability of being able to work it, he would have been slow to contradict him ; but that was not the line taken by him. The First Lord said that the Admiralty had not designed a submarine boat, and did not propose to design one, because such a boat would be the weapon of an inferior Power. But if it could be produced as a working article, the Power which possessed such an article would no longer be an inferior, but a superior Power. We, above all nations, were exposed to the attacks of this engine. He submitted that it was not a satisfactory thing to stand by and allow others to carry out this problem without making some attempt to solve it for ourselves. He admitted the tendency of the Admiralty to follow and not to lead other great nations. He hoped that one of these days we should not follow just a little too late. If we had been compelled to learn our lesson with regard to ironclads, breechloaders, and armoured cruisers in the face of an active enemy, we should have experienced the same lessons which the Austrian army underwent in 1866 when they were compelled to learn the merits of the breechloader by studying it on the field of battle. There was room for improvement in the attitude we had taken up in regard to submarine navigation."

During the short session of December, 1900, after the General Election, the Admiralty was again questioned, and the reply was that the " attention of the Admiralty had been called to the additional provision for submarine boats in the French naval programme, and a statement will be made when the estimates are laid before the House." Between this date and the introduction of the Navy Estimates endless rumours regarding the position the Admiralty would take as to the submarine boat question found their way into the daily press. While, on the one hand, it was " confidently asserted " that the Government were making secret trials with all kinds of wonderful craft, on the other hand it was stated " on the highest authority " that the Lords of the Admiralty had no intention of altering their minds as to the advisability of taking any action whatever in the matter.

The statement of the First Lord of the Admiralty explanatory of the Navy Estimates for 1901–2, published on 1 March, 1901, contained the following item :—

" Five submarine vessels of the type invented by Mr. Holland have been ordered, the first of which should be delivered next autumn. What the future value of these boats may be in naval warfare can only be a matter of conjecture. The experiments with these boats will assist the Admiralty in assessing their true value. The question of their employment must be studied, and all developments in their mechanism carefully watched by this country."

In the discussion on the Navy (Supplementary) Estimates on 4 March, 1901, Mr. Flynn asked whether the policy of the Admiralty in constructing battleships " as to the strength of which they knew nothing," when other nations were turning their attention to submarine vessels, was quite wise. This same notion as to the advisability of going in for small submarines instead of big battleships is to be found in a speech by Mr. O'Shee on 23 March, who said that if these boats were able to do half what was claimed for them, then the present gigantic expenditure for naval construction was entirely uncalled for. A submarine boat could be built for £25,000, and manned by ten men, and if it were true they were able to combat the big ships which the Government were building, those ships would be absolutely useless except for carrying the submarine boats to places where they were to work. If submarines were all that was claimed for them, it would render unnecessary the £9,000,000 which was then being expended on new battleships."

Mr. Arnold-Forster in the House on 18 March, 1901, said :—

"I will not say much about submarine vessels, but I will say that I am glad that the Admiralty, under the advice of Lord Goschen, took the view that it was wise not to be found unprepared in regard to this matter. We have a great amount of information about these boats, but we do not attach an exaggerated value to it. But we believe that an ounce of practice is worth a ton of theory, and that when we get officers and men to see these boats, they will learn more from them than from many reports which come from foreign countries. One thing stands between the submarine boat and efficiency, and that is the motor by which it is propelled. But there is no disguising the fact that if you can add speed to the other qualities of the submarine boat, it might in certain circumstances become a very formidable vessel. We are comforted by the judgment of the United States and Germany, which is hostile to these inventions, which I confess I desire shall never prosper."—(Commander Young, M.P., said that if the Admiralty built any submarine boats, all he would ask would be that he might not be ordered to serve in one.)—" But we cannot regard our position as the same as that of other nations. The United States to-morrow, if a perfect submarine were invented, would not only have more secure protection for their harbours. In Germany the harbours are no doubt carefully protected now. But we live in the narrow waters of the Channel, and our problem is not precisely that of any other nation, and I am glad that Lord Goschen did give this instruction to the Board, which has now borne fruit in the determination to put this experiment into execution, and we shall see the result of it during the next financial year."

Mr. Edmund Robertson, K.C., in the debate on the Navy Estimates on 21 March, 1901, remarked that as the building of the submarine boats was only a matter of experiment, he thought it might have been introduced upon a somewhat smaller scale. If its value was purely conjectural, he should have said that one boat would have been enough to experiment with. Two should have been quite enough, but we generally did things on a large scale, and after having refused to say one word for many years about submarine boats, we now found the Admiralty launching out into quite a little fleet of them. " What," asked Mr. Robertson, " had become of the control of the House of Commons ? What had become of that control when the Admiralty of the day, having refused to tell them their policy, come forward shortly afterwards and say they will build five of these boats ? " He could not help protesting against this, for a new departure of this nature ought not to have been made except with the sanction of the House, and at the very least it ought not to have been done without being divulged to the House.

It may be noted that Mr. Arnold-Forster, speaking in the House of Commons in January, 1902, explained that when the decision to construct submarine boats was arrived at only one type was available for purchase, that the right to build boats of this type was in the hands of one firm, and that it was therefore necessary to entrust the work to that firm.

The First British Submarines.—The first five British submarines are almost identically the same as the six Holland boats ordered by the U.S. Congress on 7 June, 1900.

. They are cigar-shaped vessels, 63 ft. 6 in. long ; beam, 11 ft. 9 in. ; and displacement submerged, 120 tons. The plating and frames are of steel, and of sufficient size and thickness to withstand the pressure at depths not exceeding 100 feet. The bulkheads are located to provide safety in event of collision, and to stiffen the hull as a whole; decks are provided throughout the whole length of the interior of the vessel, combined with beams and floors to carry the weight of machinery , the tanks are of steel, and they are braced, stiffened, riveted, and caulked absolutely tight, and manholes are located to allow access to the interior of all tanks.

When the vessel is in light condition for surface running an

above-water deck, 31 feet long, is available, and there are
means of stowing anchor and lines and of affording mooring
facilities to the vessel. Rudders of steel plates are provided,
and they are supported by skegs at the stern of the vessel.
The conning-tower is of armoured steel ; its outside diameter
is 32 inches, and its minimum thickness 4 inches ; it is provided with ports for observation by the steersman. In the

Cribb, Southsea

SUBMARINES OF THE FIRST BRITISH TYPES ALONGSIDE THE MOTHER SHIP

construction of the vessel care has been taken that all portions
of the exterior of the hull shall be free from projections of a
kind that might be entangled by ropes or other obstacles when
submerged, and the lines of the vessels have been designed so
that there shall be a minimum of resistance when it is running
at the surface.

Propulsion.—On the surface the vessel is propelled by a
160 h.p., single screw, four cylinder, Otto gasoline engine,
capable of giving a speed of 8 knots, while when submerged

it is driven through the water by a 70 h.p. electric motor giving a speed of 7 knots. The range of action at the surface is about 400 miles, while the storage batteries have sufficient capacity for a speed of 7 knots on a four hours' submerged run. Gearing is provided for the charging of the batteries by using the motor as a dynamo, and running it from the gasoline engine when at the surface, and from connecting the propeller either to the engine or the motor ; these operations are effected through clutches. Switchboards and switches are provided for the safe and efficient distribution of the electr.c current throughout the vessel. The lighting system consists of portable incandescent electric lamps, together with several ports and openings in the hull to admit the outside light. The hull is circular, in cross sections, and is divided by the watertight bulkheads into three separate compartments. There is also a thorough subdivision of the bottom, and every precaution is taken to localise any injury to the hull which might threaten the buoyancy.

In the forward compartment is one torpedo expulsion tube, located at the extreme forward end of the vessel, opening outward two feet below the light water-line. The tube is placed with its muzzle in the nose of the craft and its axis inclined somewhat to the longitudinal axis of the vessel. The muzzle of the tube is closed by a water-tight door, and this can be lifted from within for the discharge of the five White-head torpedoes, each 11 ft. 8 in. long, which are carried in the interior. One torpedo is placed in the tube, and the other four are placed side by side above the storage batteries. When the first torpedo is fired a sufficient amount of water to compensate for the loss of weight is automatically and almost instantaneously admitted into the tube, causing only a slight change of time for a few seconds. Such compensation is necessary, as the submarine boat is lighter than the amount of water it displaces, and any alteration in its weight tends to send it up to the surface or down towards the bottom. When the second torpedo is placed in the tube the water is run into a special torpedo compensating tank ; of these tanks there are four, and they are filled·as each torpedo is fired. When the last torpedo has been ejected the expulsion tube is filled with water, and is kept thus until the end of the run.

Besides the torpedo tube there is in the forward compartment a series of air flasks, a gasoline tank of 850 gallons capacity, and a trimming tank.

The central compartment contains in its double bottom the main ballast tanks and a circular compensating tank placed between the two sets of batteries. Above the double bottom and below the axis of the vessel are located the storage batteries, and above these are carried the four torpedoes, which are 45 centimetres in diameter and 11 ft. 8 in. in length. In the same compartment are a series of air flasks in which air at 2000 lbs. to the square inch pressure is stored for the purpose of keeping pure the living spaces of the crew.*

In the rear compartment is the four-cylinder gasoline engine, which is rated at from 160 to 190 actual horse-power, and at from 320 to 390 revolutions per minute. Its net weight is 1300 lb., its length over all is 9 ft. 7 in., and its total height above the crank-shaft centre is 5 ft. 6 in. In these engines, which gave satisfaction in the first Holland boat, the distribution of the cranks and the timing of the valves and igniters are so arranged that the operations in-the four cylinders alternate,· so that while one is at the expansion stroke the other three are at the suction, compression, and exhaust strokes respectively. By this arrangement·the engine is perfectly balanced and vibration is reduced to a minimum.

Submersion.—The first operation to be performed when it is desired to submerge the vessel is the admission of water into her ballast tanks. When these are full she runs " awash " with her conning-tower alone above the waves.

In order to completely submerge the boat she is steered below the surface by means of her pair of horizontal rudders at the stern. When at the required depth (normally·from.

---

* Also for firing the torpedoes and for blowing the water out of the ballast tanks when it is desired to navigate as a surface boat.

20 to 30 feet) she is brought up on an even keel by the inclination of the horizontal rudders, which may be controlled automatically (by some such arrangement as is found in the Whitehead torpedo) or by hand. All modern submarine craft go under at an angle, and are steered below the waves by rudders : the principle of submersion on an even keel by down-haul propellers, advocated by Mr. Nordenfelt, has been abandoned by all latter-day designers, as has also the submersion by the drawing in of cylinders adopted in the Campbell-Ash boat.

When running submerged the submarine is lighter than her displacement, and is only kept under by her horizontal rudders, which, of course, only act when she is moving.

The great drawback to all under-water craft has been their lack of longitudinal stability, for they have a tendency to rise or sink at the slightest provocation. In our account of the Nordenfelt boats this disagreeable quality is illustrated. In order to keep the vessel at a regular depth recourse must be had to the horizontal rudders and to the two trimming tanks and the one circular compensating tank carried.

In a general way it will probably be found possible to keep the boat on an even keel by means of her rudders, but if she shows any decided tendency either to dive to the bottom or to rise to the surface or to heel over to one side water may be admitted into the above-mentioned tanks, and the admission may be effected either automatically or by hand. A hydrostatic valve will prevent the vessel passing the safe limit of depth.

Air Supply and Ventilation.—Compressed air is stored aboard the vessel with means of allowing a supply of air into the interior of the vessel. Ventilators are provided for the circulation of outside air throughout the vessel ; the gasoline vapours from the engines and all noxious gases are carefully excluded by suitable devices ; while safety valves are provided to prevent the pressure to the vessel from exceeding that of the atmosphere.

Pumps and Pumping.—All tanks and compartments are

connected with the pumps, the valves are located to allow of quick manipulation, and pumps with independent means of operation are furnished in duplicate. The tanks can also be emptied by flowing out.

Navigating Apparatus.—In communication with the interior of the vessel there are bells and speaking tubes, while there are provided gauges, indices, and clinometers for indicating pressure, depth, positions, quantities, and weights.

Two compasses are carried, each compensated and adjusted. It is said that the first of the British submarines exhibited certain defects in its compasses, which it was thought were due to the steel conning-tower. This was replaced by a brass construction, and on being tested the compasses acted more satisfactorily. After a few trials a new steering-wheel was fixed in the boat close to the conning-tower, which could be worked from above and below alike.

The first British submarine was launched on 2 November, 1901, at Barrow, without any ceremony, although representatives of the Admiralty were present. The trials were placed under the direction of Captain R. H. S. Bacon, D.S.O.

Before launching " No. 1 " was by means of a floating dock placed on the gridiron. A crew of six men were put on board, and she was then hermetically sealed for three hours, air being supplied by compressed air cylinders. The trial was quite successful, and the men suffered no inconvenience. On her first " sea trial " " No. 1 " started from the floating dock and proceeded along the Devonshire and Buccleuch docks and back to her moorings. On subsequent trials she attained a surface speed of 10 knots.

The first submersion trials of " No. 1 " were carried out on 5 February, 1902. She went under water with some officers of the *Hazard*, t.g.b., the mother ship to the submarines (Captain R. H. S. Bacon, D.S.O.), on board, and most satisfactory results were obtained. Her appliances for the purification of the air were used to maintain atmospheric conditions without any need of her cylinders of compressed air being

R

requisitioned. The first deep sea trials of " No. 1 " took place at the beginning of April, 1902, in the Irish Sea. The submerging was accomplished in less than six seconds. From the " awash " condition she suddenly disappeared and then came again into sight some yards distant with great rapidity and ease, and the diving was continued at intervals for several hours at a time without any perceptible hitch.

Submarine " No. 2 " was launched on 21 February, 1902. Certain alterations were made in her construction, rendered advisable by defects which had been discovered during the testing of " No. 1." " No. 3," " No. 4," and " No. 5 " were launched in the same year.

The Navy Estimates for 1902–1903 provided for four further submarines of the " A " class, which are an improvement on those previously constructed at Barrow. These vessels, like the others, are all submersibles, though commonly called submarines. They are 100 feet long, are provided with two torpedo tubes, have high conning-towers, and altogether mark a great advance. A sad disaster happened to A 1 outside Spithead. Being submerged, her conning-tower struck the hull of a passing vessel, with the result that water rushed in and the boat went to the bottom, all her company being lost. After many efforts she was raised, and has been reconstructed and refitted. In some respects she differs from the other " A " boats, as may be seen in pictures in this volume. The " B " class is still larger (150 feet), and the " C " class and later boats all show great advances on their predecessors. Particulars of these have not been made public. They no longer have any resemblance to the Holland type, and are of a distinctly British class. A picture of the first of the " C " boats, given in this volume, shows that in the form of hull she differs greatly from the earlier classes. She is also very much larger.

THE UNITED STATES SUBMARINE "OCTOPUS"

APPENDIX II

THE AMERICAN SUBMARINES

" The Submarine Boat is a small ship on the model of the White-head, subject to none of its limitations, improving on all its special qualities, excepting speed, for which it substitutes incomparably greater endurance. It is not, like other small vessels, compelled to select for its antagonist a vessel of about its own or inferior power; the larger and more powerful its mark the better its opportunity"
—Mr. J. P. HOLLAND

"In my judgment, as a constructor of these boats (the new Hollands for the United States Government), and from my long experience in designing and constructing war vessels for the Government, and as the constructor of the original *Holland*, I have no doubt whatever of the endurance, habitability, durability, and reliability of these boats.

" No type of boat in the navy has received such crucial tests as the *Holland*. The submarine boat to-day is further advanced in its development than any type of naval vessels that I am aware of. I desire to say that in my opinion the *Holland*, without any improvements, is to-day the greatest vessel for harbour and coast defence ever known."—Mr. LEWIS NIXON, builder of the *Holland*.

WHEN the British Admiralty decided to experiment with submarine boats, the type chosen was that invented by Mr. John P. Holland. It is therefore fitting that some account should be given of the various stages through which the Holland boat has gone in the course of its evolution.

Although Mr. John P. Holland, of Paterson, New Jersey, U.S.A., made a number of experiments in the sixties, his first real submarine boat was not built until 1875.

Holland No. 1 may be described as an under-water canoe,

245

for there was only room for one occupant, who propelled the
vessel along by means of pedal-acting mechanism, a small
screw being fitted at the stern. The dimensions were :
Length, 16 ft. ; beam, 20 ins. ; depth, 2 ft. It was
divided into three parts ; the two end ones were used as air
reservoirs and submersion tanks, and that in the centre contained the operator, whose head was encased in a diver's
helmet. The vessel was driven by a small propeller projecting from the stern joist, and beneath this was the rudder.

Holland No. 2 was constructed in 1877 at the Albany City
Iron Works of New York. Its dimensions were : Length,
10 ft. ; beam, 3·5 ft. ; depth, 3 ft. It had a double
shell, and in the space between water ballast could be admitted for submersion. The motor was a petroleum engine

MR. HOLLAND'S EARLIEST SUBMARINE (1875)

of 4 h.p., working a screw at the stern. Two rudders, one
vertical, the other horizontal, were carried, and experiments
showed that the latter acted better when placed at the stern
than when on the side. After a series of trials on the Passaic
River, Mr. Holland removed the machinery and sank his boat
under Falls Bridge at Patterson, where it probably remains
at this day.

Holland No. 3 was commenced in 1879 in the yards of the
Delamater Iron Company of New York City, and finished in
1881. Its dimensions were : Length, 31 ft. ; beam, 6 ft. ;
depth, 6 ft. ; displacement, 19 tons. It was propelled by
a 15 h.p. petroleum engine of the Brayton type ; as armament a submarine cannon, 11 ft. long and 9 ins. in diameter, was carried, and the projectile was expelled by means
of a charge of compressed air. " She was the first submarine
since Bushnell's time," writes Admiral Hichborn, " employing

water ballast and always retaining buoyancy, in which provision was made to ensure a fixed centre of gravity and a fixed absolute weight. Moreover, she was the first buoyant submarine to be steered down and up inclines in the vertical plane by horizontal rudder action, as she was pushed forward by her motor, instead of being pushed up and down by vertically-acting mechanism. Her petroleum engine, pro-

U.S. SUBMARINE "SHARK" ON THE STOCKS

vided for motive power and for charging her compressed air flasks, was inefficient, and the boat therefore failed as a practical craft ; but in her were demonstrated all the chief principles of successful brain-directed submarine navigation. After the completion of the boat, Holland led the world far and away in the solution of submarine problems, and for a couple of years demonstrated that he could perfectly control his craft in the vertical plane. Eventually, through financial complications, she was taken to New Haven, where she now is."

Holland No. 4 was constructed in the yard of Gammon and

Cooper, of Jersey City. It was simply meant as a model, being only 16 ft. 4 ins. long, 28 ins. in diameter, and displacing a ton. The motor was an explosive engine, which was to serve for propulsion above and below the surface. The life of this model was unfortunately short, for on one occasion she was submerged with her cupola open, with the result that the water entered and she sank.

Holland No. 5, commonly known under the name of the "Zalinsky Boat," owing to its dynamite guns, was built at Fort Lafayette. It was 30 ft. long, 7 ft. beam, 7 ft. in diameter, and was armed with two Zalinsky pneumatic dynamite guns. Owing to an error in construction, she was shipwrecked on the rocks, but was afterwards rescued and used for some experiments in the docks.

Holland No. 6 never got further than the design stage ; it was not a true submarine, not being capable of total submergence. *Holland No.* 7 was known as the *Plunger*.

Whilst Mr. Whitney was Secretary of the Navy he was anxious to provide some kind of protection against gun-fire for torpedo-boats, and under suggestion he invited proposals for submarine boats. A great many designs were sent in, and two propositions to build were made by the famous Cramp firm, the designs being those of Holland and Nordenfelt. It will not be necessary to enter into any detailed comparison between the two types. Suffice it to say that while Mr. Nordenfelt screwed his boat down by using vertical screws, and held the opinion that the keel of a submarine must always be kept parallel to the surface of the water, Mr. Holland steered his boat down and up an incline by the action of horizontal rudders placed in the stern. The Holland design was accepted, because " it embodied the ideas of a fixed centre of gravity, of an exact compensation for expended weights, of a low longitudinal metacentric height, and of quick diving and rising by the effort of the propeller pushing the vessel against the resistance of her midship section only down and up inclines, the angles of which were to be determined by horizontal rudder action." Difficulties in regard to guarantees

of performance prevented the closing of a contract that year—
1888—and the next year, after all preliminaries were arranged,
a change in administration caused the matter to be put aside.
After the lapse of some years interest in submarine boats was
again aroused, and on 3 March, 1893, Congress authorised
the building of a single experimental vessel, and after a third
competition of designs and other delays a contract for a

BOW VIEW OF THE "HOLLAND"

Holland boat was signed two years later with the Holland
Torpedo-boat Company (formed in 1895). The new vessel
was to be called the *Plunger*. The long delay was owing,
Mr. Holland has said, to the opposition of a few officers of
Conservative spirit, who preferred to see the value of submarine boats fully established by their employment in other
navies, and their place in schemes of attack and defence
properly located, before they could recommend their adoption
in their own navy. The dimensions of the *Plunger* are as
follows : Length, 85 ft. ; beam, 11½ ft. ; diameter, 11½ ft;
displacement, 140 tons on the surface, 165 tons submerged ;

guaranteed speed, 15 knots on the surface for two hours, and 14 knots submerged to 1 foot with the conning-tower above water ; indicated horse-power, surface 1625, submerged 200 ; motor, steam engine on surface, fed with liquid fuel ; electric motor, completely submerged, giving speed of 8 knots for 6 hours.

Although the *Plunger* was actually launched on 7 August, 1897, she was never completed, although for three years various alterations were carried out. The steam engines were removed and were replaced by oil motors, but by the time these modifications had been effected the Holland Torpedo-boat Company came to the conclusion that the *Plunger*, when completed according to the terms of the contract, would be so inferior to the more modern *Hollands* that they offered to refund the Government all it had paid them upon the *Plunger* and all expenses connected with the contract, provided the Navy Department would enter into a contract for a new *Holland*. The proposition was accepted, and the money, some $94,000 odd, was accordingly refunded. The *Plunger* has since been broken up.

Holland No. 8 resembled very much the later types, but as she was not entirely satisfactory, *Holland No.* 9 was built. This latter vessel is generally referred to as the *Holland*. She was the prototype of the British submarines, and her performances have excited a vast deal of interest all over the civilised world.

The dimensions of the *Holland*, which was constructed at Elizabeth Port, New Jersey, by Mr. Lewis Nixon, at the expense of the Holland Company, and whilst the alterations to the *Plunger* were still in progress, are as follows : Length, 53 ft. 10 in. ; diameter, 10 ft. 3 in. ; height (bottom to superstructure deck), 10 ft. 7 in. ; displacement, 75 tons ; water ballast, 10 tons ; reserve buoyancy, 250 lb.

On the surface the motor is a gasoline engine of the Otto type of 50 h.p., giving a speed of about 7 knots an hour, and under water an electric motor, capable of giving 50 h.p. for 6 hours or 150 h.p. for 2 hours, is used. The battery of

accumulators consists of 66 cells, giving 350 amperes for 4
hours, and allowing a speed of 8 knots an hour. The radius
of action on the surface is 1500 miles at 7 knots without a
renewal of gasoline, and it can go 50 miles under water without coming to the surface. In order to dive, water ballast
is admitted until the boat is flush with the water, and it is
then steered down an incline by two horizontal rudders at

LAUNCH OF THE U.S. SUBMARINE "SHARK"

the stern, carried in addition to the ordinary vertical rudder.
It has a reserve buoyancy which tends to bring it to the
surface in case of accident. It can dive to a depth of 28 feet
in 8 seconds. The armament was intended originally to consist of three tubes—two at the bows and one at the stern ;
two were to throw aerial torpedoes and shells, while the third
was to discharge Whitehead torpedoes. The submarine gun
aft, which was worked by pneumatic power, and was capable
of throwing 80 lb. of dynamite a distance of about half a
mile, was, however, abandoned. The aerial gun at the bows is

11·25 ft. long and 8 ins. in diameter, and each of the projectiles weighs 222 lb., and carries 100 lb. of gun-cotton.
This gun can shoot these projectiles a needista of one mile.
The torpedo tube is 18 ins., and three torpedoes are carried;
they have a running capacity of more than half a mile at a
speed of 30 knots.   On the top of the boat a flat superstructure is built to afford a walking platform, and underneath
this are spaces for exhaust pipes and for the external outfit
of the boat, such as ropes and a small anchor.   From the
centre of the boat a turret extends upward through the superstructure about 18 ins.   It is about 2 ft. in diameter, and
is the only means of entrance to the boat; it is also the
place from which the boat is operated.

As Mr. Holland had been experimenting with submarine
craft for twenty-five years, and as he now considered that he
had secured a practical result, and that his newest boat
would do all that he claimed, he requested the United States
Admiralty to make a series of exhaustive trials with the
Holland.   These trials accordingly took place, and having
been found to be satisfactory, the *Holland* was purchased by
the U.S. Government on 11 April, 1900.   The price paid was
$150,000, and the Company stated that the vessel had cost
them, exclusive of any office expenses or salaries of officers,
$236,615,427.   The *Holland* was formally placed in com-
mission under the command of Lieutenant Harry H. Caldwell,
U.S.N., on 13 October, 1900, but the boat had been under
the charge of this officer since 25 June, 1900.

An Act making appropriations for the Naval Service for
the fiscal year ending 30 June, 1901, which was approved on
7 June, 1900, contained the following item :—

" The Secretary of the Navy is hereby authorised and
directed to contract for five submarine torpedo-boats of the
Holland type, of the most improved design, at a price not to
exceed one hundred and seventy thousand dollars each :
Provided, That such boats shall be similar in dimensions to the
proposed new *Holland*, plans and specifications of which were
submitted to the Navy Department by the Holland Torpedo-

boat Company, November twenty-third, eighteen hundred and ninety-nine. The said new contract and the submarine torpedo-boats covered by the same are to be in accordance with the stipulations of the contract of purchase made April eleventh, nineteen hundred, by and between the Holland Torpedo-boat Company, represented by the secretary of the said company, the party of the first part, and the United States, represented by the Secretary of the Navy, the party of the second part. Towards the completion of the equip-

THE "FULTON" RUNNING ON THE SURFACE

ment, outfit of the new vessels heretofore authorised four hundred thousand dollars."

A contract for the construction of *six* (not five) submarine torpedo-boats, Nos. 3–8, was finally concluded on 25 August, 1900, between the Holland Torpedo-boat Company and the Secretary of the United States Navy. The *Adder, Moccassin, Porpoise*, and *Shark* were constructed by Lewis Nixon, at Elizabeth Port, New Jersey, and the *Grampus* and *Pike* at the Union Iron Works, San Francisco, all being launched in 1901 and 1902. As the specification for these boats resembles in almost every particular that for the first five British submarines of the *Holland* type, details need not be given here. The contract price of the hull and machinery of each boat was $34,000.

The *Fulton* was similar to the six boats that the Holland Company had built for the United States, and was constructed at the expense of the company with the object of experimenting, to see if it was possible to get smaller engines with less weight and greater power. Mr. Holland said that he could not build his boats any longer, and could not get any more speed, simply for the reason that he could not get engines with enough power. It was his intention to subject every part of the equipment and motive power of the *Fulton* to thorough test. The boat was launched on 2 June, 1901, and in the autumn, with seven officers and men on board, she remained for fifteen hours at the bottom of Peconic Bay, whilst a bad storm was raging above, without having the air in the interior renewed. The turret-hatch was closed at seven o'clock on 23 November, and at the expiration of fifteen hours it had not been found necessary to draw off any of the compressed air contained in the four flasks taken down with the boat. The atmosphere was said to be as pure as in the cabin of an ordinary yacht. A glass of water filled to the brim stood on the cabin table during all the time of submersion, and not a drop was spilled in spite of the gale blowing above water. The *Fulton* does not, however, appear to have been perfect in every particular, for in April, 1902, she left New York for Washington, convoyed by the steamer *Norfolk*, having on board, besides stored electricity for her submarine trials, 750 gallons of gasoline for surface propulsion. She put in at Delaware Breakwater, and shortly afterwards an explosion occurred, Lieutenant Oscar Kohen, of the Austrian Navy, who was on board at the time, being severely bruised, while a lieutenant of the American Navy and several others were injured. The boat herself was not seriously damaged. It transpired that the accident was due to a slight explosion of hydrogen gas caused by the spilling of the acid from the batteries.

The experience gained was not without value, and has borne fruit in the later boats built for the United States Navy. The Naval Committee of the United States Senate in June, 1902, amended the Appropriation Bill, and provided for the purchase of five further submarines of the latest *Holland* type,

[STERN VIEW OF THE "HOLLAND"

and for investigation into other types. The five boats are the *Plunger, Cuttlefish, Viper, Tarantula,* and *Octopus,* the four last-named being built at Quincy, Massachusetts. They are enlarged *Hollands* much improved, and are not all alike, the *Octopus* being the largest (106 ft.), with a high conning-tower much resembling those of the British boats, though in other respects differing very much from them. Three additional boats were provided for in 1906, and President Roose-

velt, writing to the Chairman of the Naval Committee of the
House of Representatives in January, 1907, said that though
the strength of the Navy rested primarily in battleships, he
thoroughly believed in developing and building an adequate
number of submarines.

APPENDIX III

FRENCH SUBMARINES

"By reason of her submarine division, the navy of France is the most dread and the most powerful in the world."

A French Journalist, 1901.

"Jamais nous n'aurions trop de sous-marins."

HAD it not been for the keen and abiding interest displayed by Admiral Aube in the question of under-water warfare, it is extremely unlikely that the French Navy would be in possession of its present fleet of submarines and submersibles.

It was in 1886 that Admiral Aube, being then Minister of Marine, requested designs for submarine boats. In most quarters his ideas were received with ridicule, and the experts of the day did not hesitate to declare that such vessels would never become warships, that at best they would serve only as diving bells, and that submarine navigation was a subject more fitted for romancers like Jules Verne than for serious marine architects.

The Admiral held his own, however, and, contrary to the advice of the Director of Matériel, ordered from M. Goubet on 12 September, 1886, a small boat, and in the same year, in face of the protests of all his colleagues, he signed an order directing the Société des Forges et Chantiers de la Méditerranée to build a larger vessel from the plans of M. Gustave Zédé.

M. A. Saissy, a French journalist who has warmly advocated the construction of submarines by France, wrote a preface to MM. Forest and Noalhat's treatise, "Les bateaux sous-marins" (1900), in which he paid a tribute to the endeavours of the late Admiral to provide his country with a submarine fleet. "Had we but followed his ideas," he wrote, "had we but carried out his plans, not only would the defence of our coasts and of our colonies be assured against attack, but France would be at this hour the greatest naval power in the world."

Admiral Aube argued that in the naval war of the future France would most certainly act on the defensive, and that it was therefore the business of the nation to prepare, to organise, and to bring to the highest state of efficiency its weapons of defence. He blamed the Admiralty for spending the millions which had been voted for the navy in the creation of "mastodons" which "had neither speed, nor teeth to bite."

M. Saissy said that the Admiral's plans were put on one side and that his warnings appealed to deaf ears, but the time came when they were brought to light again.

"M. Lockroy was surrounded by officers to whom the programme of Admiral Aube was not a chimera. The study of submarine navigation was actively pushed forward, and if M. Lockroy had remained at the Ministry we should have had at this moment an important number of these weapons of naval warfare, so precious and so indispensable; but he was superseded, and, according to custom, his successor began to undo the good work of his predecessor, so that we find ourselves to-day in a most difficult situation. Our habit is always to act as if we had plenty of time before us, and the enormous budget of the Navy and its supplementary estimates will, unless we are on our guard, be wasted in a useless expenditure.

*   *   *   *   *   *

"The Ministry of Marine is aware of the gravity of the situation. - Our legislators cannot be ignorant of the facts, and yet nothing is done. Our only hope is in the individual initiative of those honest men of science who give some thought to what the morrow may bring forth."

M. Fleury-Ravarin, in a report written in November, 1900, supporting the Ministerial programme for the building of large battleships, remarked :—

" If we are now asked what a fighting navy should really be we must say that it should be capable of fighting upon the high seas with the navies of rival nations, and that it is the business of the technical boards of the Navy to indicate the nature and composition of the fleet required for the purpose. It is for the Parliament to decide if we shall be content with a modest defensive navy which would be unable, we cannot repeat too often, to do more than delay defeat in case of war, or whether, on the other hand, France is resolved to enforce her position as a great Power and to make the heavy but re-munerative sacrifices necessary to give weight to her voice in the councils of Europe, thus attracting to herself commerce and riches, and spreading throughout the world her influence and her traditional ideal of justice and generosity."

Opinion in France is divided on the question of the ship-building programme ; whilst, on the one hand, there are those who regard the construction of large battleships and cruisers as absolutely necessary, on the other, there are many who look upon this type of warship as inferior to the smaller class of fighting ship.

The former party is generally in the ascendant. M. de Lanessan contrasted the short range of the torpedo with the long range of the gun, and deduced from the conditions the necessity for two classes of vessels—(a) torpedo craft, and (b) battleships and armoured cruisers. He explained that in order that the gun should be given its full value it was essential that the platform should be stable, and that a vessel of considerable dimensions was thus called for. It was im-possible upon such a platform to place many powerful guns, but a necessary consequence was that these should be pro-tected, and hence came the need of heavy armouring. In short, the two qualities of offence and defence were indissoluble, but they were not the only qualities called for ; speed and range of action were also necessary, and these again led inevitably to the heavy battleship.

M. Fleury-Ravarin, commenting on the fact that many advocates of the *guerre de course* had asked if there did not exist a more economical means of making war than that which consisted in opposing to certain ships others of a like character, told the French Parliament that it (the *guerre de course*) had never brought an enemy to submission, and that in the existing conditions of naval warfare it was very costly, whilst speed, its essential element, was of all elements at sea the most elusive. Moreover, the organisation of the *guerre de course* required many naval bases, so that not only was it more costly in the beginning, but it demanded greater charges for maintenance. For these reasons this system of warfare could not be raised to a method ; it must remain an accessory.

The opinions of a few well-known Frenchmen upon the subject of submarines may be given here.

. M. Lockroy, in 1899, speaking in explanation of the French Navy estimates, said that whilst formerly France had but one naval rival, she then had four, and the Triple Alliance could muster but sixty-seven battleships, while England had ninety-four, and France sixty. Could France ensure superiority over her rivals ? Yes ; submarine navigation ensured her a considerable advantage. The achievements of the *Zédé* might lead to a revolution in naval equipment and warfare. Meanwhile France had a terrible weapon—just what she wanted. "Everything," said Vice - Admiral Jurien de la Gravière, "which threatens *les colosses* and tends to emancipate *les moucherons* should be warmly welcomed by the French Navy, for by such means we can double in a few years our forces and our power."

There are, however, very many who are opposed to this policy, and who believe that France would be better with more battleships and cruisers and fewer torpedo craft. In

1888 Admiral Bourgois, in his book on Torpedoes, emphatically stated that the torpedo and the torpedo-boat could not take the place of the ironclad. Said another writer : " Qu'on se rappelle les mitrailleuses de 1870. Nous souhaitons sincerement que le sous-marin après avoir inspiré la même confiance exagerée ne cause pas les mêmes déceptions que les mitrailleuses ¹ " Again the same writer reminded his countrymen that a naval battle could not be compared to a manœuvre in which everything is arranged beforehand. The submarine could not venture to sea in foul weather without exposing itself to dire accidents; but would the enemy wait until the sea was calm before commencing battle ? What would happen if he chose the moment to attack when a troubled sea forces the submarine to remain in port and no other defence can be utilised ? The submarine, he said, was still in the rudimentary condition, and the problem of submarine navigation had not yet been solved. " Other navies possess submarines and have made experiments, and we cannot be certain that we are ahead of them, although we make the most fuss. A means of defence from the attack of submarines, if ever they become really dangerous weapons, will assuredly be found, and the country which is so imprudent as to rely chiefly on such vessels will be quickly disarmed by a stronger foe. To sum up, submarine navigation, like aerial navigation, is as yet only in the experimental stage—let us follow its progress carefully and encourage experiments ; but to make a radical transformation in our Navy on the strength of certain manœuvres would be an act of imprudence both perilous and criminal."

On the other hand, Admiral Fournier, Inspector-General of the French submarine service, has made the following reflections upon the events of the Russo-Japanese War :—

" Les événements de guerre dont l'Extrême-Orient est actuellement le théâtre font ressortir d'une façon saisissante l'importance que prendra désormais le rôle militaire du sousmarin dans les guerres navales. Il est manifeste que si les

Russes avaient pu disposer à Port-Arthur de quelques sous-
marins, ces petits bâtiments auraient profité de tous les
déplacements de la flotte japonaise, nécessités par son rôle
stratégique pour détruire successivement et rapidement ses
principales unités.   Bien plus, les mouvements de transports sur les côtes même de Corée auraient été paralysés par
les incursions de quelques bâtiments de haute mer du type
actuel de nos submersibles."

M. Laubeuf also, who has designed nearly forty submersibles for the French Navy, says that the function of boats
of this class is to protect coasts and ports from bombardment; to render blockade impossible; to prevent hostile
squadrons from anchoring upon the coasts or attempting to
land troops; in narrow seas to carry the attack to the enemy's
coasts and endanger the issue of his squadrons from his ports
and their return thereto; and in European seas and in certain conditions to cut the principal maritime routes.

"Les trois premiers buts peuvent être remplis indistinc-
tement par les sous-marins purs ou par les submersibles. Les
deux derniers ne peuvent l'être que par les submersibles, car
il faut de toute nécessité pour cela des bâtiments marins,
tenant bien la mer, ce que ne sont pas les sous-marins purs.
En outre, pour être efficaces, il faut que les sous-marins soient
nombreux, car leur faible vitesse par rapport à celle des bâtiments de surface nécessite qu'ils puissent former un filet aux
mailles serrées. Il faut donc que leur prix reste peu élevé.
Enfin il faut que leur tonnage ne soit *pas trop élevé* pour qu'ils
soient très *maniables*."

But the French Ministry of Marine is pursuing a policy
of building battleships of the largest class, and the strong
advocates of the submarine and submersible have expressed
loudly their dissatisfaction. Upon this subject M. Paul
Fontin, formerly secretary to Admiral Aube, has spoken very
plainly, and he has many followers. There has been a certain relaxation in the building of the submarine flotillas, and
a purpose of experimenting with vessels of larger classes,

against which M. Laubeuf has protested, on the ground of their greater cost. France is still the leading Power in the possession of submarine boats, but the vigorous policy of the British Admiralty is rapidly diminishing her relative superiority. In relation to this subject a writer in the *Yacht* remarked a few years ago :—

" We have seriously believed that all the great modifications that have been brought about in the construction of submarines is the result of the important changes which the last fifty years of the past century have produced in the art of naval warfare. All these changes have been sought out, experimented upon, studied, and finally realised by France, who has also been the first to apply them. These results have established in a brilliant and incontestable manner the skill of our engineers , but our rivals have not only appropriated the results of our labours ; they have not been slow to place themselves on equal terms with us, and finally to excel us in the application of these discoveries. . . . We have been only the humble artisans working for them to establish their superiority."

PART I

FRENCH SUBMARINES PROPER, *i.e.* THOSE DEPENDENT ENTIRELY ON ELECTRICITY FOR MOTIVE POWER

" *Gymnote* "

The first submarine built for the French Navy was the *Gymnote*, and as the pioneer vessel it may be worth while to describe her here The original plans of this vessel were worked out by the celebrated engineer Dupuy de Lôme, but unfortunately he never lived to execute his project, for he died just when he had finished the details. Some years later M. Gustave Zédé, a marine engineer, revived the ideas of his friend, and after making some modifications in Dupuy de Lôme's original design, brought it before Admiral Aube, the

Minister of Marine, who accepted it at once, and signed a
contract for its construction by the Société des Forges et
Chantiers de la Méditerranée.

The *Gymnote* is built of steel in the shape of a cigar. It is
59 feet long, 5·9 feet beam, and 6 feet in diameter, just deep
enough to allow a man to stand upright in the interior ; its
displacement is 30 tons, a total weight a little less than the
weight of the water displaced by the boat when completely
immersed, and its speed about 6 knots ; leaden plates placed
on each side of the boat in two hollows regulate its draught
of water. The top' of the vessel affords a narrow platform,
and on this are a manhole and a little cupola, with windows.
The motive power was originally an electro-motor of 55 h.p.,
driven from 564 accumulators. It was designed by Captain
Krebs, and built in the workshops of the Société des Forges
et Chantiers at Havre. It was of extraordinary lightness,
weighing only 4410 lb., and drove the screw at the rate of
2000 revolutions a minute, giving a speed of 6 knots an hour,
its range of action at this speed being 35 knots ; reduced to
4 knots, its range of action was 100 miles. This motor was
afterwards replaced by a much simpler machine.

Immersion is obtained by the introduction of water into
three reservoirs, placed one forward, one aft, and one in the
centre. The water is expelled either by means of compressed
air or by a rotary Behrens pump worked by an electro-motor.
Two horizontal rudders steer the boat in the vertical plane,
and an ordinary rudder steers it on the horizontal. Originally
one horizontal rudder only was carried at the stern, but this
did not answer well, and was given up. The behaviour in
the sea of the boat when subjected to the influence of this
rudder was somewhat unsatisfactory. For rather prolonged
" dives," such as would be necessary, for example, in forcing
a blockade, the instability of the boat became very great, and
the man at the helm was unduly fatigued without succeeding
in retaining the mastery of his craft. On account of this instability no greater speed in submersions than 6 knots was

attained. For this speed the inclination of the axis of the boat was from 3 to 5 degrees forward. The difference in the draught of water between the bow and the stern was 0·88 metre (about 34 inches) for an inclination of 3 degrees; for 5 degrees it reached 1·50 metres (nearly 5 feet). Another system of " dip " rudder, proposed in 1891, executed in 1893, and tested towards the end of 1894, consisted in the employ-

THE " GYMNOTE "

ment of two horizontal floatboards, placed on each side of the boat at the height of the midship frame. Their use, combined with that of the stern rudder, gave better results. The boat is inclined less for the " dive," dips more regularly, and lurches or " yaws " less.

When navigating on the surface or when her hull is immersed to the water-line the *Gymnote* carries a cupola, or movable shell with sidelights. This apparatus is composed essentially of a metal shell provided with sidelights all round its circumference. Originally a cylinder of strong tarred canvas fixed on steel springs, which ensured rigidity, bound the shell itself to the upper part of the hull. Horizontal folds in front permitted this canvas to double up regularly upon itself after the style of a Venetian lantern, and in such a way that when the doubling up was complete the height of the shell (or " casque ") came exactly on a level with the upper platform of the boat. During navigation at the surface or on the water-line the whole structure could be raised or lowered by means of a vertical screw moved by a horizontal hand-wheel of which the movable nut constituted the lower part of a vertical frame formed of metallic uprights, which go to rejoin the hull. When the *Gymnote* was at the end of an upward course the canvas was completely stretched and the observatory was at its maximum height ; when, on the contrary, it was at the end of a downward run, the canvas was completely contracted and the " kiosk " had externally disappeared. The dangers of such an arrangement are obvious, and it has been changed.

But the *Gymnote* was really an experiment, and is now quite out of date. She was first tried on 24 September, 1888, in Toulon harbour. The French Press was enthusiastic about her qualities, and the *Temps* said she steered like a fish both as regards direction and depth. " She masters the desired depth with ease and exactness ; at full power she attains to anticipated speed of from nine to ten knots ; the lighting is excellent, there is no difficulty about heating. It was a strange sight to see the vessel skimming along the top of the water, suddenly give a downward plunge with its snout and disappear with a shark-like wriggle of its stern, only to come up again at a distance out and in an unlooked-for direction." At first the vessel carried no armament, but afterwards two torpedo-tubes were fitted.

" *Gustave Zédé* "

The next step was to construct a larger vessel, and M. Romazzotti, Naval Constructor, was ordered to draw up the plans for the boat and to place it on the stocks in the yard of Mourillon. During the building M. Zédé, designer of the *Gymnote*, died, and the Minister of Marine conceived the happy idea of paying a last tribute of respect to the famous engineer by giving the name of *Gustave Zédé* to the first armed submarine of the French fleet. The *Gustave Zédé* was launched at Toulon on 1 June, 1893 ; she is 159 ft. in length, beam 12 ft. 4 in , and has a total displacement of 266 tons. Her shell is of " Roma " bronze, a non-magnetic metal, and one that cannot be attacked by sea water.

The motive power, of 720 h.p., is furnished by two independent electro-motors of 360 h.p., each of the Thury type, constructed by M. Sautter-Harlé, and fed by accumulators of the Laurent-Cély type. The screw revolves at the rate of 250 revolutions a minute. In order to endow the boat with a wide range of action a battery was provided composed of 720 cells, each containing 29 plates and having an output of 400 amperes and a capacity of 1800 amperes an hour.

In the bows is a torpedo-tube, and an arrangement is used whereby the water that enters the tube after the discharge of the torpedo is forced out by compressed air. Three $17\frac{1}{2}$ Whitehead torpedoes are carried. In spite of the fact that a horizontal rudder placed at the stern had not proved serviceable in the *Gymnote*, such a rudder was fitted in the *Gustave Zédé*. With this rudder she usually plunged at an angle of about 5°, but on several occasions she behaved in a very erratic fashion, see-sawing up and down. It was therefore decided to fix a system of six rudders, three on each side. Four water-tanks are carried, one at each end and two in the middle, and the water is expelled by four Thirion pumps worked by a little electro-motor ; these pumps also furnish the air necessary for the crew and for the discharge of the torpedoes.

The successful trials of the *Gustave Zédé* resulted in stimulating the interest of the French in submarine warfare. Writers vied with one another in extolling the qualities of under-water craft, and the popular imagination saw already France supreme at sea. "Jamais nous n'aurions trop de

Photo by   M. Bar
THE "GUSTAVE ZÉDÉ"

sous-marins," wrote M. V. Guilloux in *Le Yacht*. "The twelve years of consecutive efforts and studies continued in order to obtain a solution of the question of submarine navigation have at length been crowned with success," said a writer in the *Moniteur de la Flotte*.

So great was the interest taken in France in submarine boats that the *Matin* opened a "Patriotic Subscription Fund" in 1898, to raise money for building submarine boats of the *Gustave Zédé* type. The journal itself headed the list with a subscription of 5000 francs. In a long article the *Matin* dwelt on the utility of these engines of warfare, and asked the French public to furnish the funds necessary for the construction of at least one more *Gustave Zédé*. It urged the Government to build a fleet of these boats as an effectual protection for the French ports and the harbours of the French Colonies against the most powerful navies of the world. The result of the opening of the fund was that two submarines were presented to the nation—the *Français* and the *Algérien* —and the sum of 300,000 francs, mostly in small sums, was contributed by the French nation for these vessels.

The history of the *Gustave Zédé* shows how much in earnest the French were in the matter of submarines. When it was first launched it was a failure in almost every respect, and it was only after some years, during which many alterations and improvements were carried out, that it became a serviceable craft. At first nothing would induce the *Gustave Zédé* to quit the surface, and when at last she did plunge she did it so effectually that she went down to the bottom in 10 fathoms of water at an angle of 30°. The Committee of Engineers were on board at the time, and it speaks well for their patriotism that they did not as a result of their unpleasant experiences condemn the *Gustave Zédé*, and advise the Government to spend no more money on submarine craft.

" *Morse* "

Before the *Gustave Zédé* was completed M. Romazzotti prepared designs for a smaller submarine, which should be intermediate between the *Gymnote*, displacing 30 tons, and the *Gustave Zédé*, of 266 tons. This vessel, the *Morse*, is 118 ft. long, 9 ft. beam, 8 ft. 3 ins. diameter, is made of " Roma " bronze, and displaces 146 tons. Amidships is a circular conning-tower rising about 18 ins. from the top of the boat. The sole motive power, as in the *Gustave Zédé* and the *Gymnote*, is electricity. The motor is of the Thury type, and develops 350 h.p., rotating the screw at 250 revolutions a minute. The current is derived from a battery of accumulators.

The *Morse* is submerged and steered in the same way as the *Gustave Zédé* in her most improved form. Water is admitted into three separate compartments until a certain amount of buoyancy has been overcome, and the boat is then steered below the surface by her horizontal rudders. A false keel of lead can be detached if necessary from the inside.

The armament consists of a bow torpedo tube and two special carriers on the side, each holding one torpedo. Her crew consists of a commander and eight men, and her range of action is 150 miles. Although the *Morse* was taken in hand many years previously, she was not launched until 5 July, 1899. One of the reasons for this delay was the question whether an oil-engine should be fitted in the vessel for surface navigation. She cost in all 648,000 francs. The *Morse* is steered on the surface and awash from the conning-tower, and underneath by means of a periscope. In fine weather the periscope reflects everything within its field of vision, and can be turned round so as to cover the whole horizon. The French naval authorities believed that they had in the *Morse* a vessel which fulfilled all the conditions of coast defence torpedo-boats, with the further advantage of invisibility, which made it a specially dangerous weapon of attack upon hostile vessels in day-time. The trials of the boat caused the greatest interest, and valuable experience was gained for subsequent construction.

"Français" and "Algérien"

Two sister vessels, submarines proper, the *Français* and the *Algérien*, designed by M. Romazzotti, were laid down at Cherbourg in 1900, being built with the proceeds of the subscription opened by the *Matin*. They are almost identical with the *Morse*, though in some respects they are improvements on their prototype. They are built of steel, and the

sole motive power is electricity. The cost of each was
£32.972. The *Français* was launched on 29 January, and
the *Algérien* on 15 February, 1901.

· *"Farfadet" Class*

The *Farfadet* class, designed by M. Maugas, consists of
four submarines all laid down simultaneously at Cherbourg
on 27 September, 1899, viz. *Farfadet, Gnome, Korrigan,* and
Lutin In size they are between the *Gustave Zédé* and the
Morse, the measurements being—length 135 ft. 8 in., beam
and also draught 9½ ft, displacement 185 tons. Each has
a single screw, and the sole motive-power is electricity, supplied by accumulators. On the surface the speed is 12·25,
and submerged 9 knots. The complement is a lieutenant and
eight men. The hull is of steel and not of "Roma" metal, like
the *Gustave Zédé* and the *Morse.* The cost of each of the
Farfadet class was about £32,000. The *Farfadet* was launched
on 17 May, 1901, and the last of the four was completed in
1903.

The "Perle" Class

The Budget of 1901 made provision for 23 submarines, 20
of a so-called "defensive," and 3 of an "offensive" (or submersible) class. The names of the 20 submarines are :
*Perle, Bonite, Esturgeon, Thon, Souffleur, Anguille, Alose,
Dorade, Truite, Grondin, Naiade, Protée, Lynx, Ludion, Loutre,
Castor, Phoque, Otarie, Méduse, Oursin.* All these 20 boats
(which were laid down in 1901) are constructed of steel, and
have a displacement of 68 tons, length of 77 ft., beam
of 7½ ft., and draught 8 ft. The sole motive power is
electricity supplied by accumulators, and the motor actuates
a single screw. The maximum speed is 8 knots, and
the crew consists of an officer and four men. The price of
each was about £14,600, which was less than any previous
submarine boat. Of these twenty vessels five have been built
at Cherbourg, six at Rochefort, and the rest at Toulon.

They were designed to unite all the best points of the earlier vessels, and are intended primarily for harbour and coast defence. All have been completed.

Two other submarines (*Guêpes*, Nos. 1 and 2) of a smaller class (44 tons) are in hand at Cherbourg. They belong to a series of which the rest are not to be built, and no great importance is attached to them.

PART II

FRENCH "SUBMERSIBLES," *i.e.* THOSE FITTED WITH TWO SOURCES OF MOTIVE POWER, ONE FOR SURFACE, AND ONE FOR SUB-SURFACE PROPULSION.

The "Narval" Class

In February, 1896, M. Lockroy, Minister of Marine, acting in conjunction with M. Bertin, Director of Material, invited designs for a submersible torpedo-boat from Frenchmen and foreigners. The commission appointed to examine the various projects decided in favour of the one sent in by M. Laubeuf. This decision was approved by the Minister, who ordered the construction of the vessel to be taken in hand, and awarded a gold medal to its inventor. The *Narval* was commenced at Cherbourg in 1897, and launched on 26 October, 1899, but it was not until certain modifications had been made that it was considered to be (in 1900) in a satisfactory condition to run its trials. The *Narval* can navigate in three different ways. (1) As an ordinary torpedo-boat, with water ballast tanks empty. (2) Awash, with the dome and chimney alone above the waves, carrying a certain amount of ballast. (3) Entirely submerged, with tanks full of water. She is a " sous-marin autonome à grand rayon d'action."

In designing the *Narval* M. Laubeuf aimed at producing a disappearing vessel, which should correspond with the sea-going torpedo-boat in the same way as the *Morse* is partly designed to replace the torpedo-boat for coast defence. The

Narval possesses various ranges of action. (1) On the surface and propelled by its steam-engine—252 miles at a speed of 12 knots for 21 hours; 624 miles at a speed of 8 knots for 78 hours. (2) Submerged and propelled by electricity—25 miles at a speed of 8 knots; 72 miles at a speed of 5 knots.

The hull of the boat is peculiar, being double. The interior hull is of thick steel sheets: it has a circular section, and ends in a point at its two extremities. The outer hull

Photo by]   *[M. Bar*

THE "NARVAL"

which envelopes it is of thin sheets; its form is that of the *Gustave Zédé*. The external hull is pierced with holes above and below, and at the two ends, and the sea water circulates freely between the two hulls, which should allow the vessel to receive a hail of small projectiles without suffering from them, the rents in its outer hull making no change in its situation.

The boat is brought to the awash condition by taking in water ballast, and is steered below the surface by four hori-

T

zontal float-board rudders, arranged on each side of the ship, two towards the bows and two towards the stern. These "dip-rudders" are manipulated by means of a hand-wheel placed at the centre of the ship. The *Narval* is not cylindrical in shape like the *Morse*, and her upper works are flat and form a deck. The principal dimensions are as follows : Length, 111 ft. 6 in. ; extreme beam, 12 ft. 4 in. ; displacement, 106 tons when light, 200 tons completely submerged.

The motive power on the surface is supplied by a triple-

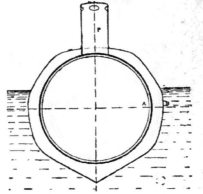

THE "NARVAL" AS A SURFACE TORPEDO-BOAT

expansion steam-engine of 250 h.p. constructed by Messrs. Brulé and Co. It has a water-tube boiler of the Seigle type, having five injectors for stoking with heavy petroleum. In the original project the boat was to have been propelled on the surface by steam machinery of 300 i.h.p., the stoking being with compressed coal, but it was afterwards decided to supply liquid fuel. Submerged the motive power is an electro-motor, the current being supplied by 158 accumulators of the Fulmen type, which can be recharged by the motor, worked as a dynamo by the petroleum motor.

Before going below the chimney has to be unshipped and all the openings hermetically closed. Sufficient time must be

allowed for the motor to cool and for the air to be cleared
of the hot gases. The steam-engine has to be replaced by
the electric motor, and water ballast has to be pumped in.
At first these operations took at least a quarter of an hour,
but the newer vessels are able to disappear beneath the waves
in some five moments only.

The armament of the *Narval* consists of four 17½-inch
Whitehead torpedoes, and there are two Drzewiecki torpedo

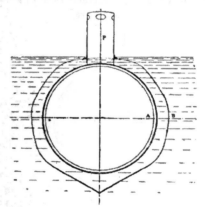

THE " NARVAL " IN THE " AWASH " CONDITION

tubes on each side and towards the upper part of the boat,
which launch the torpedoes in the direction of the beam.

"As long ago as 1893," says a French writer, "M. Drzewiecki invented a method of firing a torpedo which is quite
different from the torpedo-tubes commonly used, and which
is, therefore, peculiarly suited for submarine vessels. By it
the torpedo could be fired at any angle from 30 to 120 degrees
from the bow, and experiments with it were made in
1894 at Cherbourg. The system may be briefly explained as
follows : At the side of the boat a horizontal spar is placed,
which works on a hinge at an angle to the bow. The torpedo
is fastened to this spar by two pairs of clamps, and when not

in use lies along the side of the boat in a recess cut out inside. A swing-out rod, fastened at one end to the spar and at the other to the boat, enables the desired angle for firing to be obtained. A lever worked from inside the vessel pushes the spar and the torpedo away from the side of the boat, and the pressure of the water stiffens the swing-out rod, and by so doing frees the torpedo from the clamps, and opens the air-lever which sets the torpedo in motion. It is therefore necessary that the vessel should be under way when the torpedo is fired.

" The principle of the invention is very simple, and at the same time very ingenious ; and the experiments which were made at Cherbourg proved that torpedoes could be fired by this system with perfect precision. After 1894 Mr. Drze-wiecki made alterations in his invention. For example, he did away with the spar and the clamps, and by so doing greatly lightened his apparatus. The tail of the torpedo was seized by two claws, which gripped it firmly and held it in position. The contrivance was placed on the deck of the submarine boat, which was not submerged except on going into action. The torpedo rested on cushions fixed to the deck, with its axis parallel to that of the boat, but as soon as it was moved by a lever to the position for firing the water pressing against it freed the torpedo by opening the air-valve. The only inconvenience of the system was that it was not easy to fire at the exact angle required, but it had the great advantage of doing away with all the machinery of valves and safety appliances which were necessary when submerged tubes were employed. Further experiments will doubtless make the system still more efficacious."

Commenting on the *Narval* class, a writer in the *Temps* said : " Their range of action will be large, they will be self-controlling, and they will realise Admiral Aube's theory of the empire of the sea, invisibility, divisibility, and number. The estimate for each is 600,000 francs, which is not one-fortieth of the cost of a battleship. Are not the Mediterranean experiments calculated to lead to changes in our naval construction, and would not the present situation justify the devotion of all the efforts of the dockyards to submarine torpedo boats without stopping the programme now in progress ? "

The *Narval* class, besides the eponymous vessel, comprises four other submersibles—the *Sirène* (launched 4 May, 1901), the *Triton* (launched 13 July, 1901), the *Espadon* (launched 31 August, 1901), and the *Silure* (launched 29 October, 1901). These four resemble the *Narval* in most particulars, though in some respects they are improvements on their prototype.

The outer hull of each is made of steel, but the inner hull is of nickel steel. The choice of the metal is a matter of importance, for the difficulty is to build a hull which possesses sufficient strength to resist the pressure of the water, and yet at the same time is not too expensive. Between the two hulls in the interior of the vessel are seven compartments for water ballast. There are also four water-tanks, which are used to regulate the trim of the vessel by introducing water at the last moment.

The inconvenient points of the *Sirène* and her sister vessels are the same as those of the *Narval*. For steaming on the surface the *Sirène* uses a triple-expansion engine and a Normand boiler heated by petroleum. For submarine navigation she uses two dynamos connected with the main shaft. These dynamos recharge the accumulators, which are on the Laurent-Cély system, in less than 7 hours. The vessel can steam on the surface 21 hours at 12 knots with the petroleum engine, and 625 miles at 8 knots. Under water, making use of the accumulators, she can do 25 miles at 8 knots, or 70 miles at 5 knots. Her armament consists of four torpedoes 17¾ inches in diameter, which are fired by the Drzewiecki system. As the torpedoes are placed on the deck, the vessel must be under the water in order that they may be fired. The crew consists of twelve men, including the lieutenant-commander and his sub-lieutenant.

Much larger classes of submersibles proper and so-called

submarine boats followed. Six of the latter, displacing 400 tons, are driven on the surface by explosive motors, and below by electric motors supplied by accumulators, which can be charged afresh when the boats are navigating on the surface. These are the *Emeraude*, *Opale*, *Rubis*, *Saphir*, *Topaze*, and *Turquoise*, built at Cherbourg and Toulon, and completed in 1907. X, Y, and Z are smaller (168–213 tons). The *Omega*, a true submersible, displaces 300 tons ; and two submersibles of a special class, *Circé* and *Calypso* (350 tons), are yet in hand. The nineteen new boats, Q 51 to Q 69, were begun in 1905, and are all to be completed by 1910, and thirty other boats, Q 70 to Q 99, by 1911.

The Ministry of Marine, considering it desirable, however, to experiment with still larger boats, and in order to remove, if possible, the doubts that attended submarine warfare and navigation, issued orders that three large submersibles should be put in hand experimentally with the hope of arriving at a definite type. A competition of designs was invited among members of the Génie Maritime, and as a result two boats are to be built at Cherbourg, respectively from the designs of M. Hutter and M. Radiguer ; while another will be put in hand at Rochefort from the plans of M. Bordelle ; and possibly a fourth may be built at Toulon from the plans of M. Maurice. Of the first three, one will have a displacement of 577 tons (810 tons submerged), and will be 196 ft. 9 in. long ; the second 530 tons (628 tons submerged), length 210 feet ; and the third 555 tons (735 tons submerged), length 183 ft. 9 in. The surface speed is to be 15 knots, instead of 12 as heretofore, and the submerged speed 10 knots instead of 6 or 7 knots, while the range will be 2500 miles. Propulsion will be on the surface by means of Diesel or steam motors, and submerged by electric motors. The construction is to be hastened as much as possible, and no other boats of these classes will be laid down until the trials have taken place. There appears, however, to be a general opinion in the French Navy in favour of the *Sirène* type of M. Laubeuf.

APPENDIX IV

IT was in 1899 that Lord Goschen spoke of the submarine as the weapon of Powers that were comparatively poor and weak. No doubt in these words there was a certain truth, although it is now recognised that the submarine, or rather the submersible, may be the arm also of the stronger Powers. France has afloat or under construction 39 submarines and 45 submersibles, Great Britain 52 vessels which are really submersibles, Russia 27 submarines or submersibles, the United States 12, Italy 8, and Japan 13. Up to the present time the secondary Powers, though some of them have experimented with submarine boats, have been mostly content to observe the attitude of the greater Powers, and to await the results attained. Holland, Sweden, Norway, Denmark, Spain, Portugal, Greece, Turkey, Roumania, and Bulgaria cannot think of building the huge battleships which have been laid down by the greater Powers, and there are many who think that they would be well advised to devote more attention to the possibilities of submarine warfare. Sweden has already one submarine boat, and the Netherlands also; while other Powers, like Norway and Brazil, seem to purpose a policy of submarine shipbuilding. It appears not unlikely that within a dozen years all the secondary Powers will have entered upon the building of flotillas of submarines or submersibles.

Spain   In a survey of the work of the Powers which have not yet done much in the way of submarine construction, the first place rightly belongs to Spain, because

twenty years ago she built a submarine boat from the designs
of Lieutenant Isaac Peral, of the Spanish Navy, which was
somewhat celebrated in its time.   In reward for his labours
the Spanish Government conferred upon the designer a title
of honour and a large pecuniary acknowledgment of his ser-
vices.   The *Peral*, so-called after the designer, was constructed at the arsenal of Carraca, and launched on 23 October,
1887.   It measured 72 feet from stem to stern, and was 9 feet
in beam.   The motive power was furnished by two electric
motors of 30 h.p., each driving two screws; 600 accumulators
supplied the power for all purposes.   During its trials in 1889

THE "PERAL," SPAIN'S ONLY SUBMARINE

the *Peral* was ordered to proceed to sea to blow up an old
hull placed at a distance of some two or three miles from
shore in Cadiz Bay, running a long distance under water.
The boat was subsequently reported to have successfully accomplished this feat, and the Spanish Government would, it
was said, order several vessels of this type for the defence of
the coasts of the Peninsula.   A public subscription was
started, and for a time great enthusiasm prevailed; but
nothing further appears to have been done in the matter.

Russia   Rumours formerly gained ground that the
Russian Government intended to build a large
submarine flotilla, and it was even said that 300 boats of the

Goubet type were to be built. These statements were entirely without foundation, and it was only within recent years that Russia began to build submarine boats. A small submarine from the plans of Lieutenant Kolbassieff and Engineer Kuteinikoff was built at Kronstadt, being a cigar-shaped vessel, with side blades for sinking and raising the craft. She received the name of *Matros Piotr Koschka*. There is also a submarine boat called the *Delfin*, 77 ft. long and displacing 175 tons, which at her trials made a successful run of 36 hours, including 26 hours submerged. This was the type boat for twelve others. Money for many of these has been provided by national subscription, and one bears the name of *Field-Marshal Count Sheretmetieff*, who contributed a large sum. The particulars are unknown. The Russian Government has also purchased the Lake submarine boat *Protector*, which has received the name of *Ossetr*. She is a twin-screw boat built by the Lake Company from the designs of Mr. Simon Lake, and is cigar-shaped with a superstructure. The length is 65 feet, with 11 feet beam, and the displacement on the surface 115 tons, and submerged ·170 tons. For surface propulsion there is gasoline apparatus, and the under-water navigation is by means of storage batteries. Submersion is by water ballast, by horizontal rudders, and by hauling down to an anchor weight. The Russians have also about 8 other submarines, and the whole flotilla numbers some 29.

Italy   The first Italian submarine was the experimental boat *Delfino*, which was built of steel, and is said to have cost £12,000. The submerged displacement was about 110 tons, the length 78 feet, and the diameter 9 feet. Propulsion was entirely by means of storage batteries, and it is stated that the vessel was immersed and brought to the surface by two small screws, practically on the Nordenfelt system. There were two tubes in the bow. Five other boats have been built, the *Glauco* being the pioneer, with a surface speed of 14 knots. The others are the *Squalo*,

Narvalo, Tricheco, and *Otaria.* Some of these made their first appearance in the naval manœuvres of 1906. Several other submarine craft are to be built.

Germany The German Navy Department hesitated long before beginning the building of submarines, although it is believed that experiments took place, and that much was gained from the experience of other nations. A

THE FIRST GERMAN SUBMARINE BOAT

boat known as U was launched at the Germania Yard, Kiel, on 30 August, 1905, and one or two other boats have since been brought forward. The displacement is 185 tons, or 240 tons submerged, the length 128 feet, and the beam 8 ft. 10 in., while the surface and submerged speeds were stated to be 12 and 9 knots. U 1 was launched on 3 August, 1906, and commissioned in December, and a yearly grant of

$5\frac{1}{2}$ million marks provides for building other experimental boats.

Norway The Norwegian Government has made many inquiries into the subject of submarine navigation, and Norwegian officers have been present at the trials of many boats. It is believed that several boats will be built or purchased, and the Minister of Marine has received a grant for the purpose.

Sweden Mr. Enroth, a Swedish engineer, prepared plans for a boat which he offered to the Government. The following were the particulars : Length, 82 ft. ; beam, 13 ft. ; diameter, $11\frac{1}{2}$ ft. ; displacement (light), 142 tons ; (submerged) 146 tons ; engines 100 h.p . supplied by two boilers heated by oil ; speed, 12 knots surface and 6 submerged. The boilers did no work when the boat was submerged, the engines being then partly driven by the steam already generated and partly by compressed air stored fore and aft. A submarine named the *Hajen* underwent successful trials in 1905.

Brazil A Brazilian officer named Mello Marques prepared designs for a new type of submarine boat, which was tried as a model in the presence of the authorities. It is understood that a boat of the class has since been built.

The following are notes upon some former designs of submarine boats ; but to describe even briefly the nature of every submarine boat that has ever been constructed would necessitate a volume three or four times the size of the present work. A few, however, seem to demand some notice here.

Payerne The first inventor to propose a mode of propulsion other than by hand-operated mechanism was Dr. Payerne, who in the fifties proposed a boat which was propelled by a screw driven by a steam-engine, furnished with two boilers ; an ordinary boiler furnished steam for surface navigation, whilst the other, which he termed a "chaudière pyrotechnique," for use beneath the waves, was so arranged as to burn in hermetically closed furnaces a combustible containing in itself the oxygen necessary for its combustion. The products of combustion escaped by raising a plug so devised as to prevent water entering the fire-box. The combustibles to which Dr. Payerne gave preference were :—

Coke	165
Nitrate of Soda	835
Coke	145
Nitrate of Potash	855

The boat was known by the name of *L'Hydrostat ;* but, as its inventors were not able to work out their ideas satisfactorily, it was turned into an ordinary diving-bell, and used for submarine excavations at Cherbourg and Brest.

Riou In 1861 Olivier Riou built two models, one driven by steam (generated by the heat of ether in combustion), and the other by electricity derived from batteries. This is the first occasion on which we find electricity requisitioned for the propulsion of an under-water vessel.

Alstitt The submarine of Mr. Alstitt, constructed in 1863 at Mobile, in the U.S.A., possessed great interest in that it was the first to be fitted with two modes of propulsion—the one for navigation on the surface, the other beneath.

Bourgois and Brun The *Plongeur*, invented by Captain Bourgois and M. Brun, and built at Rochefort in 1863, was the most ambitious attempt that had up till then been made to solve the problem of submarine navigation. It was driven by an 80 h.p. compressed-air engine, and underwent numerous trials ; these did not satisfy the officials, and it was eventually converted into a water-tank. The armament of the *Plongeur* was a spar-torpedo.

Lacomme In 1869 Dr. J. A. Lacomme submitted to Napoleon III a project for a submarine railway across the Channel. Rails were to be laid on the floor of the ocean, and in the event of an accident the submarine car, by reason of its reserve of floatability, could detach itself from the track and rise to the surface. M. Goubet afterwards proposed a similar " submarine ferry."

Halstead The *Intelligent Whale* was built at Newark in 1872 from the designs of Mr. Halstead. Its novel features were two doors in the bottom through which divers could leave the boat when submerged. On one occasion the boat went down in 16 ft. of water, and General Sweeney, clad in a diver's suit, passed out through the bottom man-hole, placed a torpedo under a scow anchored there for the purpose, and after entering the boat and moving away to a safe distance exploded the torpedo by a lanyard and friction primer, and blew the scow to pieces.

Constantin During the siege of Paris, André Constantin, a lieutenant in the French Navy, built a vessel which was submerged on an entirely novel principle. Instead of admitting water to sink his boat, he immersed it by the drawing in of pistons working in cylinders.

Drzewiecki The Russian inventor, Drzewiecki, built a vessel at Odessa in 1877 which had two methods of submersion. Whilst in motion a system of sliding weights inclined the boat either upwards or downwards. To regain the horizontal position the weights were brought to the centre. When at rest submersion was obtained by the introduction of water into a central reservoir.

Campbell and Ash The *Nautilus* of these inventors was submerged on the same principle as the boat of André Constantin, viz. by the drawing in of cylinders. The submersion was effected by means of four cylinders on each side of the vessel, which were drawn in flush and pushed out beyond the side, thus altering the displacement. The *Nautilus* underwent some trials in Tilbury Docks in 1888, and the following account is from the pen of Mr. Bennett Burleigh : " A few years ago a gentleman invited a number of officials and specialists down to one of the London docks to see a new submarine boat, which, like so many gone before, was to achieve marvels. There were naval men and military men, and journalists there by the score. Among others were the present Chief Constructor of the Navy, Sir W. H. White, and Lord Charles Beresford. The writer was on board, but felt a strong natural disinclination to go below or permit any of his friends to adventure. It possibly was an excess of natural timidity. That craft was warranted ' extra special safe.' She had water tanks, a false keel that could be slipped off, and cylinders or drums which, pushed out or drawn in from her sides, added or took away from her displacement and buoyancy. Charming in theory, but hydrostatics present strange problems, so note the result. The boat, with Sir W. H. White on board, having made all tight, let water into her tanks, and sank into the profound oleaginous mud of the dock. She remained invisible beneath for a protracted period, greater, in truth, than those upon the dock knew was safe, for she had no air or oxygen storage. We could do nothing but wait and look at our watches. Finally, to everybody's intense relief, she reappeared. It happened that the boat stuck in the mud, and neither sending out the drums nor unloading the tanks made her rise. Sir William White suggested, when the light was turning blue, as were some faces, moving the crew to the higher end of the craft. It had the desired effect, the boat was lifted from the grip of the mud. Once on top, the engineer undid the manhole and shouted with elation to his friends ashore that they were going down again. Several of the visitors had had more than enough, and the gentleman was pulled down by the legs to make way for those who wished to escape upon deck and reach *terra firma*. That ' famous ' submarine craft also followed the course of its predecessors, and shortly after passed into the limbo of forgotten failures."

It appears that the cylinders declined to out-thrust because the power for working them, though amply sufficient for working in water, was not great enough to drive them into mud, and the inventors had not taken into consideration the adhesiveness of mud.

Wadding-ton   Mr. J. H. Waddington claimed that his vessel, the *Porpoise* (1886), was the first practical submarine to be propelled by electricity.   The electric motor was worked by 45 accumulators of 660 ampere-hours capacity ; the maximum current taken by the motor was 66 amperes, the e.m.f. being 90 volts, giving an electrical h.p. of 7.96   The speed was to be 8 miles an hour.

Goubet   M. Goubet constructed several submarine boats. *Goubet I* was built at Paris in 1888, and, like all the vessels designed by this inventor, its weight when submerged equalled the weight of the water it displaced.   To prevent it diving to the bottom or rising to the surface water was automatically pumped from the forward to the after tank, or vice versa.   The sole motive power of all the Goubet boats was electricity.   *Goubet I* was only 16 ft. long, and displaced one ton.   The crew consisted of two men, who sat back to back on a case containing all the machinery and the air reservoirs.   The armament was a torpedo carried on the outside of the hull and released from the interior.   By its reserve of buoyancy it rose until it caught on to the enemy's enemy's bottom by spikes ; it was then exploded electrically. *Goubet II* was 26 feet long, but its speed was only some 5½ knots.   In February, 1901, she underwent some trials in France, but the results were poor.   Her extreme range was 25 miles, her greatest speed less than 4 knots, and she never succeeded in launching a torpedo.   M. Goubet was an ingenious and persevering inventor and constructor, but none of his boats promised more than very restricted utility.

APPENDIX V

THE Right Rev. John Wilkins, from whose book, *Mathematical Magick,* some extracts have been given, was far-seeing enough to predict that a submarine vessel would prove of great value in the discovery of submarine treasures, "not only," as he expressed it, "in regard of what hath been drowned by wreck, but the several precious things that grow there, as pearl, coral, mines, with innumerable other things of great value, which may be much more easily found out and fetched up by the help of this, than by any other usual way of the Urinators." Could newspapers and magazines but find their way to the shades, Dr. Wilkins would be enchanted to find that his dream has been realised, and that a vessel has actually been constructed for the purpose of harvesting some of the treasures of the deep.

The *Argonaut,* designed by Mr. Simon Lake, of Baltimore, is a vessel designed to roll along the floor of the ocean as a carriage rolls along the highway. In this it differs from any other under-water craft either projected or constructed, for all previous inventors have attempted to navigate their boats between the surface and the bottom. In the invention of this type of submarine boat Mr. Lake elaborated an idea which the United States Patent Office described to be absolutely original, and the *Argonaut* has undoubtedly done things that no other vessel has before accomplished.

Mr. Lake built his first experimental submarine boat, the *Argonaut Junior,* in 1894. After several successful descents

288

she was abandoned at Atlantic Highlands, half-buried in the sand. Her dimensions were : length, 14 ft. ; beam, 4½ ft. ; depth, 5 ft. *Argonaut No.* 2 was a much bigger boat, and proved that Mr. Lake's theories were substantially correct. She is 36 ft. long. Her diameter amidships is 9 ft. ; her displacement when entirely submerged is about 59 tons ; her draught when at the surface is 10 ft., and when submerged 15 ft. She is built of steel plates ⅜ in. in thickness, double-riveted over strong steel frames. She is provided with a 30 h.p. "White and Middleton" gasoline engine, which propels her both on the surface and while submerged, and runs all the auxiliary machinery. She has two Mannesmann steel reservoirs for the storage of compressed air, which have been tested to a pressure of 4000 lb. per square inch. She is provided with air compressors, water-ballast pumps, and hoisting machinery for raising or lowering her two down-haul weights. She is lighted by incandescent electric lamps throughout, and carries a 4000 candle-power searchlight in her bows, all run by a dynamo. Machinery for rotating her side driving-wheels and various gauges for determining depth, rate of speed, and air pressure are also provided, together with a complete outfit for divers, who are equipped with telephones and electric lamps.

The following account of his boat was written by Mr. Simon Lake himself, and we have his permission to reprint it here :—

"The hull of the vessel is mounted on three wheels. Of these E is the rudder, for surface steering, and is also the guiding wheel when the vessel is running on the sea bottom ; and C is one of the supporting and driving wheels, of which there are two, one on each side. BB are two anchor weights, each weighing 1000 pounds, attached to cables, and capable of being hauled up or lowered by a drum and mechanism within the boat : 0000 are water-ballast compartments contained within the boat ; H is the diver's compartment, situated forward, with an exit door opening outward in the

U

bottom; while G is an airlock. When it is desired to submerge the vessel, the anchor weights BB are first lowered to the bottom; water is then allowed to enter the water-ballast compartments until her buoyancy is less than the weight of the two anchors, say 1500 lb.; the cables connecting with the weights are then wound in, and the vessel is thus hauled to the bottom, until she comes to rest on her three wheels.

THE "ARGONAUT" IN DRY DOCK

The weights are then hauled into their pockets in the keel, and it is evident that she is resting on the wheels with a weight equal to the difference between her buoyancy with the weights at the bottom, and the weights in their pockets, or 500 lb. Now this weight may be increased or diminished as we please, either by admitting more water into the ballast tanks or by pumping some out. Thus it will be seen that we have perfect control of the vessel in submerging her, as we may haul her down as fast or as slow as we please, and by

having her rest in the bottom with sufficient weight to prevent the currents from moving her out of the course, we may
start up our propeller or driving-wheels and drive her at will
over the bottom, the same as a tricycle is propelled on the
surface of the earth in the upper air.   In muddy bottoms,
we rest with a weight not much over 100 lb. ; while on hard
bottoms, or where there are strong currents, we sometimes
rest on the wheels with a weight of from 1000 to 1500 lb.
Thus the effect of currents and wave motion, and the maintenance of trim and equilibrium are not factors in the successful navigation of the vessel ; in fact, navigation becomes surer
than on the surface, as one is travelling in a medium which
does not constantly change like the surface water from the
effects of winds, waves, and currents.   When the divers desire to leave the vessel they go into the diver's compartment,
located in the forward portion of the ship, and close the door
communicating with the living quarters.   This door closes
on rubber packing, and is air-tight.   Air is then admitted
into the compartment from compressed-air reservoirs, until
the pressure of air equals that of the surrounding water.
The bottom door may then be opened, and no water will
come into the boat, as the pressure of air contained within
the compartment offers an invisible barrier to its entrance,
and the divers may pass in and out as frequently as they
please.   The *Argonaut* is fitted with a White and Middleton
gasoline engine of 30 h.p., which operates the screw, the
driving wheels, the dynamo, the air compressors, anchor
hoists, and derrick-operating machinery.   She is provided
with two Mannesmann steel tubes, in which sufficient air may
be stored, with what is contained in the boat, to last the crew
for twenty-four hours without obtaining a fresh supply from
the surface.   In the *Argonaut*, however, and probably in all
such craft used for commercial pursuits, as a usual thing,
there will be a connection with the surface, through which a
constant supply of air may be drawn, either by the masts,
as shown in the views, one of which supplies air to the in-

terior of the vessel, the other being utilised as an exhaust from the engine, or through suction hose extending to a buoy on the surface. While the engine is running there is about fifty cubic feet of air flowing into the boat per minute; and when the engine is closed down there may be a flow of air maintained by an auxiliary blower, so that it is possible to remain below for days, or even weeks, at a time.

" The course is directed by an ordinary compass when on the bottom, and it is found that the needle responds as quickly and is as accurate as when on the surface. Notwithstanding the fact that the *Argonaut* is quite a small vessel, a crew of five men have lived aboard her during an experimental cruise extending over two months, during which she travelled over 1000 miles under her own power, partly on the surface and partly on the bottom. The trip was made to demonstrate the practicability of vessels of her type travelling on various kinds of bottoms; also to demonstrate her seaworthiness and capabilities in searching the bottom, in working on sunken wrecks, finding and taking up submerged cables, &c.

" We have been in some pretty rough weather, and found that she was perfectly seaworthy. Of course, being so small and of such weight, the seas at times would wash clear over her decks. This, however, caused no inconvenience to those below, as her stability was such that she would roll or pitch very little, even though the seas were breaking over her in great volume. We have been cruising on the bottom in rivers, in Chesapeake Bay and beneath the broad Atlantic. In the rivers we invariably found a muddy bed; in the bay we found bottoms of various kinds, in some places so soft that our divers would sink up to their knees, while in other places the ground would be hard, and at one place we ran across a bottom which was composed of a loose gravel, resembling shelled corn. Out in the ocean, however, was found the ideal submarine course, consisting of a fine gray sand, almost as hard as a macadamised road, and very level and uniform.

" During this trip we investigated several sunken wrecks, of which there are a great many in Chesapeake Bay and on the coast adjacent thereto. The vessels we boarded were coal-laden craft, and of themselves not of much value ; but the coal would pay handsomely for its recovery, which could be readily accomplished with the proper equipment. We found

THE "ARGONAUT" AWASH

one old wreck, said to have gone down some forty years ago near the mouth of the Patuxent River. There was nothing in sight except a few timbers and deck beams, and these were nearly consumed by the teredo—a boring worm which completely honeycombs any timber it may attack. We pulled up some of the planks of this vessel, which had a numerous growth of oysters, mussels, and several kinds of submarine vegetation clinging to them. The portion of the

timbers not eaten by the teredo was found to be almost as
hard as iron, and thoroughly imprégnated with the dark blue
mud in which the hull lies buried. After the timbers were
hauled to the surface, in sawing them in two, we noticed
a very strong odour of yellow pine, and so learned that they
must be of that wood, though they were as black as ebony.
Toad-fish had evidently found this old wreck a congenial
habitation, and when the diver's hand comes in contact with
the slimy back of one of these horrible-looking, strong-jawed,
big-mouthed fish, he pulls it back pretty quickly. The piece
we pulled up had within it three of these fish, which had taken
up their abode in portions of the timber that had been eaten
away, and one was a prisoner in a recess which, evidently,
he had entered when small, and had grown too large to get
out. In a wreck near Cape Henry, fish were very numerous,
principally bass and croakers, though two or three small
sharks were seen in the vicinity.

" It might prove interesting to copy one day's experiences
from our log-book. This day we submerged for the purpose
of discovering how much weight was necessary to prevent
the current from moving the *Argonaut* in a strong tideway
(Hampton Roads), and also to discover if there was any
difference in starting our machinery again under water after
it had been shut down for several hours. I copy verbatim
from the log-book under date of 28 July, 1898 :—

" ' We spent some hours with Hampton Roads as head-
quarters, and made several descents in the waters adjacent
thereto ; we were desirous of making a search for the cables
which connected with the mines guarding the entrance to the
harbour, but could not obtain permission from the authorities,
who were afraid we might accidentally sever them, which
would, of course, make their entire system of defence useless.
It was, therefore, necessary for us, in order to demonstrate the
practicability of vessels of this type for this purpose, to lay
a cable ourselves, which we did, across the channel leading
into the Patuxent River. We then submerged, and taking

our bearings by the compass, ran over the bottom, with the
door in our diving compartment open, until we came across
the cable, which we hauled up into the compartment with a
hook only about 4½ feet long, and we could not avoid the impression that it would be a very easy thing to destroy the
efficiency of the present mine system   And how many lives
might have been saved, and millions of dollars besides, had
our navy been provided with a craft of this type to lead the
way into Santiago, Havana, or San Juan, off which ports
squadrons were compelled to lie for weeks and months owing
to fear of the mines ! '

"I have frequently been asked my sensations on going
beneath the water—whether I had any fear of not being able
to come up again, and whether it did not require a lot of
courage. I usually replied that I have always been too busy
and interested for fears or sensations, and that it does not
require any courage on my part, as I am so thoroughly satisfied of the correctness of the principles upon which the
Argonaut is constructed and the strength of the structure as
to have no doubts or fears of any kind ; but I do think it
requires courage on the part of those who do not understand
all the principles involved, and who simply trust their lives
in my hands. Quite a number of people have made descents
in the vessel, but in only one or two instances have I seen
them show any signs of fear.

"In one instance, during our trials in the Patapsco, several
gentlemen were very importunate in requesting the privilege
of making a descent the next time we were to submerge.
They were accordingly notified when the boat was to go
down. At the appointed time, however, some of them did
not appear, and of those who did not one at the last would
venture. I have no doubt had we made the descent at the
time they made the request all would have gone, but thinking
about it for a couple of days made them change their minds.

"On another trip we had a college professor on board who
could not understand exactly how our men could get out of

the boat. I told him to come into the diver's compartment and I would explain it to him. Accordingly he reluctantly, as I thought, entered the compartment, which in the *Argonaut* is a little room only four feet long and a little wider. After closing the door I noticed that the colour was leaving his face and a few beads of perspiration were standing out upon his forehead, and had he been any one else than a professor or, possibly, a newspaper man, I would not have gone any further with the experiment. The door, however, was closed and

THE "ARGONAUT" ON THE SEA BOTTOM

securely fastened. I then opened the valve a full turn, and the air began to rush in with a great noise. He grabbed hold of one of the frames and glanced with longing eyes at the door we had just entered. I then turned off the air and said, ' By the way, Professor, are you troubled with heart disease ? ' He said, placing his hand over his heart, ' Why, yes, my heart is a little affected.' Remarking, ' Oh, well, this little depth will not hurt you,' I turned on the air again after saying to him, ' If you feel any pain in your ears swallow as if you were drinking water.' He immediately commenced swallowing, and during that half-minute or so we were getting the

pressure on I believe he swallowed enough to have drunk
a bucketful of water. After getting the desired pressure I
stooped down and commenced to unscrew the bolts, holding
the door which leads out into the water. Our professor said,
'What are you doing now?' I answered, 'I am going to
open this door so that you can see the bottom.' Throwing
out his hands he said, 'No, no. Don't do that. I would not
put you to that trouble for the world.' However, about that
time the door dropped down, and as he saw the water did
not come in the colour returned to his face, and he exclaimed,
'Well, if I had not seen it I would never have believed it!'"

Mr. Lake declares that as a submarine torpedo-boat his
vessel will be practically invincible. She could, he claims,
approach a stationary enemy on the bottom and rise up under
the water and secure a time-fuse torpedo to her bottom, and
she could be fitted with tubes to fire automobile torpedoes.
She could also find cables to repair or cut them, and could be
used for countermining purposes. The *Argonaut* is, however,
intended not so much for warfare as for recovering treasures
from the deep, and for the coral, sponge, pearl, and similar
industries. It has been calculated that of the cargoes, treasures, and vessels lost in the merchant service the aggregate
amounts to over one hundred millions of dollars per year,
and the loss has, of course, been going on for many years.
"There is every reason to believe," says a writer, "that
the sea is even richer than the earth, owing to the millions
of shipwrecks which have swallowed up so many a royal
fortune; the wealth lying at the bottom of the ocean tran-
scends the fabulous riches of the Klondyke."
The recovery of sunken treasure has always exercised a
great fascination over certain minds, and much money has
been spent in devising means whereby it might be brought
again to the surface. Hitherto the results have not been
such as might have been desired, but the *Argonaut* seems to
promise success in the future.

Mr. Lake believes that the majority of the great losses on the ocean occur in waters in which it will be practical to operate with submarine boats of the *Argonaut* type. The bottom around the coast lines of the United States is principally composed of a hard white or grey sand, and is very uniform. The depth increases from the shore at the average rate of about 6 feet per mile, and the bottom forms " an ideal roadway." The *Argonaut* can descend to 100 feet below the surface. Needless to say, there are ocean depths where the pressure would be so great that man could never live, but Mr. Lake appears to think that exploring the ocean bed, within certain limits, will become in the near future almost as common as travelling on the surface.

Mr. Lake's third under-water vessel, *Argonaut No. 3*, is built of steel, is 66 feet long and 10 feet wide, and displaces 100 tons ; the motive power is gasoline, and the air chambers contain 13,000 cubic feet of air. She has four large wheels for running on the bottom, and also twin screws for the surface.

The following is taken from a New York paper, and relates to an entertainment given on *Argonaut No. 3* : " Captain Lake, the inventor of the submarine boat *Argonaut*, participated yesterday with thirteen other guests in one of the most novel summer entertainments ever devised by the brain of man. The party embarked at Bridgeport on Long Island Sound in the boat, which was then submerged, and travelled along the bottom of the sea for several miles. While running at a depth of 35 feet a dinner prepared and cooked on board was served. After dinner Captain Lake had the door of the diving compartment opened, and two divers went out and exhibited the patent diving suits. Captain Lake then gave an exhibition of his suction pump, which is designed to raise sunken wreckage. The *Argonaut* stopped near a sunken coal schooner, and by means of the pump four tons of coal were sent up through the water to a coal barge above. The coal was transferred at the rate of a ton a minute. A crew of five men navigated the *Argonaut* under the inventor's direction.   Slight headaches were experienced by some of the guests, otherwise no inconvenience was suffered from the submarine voyage."

The following is from the *Proceedings* of the United States Naval Institute, June, 1906, relating to a new Lake submarine: "The submersible torpedo-boat *Lake* has been launched at Newport News and appears to be a very powerful craft, supposed to be capable of crossing the ocean with her own engines.   The armament is three torpedo-tubes. The boat is submerged by sinking on an even keel, and running at any desired constant depth parallel to the surface by means of a system of rudders, a great reserve of buoyancy, and great longitudinal stability.   There is a large and high conning-tower, and a wide and high superstructure in which the gasoline is to be stored.   There is a diving compartment forward through which a diver can leave the vessel and pick up cables, mines, or counter-mines, or to establish telephone communication with fortifications on shore.   There is a 5-ton drop emergency keel, which would cause the vessel to come to the surface immediately, and the keel, drop anchors, and diving chamber are said to provide absolute means of escape for the crew."   This vessel, which is 85 ft. long, with 220 tons submerged displacement, has been put under trial against the United States Submarine *Octopus*.   Another Lake boat, the *Protector*, has been purchased by the Russian Government.

Mr. Simon Lake is a firm believer in the value of submarines both in peace and war.   At the meeting of the Institution of Naval Architects, March, 1907, he read a paper on " Safe Submarine Vessels and the Future of the Art." He placed safety at the head of the list of fundamental requirements, as it gave confidence and added greatly to the efficiency of the crew ; consequently better results were secured when navigating below the surface.   Longitudinal stability was next in importance to safety. There were official records of twenty-four accidents to submarine vessels belonging to various countries, and these had resulted in the loss of 117 lives. Mr. Lake thought it was to be regretted that full and complete official information had not been given in all cases where disasters had occurred, as designers had consequently been compelled to rely on their own experience or assumptions to provide in future designs for a larger measure of safety. A submarine should be valued in proportion to the number of torpedoes which she has ready for instant firing. The submarine had been decried by some representatives to The Hague Tribunal on the ground that it is barbarous and unfair, and a method of fighting which is effective because it strikes below the belt—the armour belt. He did not think he was betraying any secrets when he stated that the technical authorities of a great nation, after recent extensive experiments, had just become convinced that the submarine is to bring about a new era in naval construction, and, as the old wooden ship of the line has been displaced by the heavily armoured ironclad, so these great Goliaths will in turn be displaced by the little Davids, which may approach entirely unseen and strike a death-blow into the vitals of the surface monsters from a direction entirely unknown. The new method of taking sights made the submarine invincible. It was impossible to fire against things unseen. The result of the general adoption of the submarine would be a universal peace. Where submarines exist it would be foolhardy to attempt to land an invading army by sea. No transport ships would dare approach a coast-line for the purpose of landing an army if submarine torpedo-boats were known to be protecting the coast. The Hague Tribunal, instead of opposing submarines, should welcome them, as the first great battle where submarines are employed may possibly prove that the future of the mighty surface vessels is behind them.

A SHORT BIBLIOGRAPHY OF
SUBMARINE WARFARE

France

"Les Torpilleurs autonomes et l'avenir de la Marine," by
G. Charmes. Paris, 1885.
"Les Torpilleurs, la Guerre Navale et la Défense des côtes,"
by Vice-Admiral Bourgois. Paris, 1888.
"La Navigation Sous-Marine," by G. L. Pesce. Paris, 1897.
"Les Bateaux Sous-Marins," 2 vols., by F. Forest and H.
Noalhat. Paris, 1900.
"La Navigation Sous-Marine," by M. Gaget. Paris, 1901.
"La Navigation Sous-Marine à travers les Siècles," by M.
Delpeuch. Paris, 1902.
"Les Sous-Marins et l'Angleterre," by Paul Fontin. Paris,
1906.
"Notre Marine de Guerre," par un Marin (Admiral Fournier).
1906.

Belgium

"La Guerre Sous-Marine," by L. G. Daudenart. Brussels,
1872.
"Les Mines Sous-Marines dans la défense des Rades," by
C. Huët. Brussels, 1875.

Germany

"Die Unterseeische Schifffahrt," by L. Hauff. Munich, 1859.
"Geschichte der Seeminen und Torpedoes," by F. von
Ehrenkrook. Berlin, 1878.
"Die unterseeboote der Gegenwart" ("Jahrbuch für Deutsch-
lands Seeinteressen," by "Nauticus"), 1902.

Great Britain

" Submarine Boats," by G. W. Hovgaard. London (Spon), 1887.

" Submarine Mines and Torpedoes as applied to Harbour Defence," by Major J. T. Bucknill. London, 1889.

" Notes on Submarine Mines, commonly called Torpedoes," by Capt. H. Steward, R.E. London, 1886.

" Torpedoes and Torpedo Warfare," by Lt. C. W. Sleeman (2nd ed., 1889). Simpkin, London.

" Torpedoes and Torpedo Vessels," by Lt. G. E. Armstrong, London (2nd ed.), 1901.

" Submarine Navigation," by Alan H. Burgoyne. 1904.

United States

" Torpedo War and Submarine Explosions," by R. Fulton. New York, 1810.

" Submarine Warfare," by J. S. Barnes. New York, 1869.

PLYMOUTH
WILLIAM BRENDON AND SON, LTD., PRINTERS